Beyond Lisbon

A European Strategy For Globalisation

P.I.E. Peter Lang

Bruxelles · Bern · Berlin · Frankfurt am Main · New York · Oxford · Wien

Laurent Cohen-Tanugi

Beyond Lisbon

A European Strategy For Globalisation

Éditions scientifiques internationales
Brussels, 2008
1 avenue Maurice, 1050 Brussels, Belgium
info@peterlang.com; www.peterlang.com

ISBN 978-90-5201-461-6
D/2008/5678/50

Library of Congress Cataloging-in-Publication Data
Beyond Lisbon : a European strategy for globalisation /
Laurent Cohen-Tanugi.
p. cm.
Includes bibliographical references.
ISBN 978-90-5201-461-6
1. European Union countries--Economic policy. 2. Europe--Economic integration.
3. Globalization--European Union countries. I. Title.
HC241.2.C554274 2008 337.4--dc22 2008037535

CIP also available from the British Library, GB

Bibliographic information published by "Die Deutsche Bibliothek". "Die Deutsche Bibliothek" lists this publication in the "Deutsche National-bibliografie": detailed bibliographic data is available on the Internet at <http://dnb.ddb.de>.

TABLE OF CONTENTS

Preface

by
Christine LAGARDE and Xavier BERTRAND

Since we took office, we have been struck by the paradoxical situation of France in relation to Europe's collective ambition, as expressed by the Lisbon strategy.

Certainly, citizens, economic and social actors and political leaders are in very broad agreement on the objective of making Europe the most competitive society in the world, increasing to 3% of GDP our investment in research and achieving an employment rate of 70%. At the same time, we should recognise that scepticism is very often expressed regarding the means committed to attaining these objectives, the reality of the advances that have been made since 2000, and even the very existence of a political will to include our national policies within the European framework. As noted by Laurent Cohen-Tanugi, France is experiencing greater difficulty than other countries in appropriating the Lisbon strategy.

This observation was all the more frustrating that, since Nicolas Sarkozy's election, we have undertaken an effort of unprecedented scale in structural reform, aiming to make our country more competitive and more innovative, strengthen its potential for growth to bring it up to the level of the best European countries, and to release the energies of a relatively inflexible labour market while providing new guarantees for salaried employees and job seekers.

In a few months, we have achieved the adoption of university reform – begun in the summer of 2007 and seeking to endow universities with the autonomy they require –, an R&D tax credit that is among the most attractive in the world, the merger of the Agence nationale pour l'emploi (ANPE) and the Association pour l'emploi dans l'industrie et le commerce (ASSEDIC) to make our labour market more efficient and other key measures, taken within the framework of the law for employment, labour and purchasing power, to put work back at the core of our economy. An agreement on the modernisation of the labour market, signed by four of the five major union confederations, has been concluded and will be extended. A law enforcing the compulsory measures it requires was adopted on first reading at the National Assembly and the Senate. The law and the decrees implementing the agreement should be promulgated before the summer of 2008.

Each of these reforms falls fully within the scope of the Lisbon strategy and that is precisely how they are perceived by our European partners to whom they have been regularly presented.

Faced with this picture that is both mixed and promising – and at a time when the second cycle of the Lisbon strategy is commencing –, it seems vital to us to open up a wide-ranging debate on the future of this strategy and the role that France should play within it. The stakes are indeed critical. What economic and social policy and what medium-term objectives do we want for Europe? How can we really encourage innovation on our continent? How can we provide our industries with the best possible environment? For what transformations should we prepare our labour markets? And, no less important, how should we work together, among Europeans, to reach these objectives in such a way that they do not remain merely slogans but are subject to monitoring and full ownership?

With this in mind, we have encouraged Laurent Cohen-Tanugi to reflect without prejudgement, taboos, preconceived ideas or hesitation and to make a frank diagnosis of both our shortcomings and our successes. We also asked him to work in full collaboration with the social partners, without whom the renovation of the Lisbon strategy would be fruitless. Finally, we wished him to make a broad use of the experiences of our European partners and of the thinking conducted outside Europe on defining medium- and long-term economic and social policies.

The report he has delivered to us lives up fully to these expectations.

We believe it is an essential contribution to our collective thinking at a time when France is getting ready to preside over the EU Council for six months, and when the European Council meeting of March 2008 – at France's request – has invited the Member States and the Commission to reflect on what a post-Lisbon strategy might look like. We are particularly proud of the fact that our country is among the first to launch this debate. Our ambition is for it to be as broad and open as possible, marking a genuine turnaround and making France a resolute and fully committed player in a European economic and social strategy for globalisation.

May 2008

Foreword

This book is the outcome of the "Europe in the Global Economy" Mission – relating, more specifically, to the future of the European strategy launched in Lisbon in March 2000 – that was entrusted to me by Mrs. Christine Lagarde, French Minister for the Economy, Industry and Employment, and Mr. Xavier Bertrand, French Minister for Labour, Labour Relations, Family and Solidarity, in November 2007, ahead of the French presidency of the European Union.

It is the product of six months' work, including extensive consultations conducted in France and throughout the European Union. We have benefited from valuable input by a Steering Committee composed of some fifteen experts from varied backgrounds, regular dialogue with the French social partners represented on the Comité du dialogue social pour les questions européennes et internationales (CDSEI), and numerous meetings and interviews within the European institutions and six Member States: Germany, Italy, the Czech Republic, the United Kingdom, Slovenia and Sweden, as well as Israel, a leader in the knowledge economy that participates in most EU research programmes.

This wide-ranging concertation process allowed us to devise a middle way between an indispensable European "reality principle" and the need to update certain ways of thinking prevailing in Brussels and elsewhere, in response to the changing world and the necessary "outward-looking" perspective of the European project in the years to come. It also confirmed my strong view that the central challenge facing European unification today – and the key to its revival – is about how to create European added value in a globalised world.

The broad scope of the subject prevented us from going as deeply as we would have liked into some important issues in the time available to us. But we did our best not to remain silent on any essential aspect, and to express our views clearly on each of them.

This report is not intended as a catalogue of proposals (although it does include many), but rather sets forth a coherent strategic vision for tomorrow's Europe in the global economy. It aims at contributing to the success of the French EU Presidency and, beyond that, to the 2009 European electoral debate and the revival of the European project. To facilitate access by a wider audience, it is the subject of two dedicated websites:

www.euromonde2015.eu (French speaking), and
www.euroworld2015.eu (English speaking).

Following our interim recommendation, supported by France and other Member States, the spring 2008 European Council has officially invited the Commission, the Council and the national Lisbon coordinators to start reflecting on a post-2010 globalisation strategy. The French presidency will launch this process within the group of the national Lisbon coordinators in the fall of 2008. This book represents the first substantive contribution to this exercise, which should lead us from the current, imperfect Lisbon process to the more ambitious globalisation strategy Europe needs and can afford.

My warmest thanks to Yves Bertoncini, Olivier Ferrand (general *rapporteurs*), Virginie Parizot, Fausto Rotelli, and Marie-Christine Moison for their contribution to this work, their team spirit, dedication and enthusiasm, and also to the members of the Mission Steering Committee, the CDSEI, the Centre d'analyse stratégique (CAS), the French economic missions in the countries visited, and the many personalities listed at the end of this book for their valuable input. Shortage of time prevented us from making full use of the wealth of these consultations, but they will be useful in the future.

I also wish to warmly thank Adrian Mathews and Anne Castiglione-Minischetti, our translators, as well as Caroline de Jessey, Yves Bertoncini, Ann Pollock, Delphine Qui and Marie Madelpuech for their contribution to this English edition.

Lastly, I would like to thank Mrs. Christine Lagarde and Mr. Xavier Bertrand for their trust, as well as Mr. Jean-Pierre Jouyet, France's Secretary of State for European Affairs, for his unfailing support. Needless to say, the Mission team assumes sole responsibility for the substance of our report.

Laurent COHEN-TANUGI
August 2008

Introduction

Is the European project still relevant in the globalised economy of the early 21st century?

There are two conflicting views on this question, the resolution of which is critical for restoring full public support for the European enterprise and, indeed, for the future of the Old Continent itself.

The first one holds that the European enterprise is confronted with a twofold challenge, from the accelerating process and dilutive effect of globalisation on the one hand and, on the other, from the enduring reality of the Nation State as the locus of social cohesion and the exercise of democracy.

The second view claims, on the contrary, that globalisation can only strengthen the original objective of European unification, which – beyond establishing lasting peace – consists in restoring the Member States' ability to exert influence at the international level by providing them with a critical size and a common will to face up to the continental scale nations of the global economy.

Even though we may not endorse it, the first argument is based on a realistic assessment of a major challenge to the European project. As for the second, its validity can no longer be presumed, which takes us back to the means and ambitions that the European Union may or may not be prepared to adopt in order to prove it right.

Europe's official response to globalisation is today embodied in the "Lisbon strategy". This initiative was launched in March 2000, at the height of the Internet boom and in response to the risk of Europe falling behind in relation to America's economic performance. Its aim was to make Europe "the most competitive and dynamic knowledge-driven economy in the world by 2010". After several years of immobility and an initial clear-sighted assessment established by the 2004 Kok report, the Lisbon strategy was relaunched in March 2005 and refocused on "growth and jobs". Today it has become the central and consensual strategy of the EU-27 in economic, social and environmental matters, the "European response to globalisation". The European Council of 13-14 March 2008 has just adopted the latest cycle of the Lisbon strategy for the 2008-2010 period, a continuation of the previous cycle.

Assessing Europe's ability to confront globalisation requires, therefore, an evaluation of the Lisbon strategy by the same yardstick. The question is politically sensitive. For the current European Commission, which has made it its key project, the Lisbon strategy (in its 2005 relaunched form) is now a success and should be pursued as it stands until 2010 and beyond. As evidence of this, the Commission cites, in particular, the European Union's improved global economic performance in 2006-2007 and the 6.5 million jobs created in the course of that period. The American economy's present difficulties also contributed to boosting Europe's fortunes in terms of growth and productivity. However, the reality is less clear-cut and the durability of Europe's economic resilience is uncertain.

This report begins with an assessment of the Lisbon strategy that is meant to be as comprehensive and nuanced as possible. To our knowledge, it is the first evaluation of this process to be established at the initiative of a Member State since its 2005 relaunch. The exercise was delicate for two reasons: we are talking about a process that is itself intended to evaluate the performances of Member States according to a number of predefined criteria, and it is even more difficult if the evaluation is made by a Member State whose own performance in relation to those criteria has so far been disappointing.

No doubt there will be further assessments of this kind in Europe as we near 2010 – the deadline set when the strategy was launched in March 2000 –, with important political stakes. But let one thing be stated right away: *with only two years to go before this deadline, Lisbon is neither the success story the Commission declares it to be, nor the manifest failure it is sometimes wrongly depicted as being*. It has had mixed results, depending on country and objective, and its success has been largely tempered for the whole European Union by the mediocre performances of the major Eurozone economies (France, Italy, Germany). Its implementation process – the "open method of coordination" (which is non-binding and relying mainly on the reforming good will of Member States) – is a weak engine and leaves too much scope for bureaucracy. As a result, even when economic performance is strong, one can justifiably question the extent to which this is attributable to the Lisbon strategy rather than macro-economic cycles or autonomously conducted national reform programmes.

Nonetheless, the Lisbon strategy has gradually become a consensual agenda for adapting the European economies to the challenges of globalisation. In particular, its great merit is that it has introduced European coordination in largely national areas of competence (higher education, research, employment, social issues, etc.), helping minds focus, develop and advance in the same direction throughout Europe. Its objectives remain valid but are still far from having been achieved.

These mixed results lead us to support the directions proposed by the Commission and decided upon by the European Council for the 2008-2010 cycle of the Lisbon strategy, which are consensual in Europe and centred on improved national implementation of the objectives defined in 2005-2006. *The prescription is particularly important for France, where structural reform has suffered delays for several years and should be vigorously pursued in the next couple of years.*

However, the justifiable short-term continuity advocated by the Commission should not eclipse a deeper reality: *in the medium and long term, the Lisbon strategy does not constitute an adequate response to globalisation.* There are at least three reasons for this.

First, the "performance" of the Lisbon strategy – as a framework to adapt the European economies to globalisation – is insufficient in the face of intensifying global competition. Far from having bridged the gap that separates it from the United States, Europe is now also threatened with a drop in status caused by the rise of the Asian economic giants.

Furthermore, the European Union is being confronted with *new challenges*, both within and outside its borders, the existence – or at least the extent – of which was not perceived in 2000, or even in 2005: high-end competition from emerging countries, the energy/climate issues, the effects of enlarging to 27 members, the international financial crisis and the increasingly geopolitical character of globalisation. These challenges also bring with them *new opportunities* that Europe must learn to seize: dynamic global growth, greater mobility for skilled and talented workers, the rising influence of the euro as an international currency, etc.

Lastly and most importantly, *the Lisbon strategy is only about adapting European economies and societies to globalisation.* Yet, Europe cannot adapt successfully on its own – that is, without linking this process to *an external economic strategy that rely on common policy instruments and aim at shaping globalisation.*

At the initiative of France, the European Council of 13-14 March 2008 has acknowledged this reality by launching the reflection on the future of the Lisbon strategy after 2010 without delay.

* *
*

The foregoing analysis outlines the required evolution for the Lisbon strategy, which is the subject of the third part of this report. Internally, we should pursue the direction traced since 2000 by the Lisbon strategy, but with a refocused agenda and a stronger engine. Externally, the European Union needs to be equipped with a complete panoply of external economic policy instruments, some of which are already in place and need to be strenghtened while others have yet to be developed.

We suggest calling the *internal component* of this new strategic vision "*Lisbon Plus*", to mark both the continuity with the agenda of the 2000 decade and the need for *refocusing accompanied by a change in pace and intensity*. Lisbon Plus must focus on *competitiveness through innovation* and, with increasingly strong and global economic competition, Europe must learn to make innovation its speciality.

In light of the growing and counter-productive tendency of the Commission and certain Member States to subsume all European policies under the "Lisbon" label, this refocusing is critical to provide legibility, effectiveness and meaning: the Lisbon strategy was never intended to absorb the entire European agenda in the first place and it is certainly not the right vehicle to do so. Faithful to the original spirit of the 2000 decade, *Lisbon Plus will interlink the economic, social and environmental dimensions of a knowledge and innovation-driven economy and society, without monopolising all national and European social and environmental policies, which should preserve their autonomy.*

As far as social affairs are concerned, education, training, mobility, globalisation adjustment policies, integration policies, dealing with an aging population and relaunching the European social dialogue should be at the heart of Lisbon Plus. Other realms of social policy can be dealt with by other institutional processes, particularly the European Social Agenda, which we call upon the French EU presidency to promote.

As for the *external dimension* of Europe's post-2010 globalisation strategy, it should be distinguished from Lisbon Plus to the extent that it does not come under the open method of coordination (even in its "strengthened" form) and the mainly national competences that characterize the Lisbon strategy. *This external dimension should instead be based on common policies that correspond to competences that are exclusively Community-centred or at least broadly shared with Member States.*

In fact, the EU only really matters in the globalised economy when it is endowed with such competences and policies. This is the case with the Common Trade Policy, the Common Agricultural Policy, the international dimension of the Internal Market and the Economic and Monetary Union, the Cooperation Policy. To this arsenal – which is already old and partly under challenge – should be added new common external policies: an energy and environmental diplomacy, a European immigration and co-development policy, an international normative strategy, and a Community instrument for monitoring non-EU takeovers in sensitive sectors.

The combination and interaction of these two dimensions – one internal, the other external – aim to produce a more comprehensive and ambitious strategy than the current Lisbon agenda, that we propose to name "EuroWorld 2015".

To respond to accelerating changes in the world around us, we propose setting a five-year term for the implementation of this new strategic vision. This corresponds to the mandate of the Commission that will result from the June 2009 European elections. As such, this implementation could constitute the European Union's *main economic and social roadmap for the first half of the 2010 decade.*

The political, doctrinal, institutional and financial conditions required for this more ambitious strategy to succeed are outlined in the last chapter of this book. The importance given to the external dimension signals the fact that European unification has entered a new phase in its history, centred no longer on its own making but on its relationship with the rest of the world. This new phase represents a genuine *paradigm shift*, the implications of which we have attempted to explore.

PART I

EUROPE IN THE GLOBAL ECONOMY: THE STATE OF PLAY

CHAPTER I

The Lisbon Strategy: A Mixed Balance Sheet

It was more than eight years ago, in Lisbon, that the EU set itself "a new strategic goal for the next decade: to become the most competitive and dynamic knowledge-based economy in the world, capable of sustainable economic growth with more and better jobs and greater social cohesion"[1].

For many Europeans, the Lisbon strategy is still identified with this initial, unrealistic and even immodest phrase which – by rapidly transforming into a pious hope – has done lasting harm to the ambition it was supposed to serve. However, the Lisbon strategy has developed over the years and now covers a complex and positive reality, a brief reminder of which may be useful to start with.

The Objectives

The Lisbon strategy was initially implemented on the basis of a *series of figure-based objectives defined and adopted by EU heads of State and government* at the spring European Council each year.

The European Council first set three "final" figure-based objectives for the Lisbon strategy, between 2000 and 2002, before refocusing on the first two of these in March 2005 ("growth and jobs").

1 European Council of Lisbon, March 2000, Presidency Conclusions.

The "final" figure-based objectives to be met by 2010, set by the spring European Council meetings

Subject	Figure-based objective	European Council
Growth rate	3% per year[2]	Lisbon 2000
Employment rate	70% of the economically active population	Lisbon 2000
	60% of the economically active female population	Lisbon 2000
	50% of workers over 50	Stockholm 2001
Greenhouse gas emission rate	8% reduction compared to the 1990* level (to apply the Kyoto Protocol)	Barcelona 2002

* The March 2007 European Council set an EU objective of at least a 20% reduction in greenhouse gas emissions by 2020 compared to 1990 levels (or even 30%, depending on the conditions under which the Kyoto Protocol is adapted beyond 2012).

On this basis, the European Council also identified around ten "intermediate" figure-based objectives which, if pursued, should make it possible to attain the growth and employment objectives: some of these have become emblematic (*e.g.*, the one relating to R&D expenditure).

The intermediate figure-based objectives to be met by 2010, set by the spring European Council meetings

Subject	Figure-based objective	European Council
Education	85% of each class group up to Baccalauréat level	Lisbon 2000
Stability and growth pact	Public deficit lower than 3% of GDP * Public debt lower than 60% of GDP	Stockholm 2001
Internal Market	98.5% of directives transposed on deadline ** Overall reduction of State aid as percentage of GDP by 2003	Stockholm 2001
R&D expenditure	3% of GDP, including 2/3 private expenditure	Barcelona 2002
Effective retirement age	To be raised by approximately 5 years	Barcelona 2002
Subsidised reception centres for children	90% of children between 3 years of age and compulsory school age 33% of children under 3	Barcelona 2002

2 The Conclusions of the Lisbon European Council state that "If the measures set out below are implemented against a sound macro-economic background, an average economic growth rate of around 3% should be a realistic prospect for the coming years".

Youth unemployment (18-24 years of age)	Education drop-out rate lower than 10% Offer of employment, training or work experience placement within a maximum period of 4 months	Brussels 2006

* The Conclusions of the Stockholm European Council meeting even mention the objective of "achieving public finances close to balance or in surplus" ** The March 2007 Brussels European Council meeting set a new objective of 99% of directives implemented on time by 2009.

The new objectives set by the March 2007 European Council meeting

The March 2007 European Council meeting identified new "intermediate objectives" for EU countries that go beyond the 2010 deadline selected at this stage for the Lisbon strategy:

- an objective relating to the regulatory environment of the economy: to reduce "administrative burdens arising from EU legislation by 25%" by 2012, and, for each Member State, to set "national targets of comparable ambition within their spheres of competence" by 2008;
- objectives relating to the energy situation of EU countries, to be met by 2020: "saving 20% of the EU's energy consumption compared to projections for 2020"; "a binding target of a 20% share of renewable energies in overall EU energy consumption by 2020"; and, lastly, "a 10% binding minimum target to be achieved by all Member States for the share of biofuels in overall EU transport petrol and diesel consumption".

The Integrated Guidelines

With a view to achieving the above-mentioned figure-based objectives, the implementation of the Lisbon strategy is also based on 24 "Integrated Guidelines for growth and jobs"[3] adopted by the March 2005 European Council. These guidelines formalize the "pacts", "processes" and guidelines that pre-existed the launch of the Lisbon strategy and their purpose is to simplify and coordinate them, while setting them within a three-yearly operational framework.

The "Integrated Guidelines" (IGs) are commonly divided into two categories:

– The "Broad Economic Policy Guidelines" (BEPGs) encompass the whole range of macro-economic and micro-economic policies, as well as employment policies insofar as they interact with the former. BEPGs are based, to a limited degree, on the "Stability and Growth Pact" (SGP) and other coordination processes already begun at Community level;

[3] See http://ec.europa.eu/growthandjobs/pdf/integrated_guidelines_en.pdf.

– The "Employment guidelines" (EGs) form part of the EU's "Social Agenda"[4]. The principle of these Community guidelines was first adopted by the 1997 Luxembourg European Council and their content then revised and updated.

The "Open Method of Coordination" (OMC)

Since its launch, the implementation of the Lisbon strategy has been based on *mobilising the players concerned and, in the first place, national governments*, since improved EU growth and competitiveness cannot by nature ensue from Community decisions alone.

The recourse to the "open method of coordination" was confirmed in principle and detailed in its procedures by the March 2005 European Council, which sought to clarify the role – and improve the mobilisation – of the different players whose involvement had proved very uneven during the 2000-2005 period. By instituting a "partnership for growth and jobs", this "relaunch" introduced the main instruments presently used to implement the Lisbon strategy:

– the "Community Lisbon Programme" (CLP), which makes an inventory of the measures and decisions planned by the EU for a period of three years;

– the "National Reform Programmes" (NRPs), which present the measures envisaged by Member States for the same period.

* *
*

When assessing the Lisbon strategy's track record, one should first note that it still forms part of the EU's main priorities – which was not necessarily self-evident – and that it was even successfully restructured and relaunched in mid-term to encourage increased mobilisation of Community institutions and governments.

Beyond this observation, the Lisbon strategy's track record can be summed up in three points:

– the economic and social performances of EU Member States with regard to the set objectives have been mixed;

– this mixed track record does not call into question the validity and relevance of the Lisbon agenda's economic and social foundations;

---

4 Besides the "Employment guidelines", the EU's Social Agenda gives rise to other types of European coordination, *e.g.* concerning social protection and inclusion. Since the 2005 refocusing of the Lisbon Strategy, these other areas are tackled in parallel with the latter.

– it is, above all, the effectiveness of the method chosen to implement it that is called into question.

I. Positive but Uneven Results

Before analysing the results of the Lisbon strategy, a few precautions need to be taken.

First, it is advisable to specify the objectives or indicators on which the analysis is based: in this respect, the Mission considered that the figure-based objectives selected by the European Council were of particular political importance and should be the preferred basis for evaluation, despite their heterogeneous nature and although they only partially match up with the limited list of indicators chosen by the European Commission.

Furthermore, it is important to distinguish clearly between analyses of the EU's overall performance and that of the different Member States: this distinction is all the more important given that the implementation of the Lisbon strategy gives Member States wide-ranging autonomy within the framework of the OMC; it is all the more necessary because the EU is, to a great extent, a "statistical illusion" whose performance is in fact largely marked by the individual performances of a few countries (as a rough guide, France, Germany and Italy represented 48% of the EU's GDP in 2006).

Once these precautions have been taken, we can start evaluating the results of the Lisbon strategy with regard to its final objectives for growth and jobs and its intermediate and related objectives, while distinguishing the performances of Member States according to these objectives (see Annex 1 for a complete presentation).

A. Growth rates: often disappointing, despite a recent upturn

Though the objective of a 3% growth rate was not achieved by the EU for the 2002-2006 period, the performance of more than half its Member States was higher than 3%.

GDP volume growth in the EU (in %)

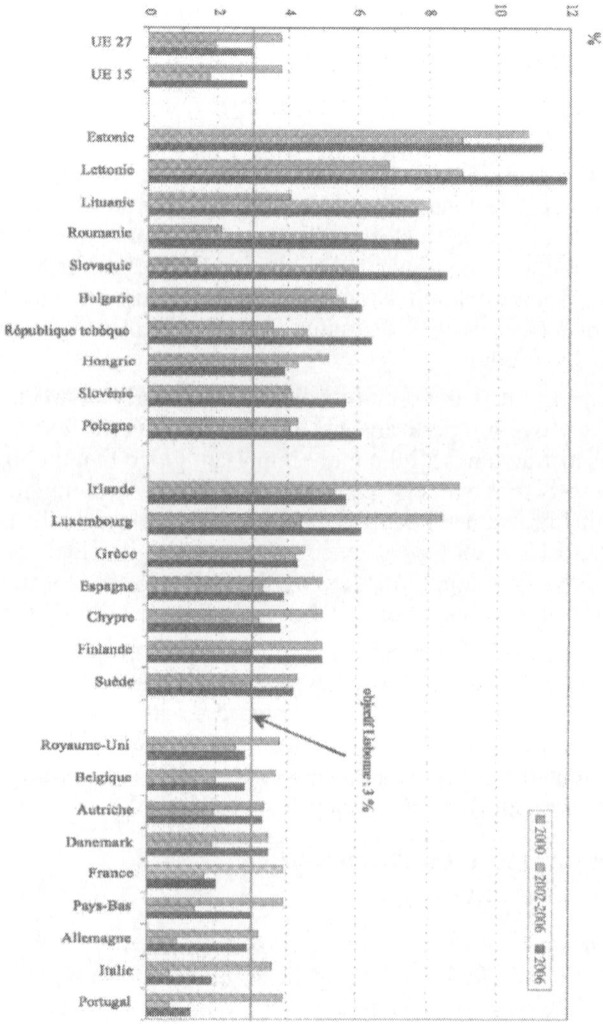

Source: Eurostat data – Chart produced by the Centre d'analyse stratégique.

Closer analysis shows that:

– the growth rate of 17 countries was higher than 3% for the 2002-2006 period: on the one hand, the 10 Central and Eastern European countries that joined the EU in 2004 and 2007 and who were carried along by a catch-up dynamic and, on the other, 7 countries with very different characteristics but all with a certain economic dynamism;

– the performance of France, Germany and Italy – the three largest continental economies – was relatively mediocre for the 2002-2006 period: this was largely because of the decline in average growth rates for the EU-27 (1.9% over this period).

Furthermore, it is important to emphasise that:

– 2006 was a recovery year for the EU-27 with an estimated growth rate of 3%, *i.e.*, the highest since 2000;

– for the same year, 20 of the EU-27 countries had a growth rate that was higher than 3%, and four others had growth rates higher than 2.5%;

– forecasts for 2007 seem to confirm this upturn in growth rates (2.9% forecast for the EU-27), which would ensue from the recovery that has already begun in employment. Nevertheless, it is difficult to extrapolate for the coming period, given the uncertainties surrounding the world economy with the deepening of the American and international financial crisis.

B. Substantial progress in employment rates

Though it is still for the time being below European Council objectives, *the situation for overall employment rates has undergone positive change since the launch of the Lisbon strategy*. This rate has now reached 65%, *i.e.*, an increase of 2.1 points in the EU-27 between 2000 and 2006 and this increase reflects different developments in several "groups of countries":

– 5 EU countries have already reached and exceeded the objective of a 70% employment rate (Denmark, Sweden, the Netherlands, the United Kingdom and Austria);

– 9 others exceeded 65% in 2006, the next 6 crossed the 60% threshold, whereas the employment rate of 7 EU countries was less than 60% in 2006;

– moreover, if trend developments are analysed, it is observed that 7 countries with low employment rates advanced by more than 3.5 points between 2000 and 2006, and sometimes this advance exceeded 5 points (Spain and Latvia); and only 3 countries in the EU-27 experienced a decline in their overall employment rate for the period (Poland, Portugal and Romania).

Total EU employment rate in %

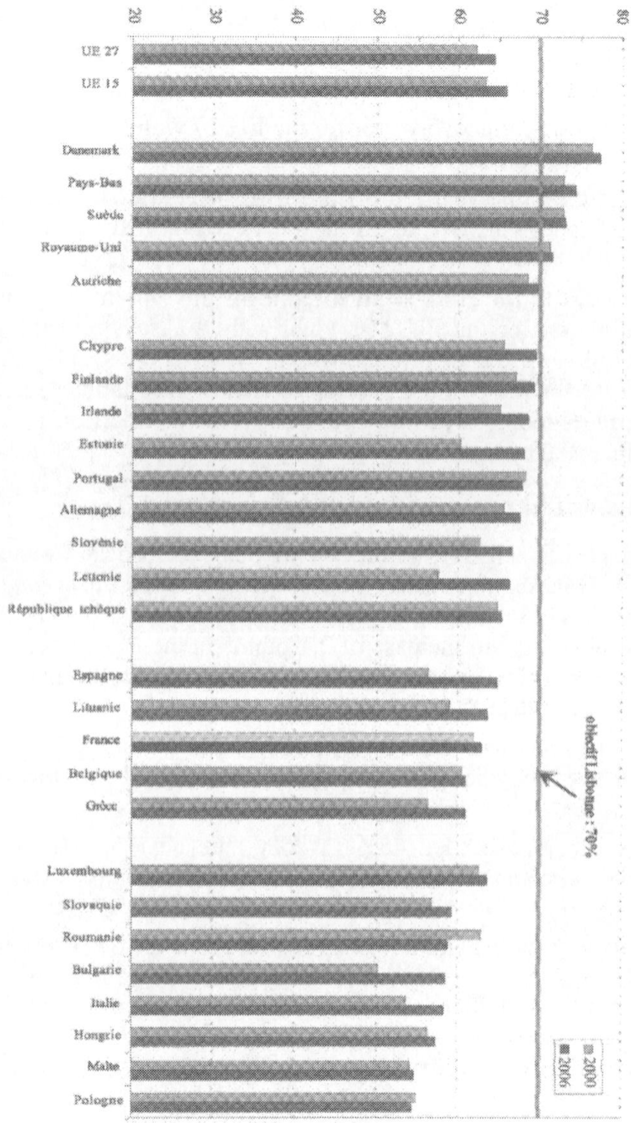

Source: Eurostat data – Chart produced by the Centre d'analyse stratégique.

C. Very diverse results in relation to the Lisbon strategy's intermediate figure-based objectives

An evaluation of EU countries' results in relation to all of the Lisbon strategy's intermediate objectives (see Annex 1) reveals an equally diverse reality. As the promotion of a "knowledge-based economy" founded on education, training, R&D and innovation is at the heart of the Lisbon strategy, it is particularly worrying that the results for this objective were highly ambivalent for the 2000-2006 period.

1. An overall erosion in R&D expenditure

The Lisbon strategy set an overall objective of 3% of GDP to be invested in R&D. However, European public expenditure is still very far short of this objective, at 1.8% of GDP, and even appears to have declined since 2000.

On closer inspection, the analysis of developments in national R&D expenditure shows that:

– in 2006, only Finland and Sweden exceeded the objective of 3% of GDP and 4 countries were between 2% and 2.5% (Denmark, Germany, Austria and France), whereas the expenditure level of 11 other countries was less than 1%;

– for the 2000-2006 period, 17 countries increased their internal R&D expenditure, while 10 others (including France and the United Kingdom) saw a drop or stagnation in expenditure;

– taking into account the absolute and relative importance of the R&D expenditure of these two last countries, this performance explains why the EU's overall average investment decreased slightly between 2000 and 2006, which – without a doubt – contravenes the commitments made in Lisbon, then in Barcelona in March 2002.

R&D expenditure as % of GDP

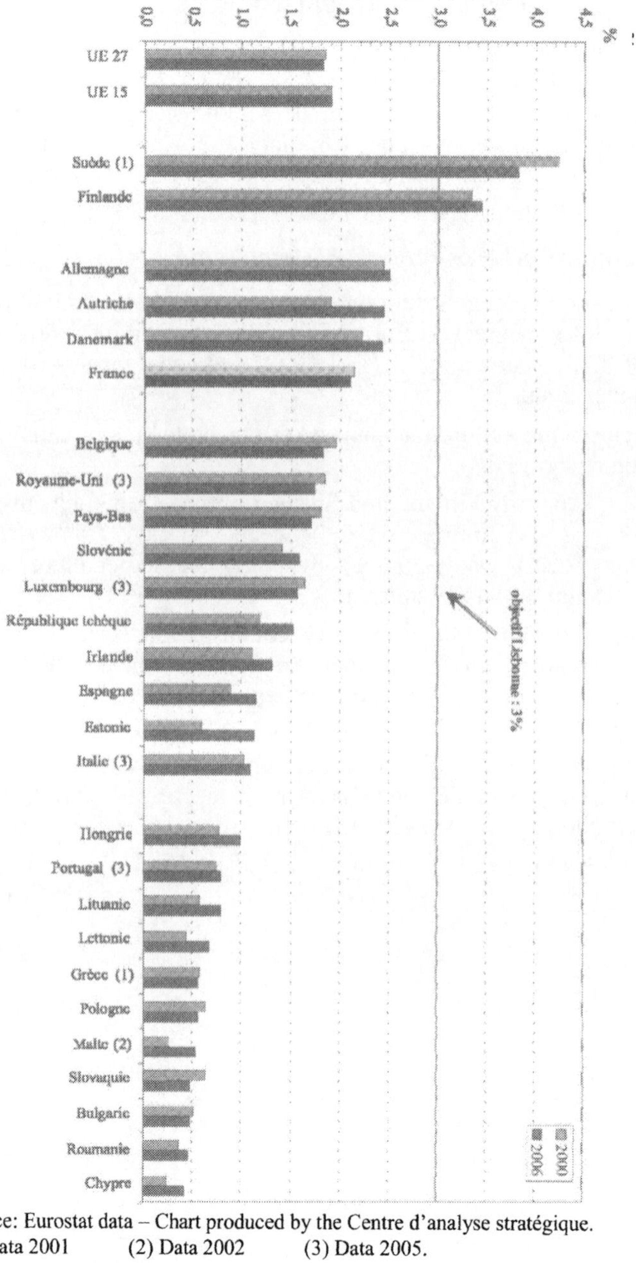

Source: Eurostat data – Chart produced by the Centre d'analyse stratégique.
(1) Data 2001 (2) Data 2002 (3) Data 2005.

2. *An improved level of education*

However, as far as the level of education in EU countries is concerned, it can be observed that:

– 8 of the EU-27 countries have already reached or exceeded the objective of 85% for an age group at higher secondary education level, and 9 others exceeded the 80% threshold;

– *the level of education in 21 of the EU-27 countries advanced between 2000 and 2006*, sometimes substantially (Lithuania, Malta, Greece, Portugal);

– 3 of the countries that did not reach the 85% target recorded a significant decline for the same period (Germany, Spain and Luxembourg), whereas Finland seems to have slipped below the 85% target;

– the relative population size of Germany and Spain within the EU explains the limited increase in the percentage of those in the 20 to 24 age-group reaching at least higher secondary education level, which nonetheless rose from 76.6% to 77.8% between 2000 and 2006.

Populations of 20-24 year olds reaching at least higher secondary education level (in %)

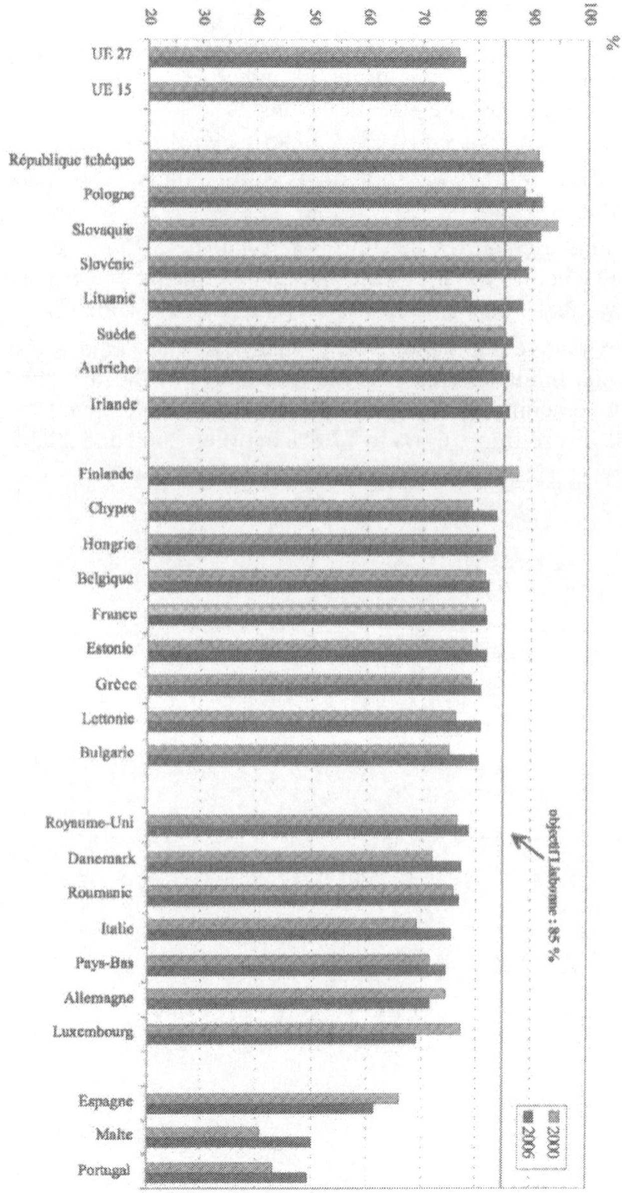

Source: Eurostat data – Chart produced by the Centre d'analyse stratégique.

II. The Foundations: Still Valid

The Lisbon strategy has produced mixed results, but this does not in any way detract from its relevance: the strategy's foundations, taken as a whole, remain valid eight years after it was launched.

A. A strategy targeting Europe's gap in wealth, productivity and innovation

According to the analysis made when the Lisbon strategy was launched, the EU's main competitors – other than Member States themselves (owing to strong intra-European competition) – are countries that have reached a comparable stage of economic development, particularly the United States and Japan. That analysis was strongly influenced by the economic context at the turn of the millennium, characterised by the emergence of a "new economy" based on knowledge and information and communication technologies, but it still seems valid in the run up to 2010, as do the paths of structural reform to which it has given rise.

1. The European gap in terms of wealth, productivity and innovation (see Annex 2)[5]

• *As far as wealth is concerned,* it was observed in 2000 that Europe had gone through a catching-up period in relation to the United States in the post-war period through to the mid-1970s but that, since the 1990s, the catching-up dynamic was regularly running out of steam (see table).

Breakdown of GDP/inhabitant in 2006

	GDP/inhabitant as a percentage of the US level	Hourly productivity as a percentage of the US level*	Number of hours worked per inhabitant
France	72%	101%	617
EU-19**	67%	79%	726
US	100%	100%	865

Sources: OECD (Labour productivity report, 2006) and European Commission (Competitiveness report, 2006) *GDP per hour worked; **EU Members belonging to the OECD.

The gap in GDP level is due, first of all, to a "quantitative" gap due to the lower average number of hours worked by Europeans and the lower employment rate. This observation was largely responsible for the Lisbon strategy's call to increase Europe's employment rate, based on

5 For a deeper analysis of this gap, see in particular Aghion P., Cohen E. and Pisani-Ferry J., (2006), "Politique économique et croissance en Europe", Paris, Conseil d'Analyse Économique Report, No. 59, La Documentation Française.

the presupposition that Europeans wish to maintain or increase their relative level of wealth and that achieving this involves increased mobilisation of the labour market.

• According to the analysis at the time, the gap in GDP level was also due to more "qualitative" factors, particularly a discrepancy in hourly productivity: the growth in European productivity, which was more dynamic up to then, has thus been lagging behind that of the United States since the mid-1990s (see table below). Though this productivity gap appeared at a particular moment in the economic cycle, most economists now agree that it is structural in character.

Hourly labour productivity in the United States and Europe, 1950-2003

	Average annual growth rate for productivity		The EU as a percentage of the US	
	US	EU-15		
1950-1973	2.77	4.77	1973	79
1973-1995	1.48	2.25	1995	94
1995-2003	2.33	1.15	2003	85

Source: Conseil d'analyse économique / Gordon, 2004.

• Europe's disappointing productivity performance in the course of the recent period is also explained by an innovation gap.

Generally speaking, economic literature grants a central role to *innovation, which largely determines the overall productivity of production factors*. That Europe has fallen behind in terms of innovation can be observed at two levels: a lower volume of investment (in R&D, in the means available for higher education, information and communication technologies ICTs), and lower "results" as measured by certain intermediate indicators (publications and scientific prizes, patents, the growth of certain innovative industrial sectors, the number of new products and new companies, reorganisation and reallocation operations for the means of production). This twofold gap in the EU's performance explains why the Lisbon strategy places education, training, R&D and innovation centre-stage.

2. *The need to undertake structural reforms*

To remedy the EU's triple shortfall in productivity, employment rate and innovation, the Lisbon strategy recommends a set of structural reforms: essentially, the EU has to stress "supply policies", since the shift to the Economic and Monetary Union profoundly changed the conditions under which demand policies (monetary and budgetary) are implemented. This requires supplementing the traditional approach of opening markets to European competition set in motion by the Treaty of Rome with national reforms, because it is at the national level that "supply policies" are mainly implemented (labour market, R&D, education, regulatory policies, etc.). A European political consensus on these issues was reached to implement structural reforms falling mainly into two categories:

a) The liberalisation of national and European markets

The promoters of the Lisbon strategy consider that Europe's growth and competitiveness suffer from a lack of market liberalisation. To support this view, they use a set of principles and analyses to show that, essentially:

– a bigger market enables economies of scale and greater price competition, both of which generate gains in growth and productivity: this credo, which was that of the promoters of the Treaty of Rome, inspired the European strategy that sought to establish an Internal Market, then a "Single Market". A whole section of the Lisbon strategy is simply the logical extension of this view;

– administrative restrictions on the goods market[6] result in slowing down the adjustment process by which the most advanced production techniques, particularly ICTs, spread beyond borders and are incorporated into the productive activity of the national economy;

– there is a correlation between a given market's degree of competitiveness and the vigour of the innovation process deployed in it.

b) Support for education-training, R&D and infrastructures

So-called "endogenous growth" theories give prominence to key "externality-producing" factors that influence an economy's rate of growth: public infrastructures, R&D and the accumulation of human capital. The driving force of growth is no longer sought exclusively through increased market integration (even if this is still a topical factor, particularly for services), but also through the accumulation and dissemination of knowledge. Since the private return on investment is less than its social return, governments are called upon to create an environment that promotes growth through public equipment and training spending in addition to an R&D support policy and the creation of a favourable environment for innovative companies.

These theoretical factors have been all the more fruitful for the Lisbon strategy in that they tally with the empirical analysis of the gaps that

---

6 See, for example, Conway P., Rosa D., Nicoletti G. and Steiner F., (2006), "Regulation, Competition and Productivity Convergence", OECD Economics Dept Working Paper No. 509, September 2006.

the EU has to make up for: in this context, the per capita GDP shortfalls for employment and productivity are, in the end, perceived as different facets of the same problem, namely a gap in technological adaptation rooted in a situation of insufficient competition and under-investment. This dual vision is particularly representative of the double economic foundation for the structural reforms recommended by the Lisbon strategy, which lie at the heart of the political agenda set up to implement it.

3. Reform priorities codified in the form of Integrated Guidelines for growth and jobs

Along with the previously mentioned adoption of a series of figure-based objectives by the European Council, the implementation of the structural reforms provided for by the Lisbon strategy also led to the adoption of the 24 "Integrated Guidelines for growth and jobs" in March 2005 (see Annex 3).

For the most part, these "IGs" are a formulation of the "pacts", "processes" and guidelines that pre-existed the launch of the Lisbon strategy and their purpose is to simplify and coordinate them, while setting them within a three-year operational framework. They are commonly divided into two categories:

– *the "Broad Economic Policy Guidelines" (BEPGs)* encompass the whole range of macro-economic and micro-economic policies, as well as employment policies insofar as they interact with the former. BEPGs are defined by article 99 of the Treaty instituting the European Community and are decided upon by the Council of Ministers by qualified majority vote;

– *the "Employment guidelines" (EGs)* form part of the EU's "Social Agenda"[7]. The principle of these guidelines at the Community level was first adopted by the 1997 Luxembourg European Council and their content then revised and updated. EGs are mentioned in article 128 of the Treaty instituting the European Community and are also decided upon by the Council of Ministers by qualified majority vote.

B. A strategy the economic foundations of which have nevertheless given rise to several controversies

Successive figure-based objectives and IGs constitute the economic and social roadmap for the EU and its Member States in the run up to

[7] Besides the "Employment guidelines", the EU's Social Agenda gives rise to other types of European coordination, *e.g.* concerning social protection and inclusion. Since the 2005 refocusing of the Lisbon strategy, these other areas are tackled in parallel with the latter.

2010 and are not really fundamentally challenged. In fact, the main criticisms made to the Lisbon strategy focus rather on its imperfect implementation, which amounts to an implicit recognition of the validity of its objectives and guidelines. However, a few substantive criticisms are made of the latter, too.

1. The issue of macro-economic support for structural reform

The Lisbon strategy stresses "supply policies" (largely conducted at the national level), since the shift to the Economic and Monetary Union profoundly changed the conditions under which demand policies (monetary and budgetary) are implemented by giving central importance to the European level (the ECB, the Stability and Growth Pact). This apparent disconnection has given rise to two types of questions about the link between these two levels:

– *A question of principle.* As early as March 2000, the maintenance of a sound macro-economic framework was mentioned as an essential component of the Lisbon strategy, but it was not among the four priority issues identified after the 2005 relaunch, as if it was taken for granted and did not fall within the scope of the strategy. However, do the objectives of 2% inflation (set by the ECB) and those relating to public deficit and debt (set by the Stability and Growth Pact) not have a major effect on the economic and social field, both from a legal point of view (they do not fall under the OMC) and with regard to their concrete impact on the policies conducted? Is this impact positive or negative? Shouldn't these interrelations be more strongly stressed, since the three objectives – inflation, deficit, debt – are not commonly thought of as an integral part of the Lisbon strategy? *We shall consider here that the maintenance of a sound macro-economic framework is, in fact, indispensable from an economic and social point of view and that the corresponding objectives need not be stated systematically among the components of a structural reform agenda.*

– *A question of method.* Since the structural reforms provided for by the IGs are easier to implement in periods of growth, should the Lisbon strategy be subject to specific support measures both at the budgetary and monetary levels? In a way, this question has already been answered by the reform in the implementation of the Stability and Growth Pact and the trend towards taking long-term investment expenditure into account when calculating national deficits. More generally, would it be advisable to authorise cyclical interventions to support a large wave of reforms (like those for retirement or labour law), favouring the repayment of their social cost – and, hence, increasing their acceptability – over a limited transition period?

2. *Internal contradictions between the objectives*

a) How to combine an increase in employment rate and productivity gains?

In other respects, one might wonder about the compatibility between the objectives of increasing the employment rate and productivity, at least in the short term (cf. IG 19 & 17). In the first place, integrating the underqualified unemployed into the labour market may automatically lower productivity (integrating a relatively unqualified population into jobs with low productivity). To resolve this potential dilemma between productivity and employment, some people have emphasised the need for a marked increase in investments in human capital (education, training) and an improvement in their quality. This approach takes us back, in particular, to the way in which we manage transition periods (and the mass of relatively unqualified, or inappropriately qualified, workers), or the improvement of services productivity, in Europe.

b) How to connect the Internal Market, innovation and competition policies?

Are innovations produced by companies that are already established or rather by newcomers to the market? The outcome of this debate can influence public policy targeting. Should the priority be supporting investment (IG 7 to 10) – particularly for major existing R&D centres? Or should it be competition and liberalisation (IG 12 and 13), combating the entry barriers (see also IG 15) that would slow down the game of "creative destruction"?

While "flexicurity" (IG 21) is a good response to a context in which production structures undergo accelerated change, would it not be better if the more explicit link between an innovation dynamic – which requires mobility of resources and stability of key resources – and "flexicurity" were given more substance (possible link between IG 7 and IG 21)?

Since the direct objective of competition policy is not innovation but consumer protection, should not a more systemic approach to innovation be planned for? From this perspective, aid for innovation, public procurement and intellectual property would seem to be the most crucial levers for action; however, they are based on a recognition of market weakness and encroach on the manner in which competition policy can be enforced.

3. An inadequate external dimension?

Since the Lisbon strategy aims to define the path European countries must follow in a globalised world, it rightly concentrates on all the structural reforms that must be accomplished to preserve those countries' growth and competitiveness – which are first and foremost national – by emphasising that globalisation is not the only structural challenge confronting the EU (an aging population is also often cited and it is important to bring out more clearly what is attributable to this factor). That said, globalisation does constitute the major prospect to which even the aging population problem could be linked (through the implications of migration).

In this context, it might seem paradoxical that the Lisbon strategy does not refer more broadly to the external policy stakes associated with the EU's growth and competitiveness objectives, apart from an inevitable reference to the Common Trade Policy and the desired conclusion of the "Doha round", in addition to an increasing reference to energy and climate issues, then migration. That being the case, it is relevant to ask whether this external component should not be developed more extensively, or even structured as such. After all, besides the three previously mentioned areas, it tallies with a whole series of factors that are social (Adjustment Fund and Core Labour Standards), environmental (Kyoto, but also "positive economics"), industrial (intellectual property – sovereign wealth funds), political (EU enlargement) and diplomatic (the euro's international role, the impact of CFSP-ESDP on the EU's capacity to exert influence at the international level, including on economic and social matters). *However, as we shall demonstrate in Part III of this volume, the recent trend of integrating these external policies into the Lisbon strategy is mistaken.*

4. What place for the environment in the Lisbon strategy?

The March 2000 European Council meeting was quick to mention the "sustainable growth" objective, which was subject to specific developments right from the Stockhom European Council meeting the following spring. These developments found full expression in the EU Sustainable Development Strategy (EU SDS) adopted in Göteborg in June 2001[8], the implementation of which is intended to be linked with that of the Lisbon strategy. When the Lisbon strategy was "refocused" by the March 2005 European Council, it was confirmed that "the Strategy's

---

8 The Stockhold European Council specified that the EU Sustainable Development Strategy will "complete and build on the political commitment under the Lisbon Strategy" and that "All dimensions of sustainable development should be reviewed in the context of the annual Spring European Council".

three dimensions (economic, social and environmental)" should be tapped into "in a general context of sustainable development".

Consequently, the guidelines and objectives related to environmental protection occupy an important, but not central, place in Lisbon strategy implementation:

– reducing the greenhouse gas emission rate could be considered as one of the main figure-based objectives identified by the European Council, which recently pronounced in favour of increased EU mobilisation by 2020[9]: beyond a reduction of at least 20% in the greenhouse gas emission rate compared to the 1990 level, the Conclusions of the March 2007 European Council meeting provide, in particular, for a "binding target of a 20% share of renewable energies in overall EU energy consumption by 2020";

– only IG 11 specifically relates to the environment in its appeal to "encourage the sustainable use of resources and strengthen the synergies between environmental protection and growth";

– 3 of the 14 Lisbon strategy monitoring indicators chosen by the European Commission have an environmental dimension.

From the outset, it has been emphasised that the environmental objectives set by the EU could sometimes have negative consequences on the competitiveness of its companies when the latter have to meet standards and requirements to which their competitors are not subject (*e.g.*, in applying the Kyoto Protocol). This tension is all the more relevant because the EU makes those companies exposed to international competition (Kyoto 1) bear the greater part of the burden to reduce greenhouse gas emissions, while their competitors do not participate in this effort and while other sectors (such as housing) are equally significant emission producers.

The environmental issue was revisited in the framework of the new integrated Energy-Climate policy launched by the March 2007 European Council. This integration demonstrated the desire to reconcile the two dimensions and emphasise the "new energy economy" (as Lisbon 2000 emphasised the new digital economy).

III. An Essential Social Dimension

Since the launch of the Lisbon strategy, its social dimension has contributed to important debates that have been revived by the 2005 refocusing on the objectives of "growth and jobs".

---

9 See its conclusions at: http://www.consilium.europa.eu/uedocs/cms_Data/docs/pressdata/en/ec/93135.pdf.

The Lisbon strategy is often criticised in this respect, especially in France: it is seen as an essentially "liberal" growth programme, based on intensified economic competition that is incompatible with maintaining European social standards. It is true that this vision was held by certain governments. It undoubtedly also contributed to the 2005 refocusing on a growth programme, even though effectiveness considerations predominated.

Nevertheless, the reality of the Lisbon approach is, paradoxically, quite the reverse: it outlines a European development model that specifically aims for the highest levels of social (and environmental) standards. For example, this model incorporates the new need to support education and R&D expenditure. Thus, the Lisbon strategy is based on the compatibility between economic competitiveness and social standards.

A. A clear resolve to preserve European social standards

1. A strategy for social cohesion

As the Conclusions of the European Council spring meetings frequently remind us, preserving European social standards is the Lisbon strategy's final objective. These Conclusions are an appeal "to undertake both economic and social reforms as part of a positive strategy which combines competitiveness and social cohesion". The reforms should promote growth, competitiveness and employment rates that make it possible to maintain the European social model. Consequently, one can consider the ultimate aim of the Lisbon strategy to be the preservation of "European social standards" by adapting European economies facing several dynamics, principally globalisation, aging populations and technological change.

2. Reforms based on components of the European social model

As early as 2000, heads of State and government asserted that the EU should shape economic changes in progress "in a manner consistent with its values and concepts of society". "The European social model, with its developed systems of social protection, must underpin the transformation to the knowledge economy." Since then, they regularly insist on the fact that the Lisbon strategy must strive to reconcile the economic, social and environmental dimensions of growth, a reconciliation that does not seem to be such a strategic priority for the United States or emerging countries.

B. A broader vision of "social Europe"

It seems simplistic to have considered that the Lisbon strategy would be founded in a compartmentalised fashion on three separate "pillars" – economic, social and environmental – and that the "social" pillar, mainly structured by the employment guidelines, would alone narrowly embody the social dimension of the strategy. In reality, such social dimension is much more wide-ranging. *The Lisbon strategy is in fact based on a broad social vision: it incorporates the social dimension of economic policies* (liberalisation, the Stability Pact, etc.) *and is the expression of a social approach founded on the primacy of employment questions* which, unlike other social issues, commanded European consensus. In this context, the 2005 refocusing appears to reflect a desire to concentrate on structural reforms that promote growth and employment for reasons of effectiveness rather than a deliberate determination to lessen the importance of the Lisbon strategy's social (and environmental) ends.

1. The social dimension of the Economic guidelines

The resolve to defend high social standards is expressed through the different instruments of the Strategy's social pillar (the Social Agenda, Employment guidelines), but also through certain economic guidelines.

– in effect, the liberalisation of trade at the European level (*e.g.* air transport and telephony) and at the international level (*e.g.* mass market electronics and textiles), in addition to the competition policy, include a not insignificant social dimension: they may be considered to target *the protection/promotion of European consumer purchasing power* (a timely point, when purchasing power is currently a key European preoccupation). However, these policies can conflict with preserving jobs and labour conditions in the liberalised sectors concerned or have a fairly limited impact on price decreases (*e.g.* energy);

– the intergenerational social dimension of the Stability and Growth Pact put forward by the Lisbon strategy and the Integrated Guidelines for growth and jobs should also be noted: these instruments aim to *protect present and future taxpayers* against an excessive burden of debt. This point is particularly important in a country like France, where the repayment of interest on debt is the State's second biggest budget item, whereas VAT (a non-progressive tax, paid by all) is by far the leading resource.

It is not a question of claiming that all the Lisbon strategy's guidelines are necessarily positive from a social point of view, but simply of emphasising that many of them have a strong social content which cannot be reduced to a separate, hermetic "social pillar" opposed to an "economic pillar".

2. *Common social guidelines centred on the primacy of employment*

Moreover, the Lisbon strategy proposes reforming social policy around a new vision, centred on a return to employment (*workfare* rather than *welfare*). On the basis of flexicurity, it promotes a shift from passive social protection focused on job protection and unemployment benefits towards active social protection that aims to make professional career paths secure and provide dynamic support for job seekers. As far as *welfare* is concerned, it emphasises an upstream approach (early childhood, education) to avoid the *ex ante* creation of inequalities, rather than the traditional downstream approach of the welfare state (redistribution) which seeks to correct these inequalities *ex post*.

While promoting employment appeared to be a consensual objective in Europe (hence the Employment guidelines), the collective social preferences of EU countries would seem to be much more heterogeneous as they involve other social issues. General objectives can certainly be set, but it would appear difficult to link them to European legislative harmonisation.

The launch of the euro contributed to setting up the Stability and Growth Pact and establishing multilateral monitoring mechanisms because Eurozone countries were prompted to cooperate with each other to manage what economic theory describes as a common "public good". The Member States (France included) do not seem to consider that the way in which they manage their labour laws or their model of social protection can emerge from a Community approach of this kind.

Very different social situations exist in EU countries and disparities in level of development increase the difficulty of setting consensual objectives at the Community level (*e.g.* for the unemployment rate), leading Member States to have social priorities that are not necessarily convergent.

In the final analysis, it is up to each EU State to establish at the national level the social guidelines it wishes to promote and which best correspond to its characteristics and economic history. Moreover, several types of social model can be observed to coexist in the EU (see the typology produced by Esping-Anderson and completed by Boeri) and countries that perform well in relation to the Lisbon strategy objectives may have made quite different social choices (for example, Sweden and the United Kingdom).

In this context, the thesis that economic competitiveness and high social standards are incompatible should in any case be rejected for the aforementioned reasons of principle and for empirical reasons, considering, for example, the Nordic countries' successful experience with regard to both the economic and social objectives of the Lisbon strategy.

C. A social dimension which remains perfectible

1. Insufficiently visible social goals

The idea that the goal of the Lisbon strategy is essentially economic would seem to arise from two factors:

– *The existence of a legal hiatus.* The Integrated Guidelines for growth and jobs are not really integrated because, in reality, they hinge on two legal bases: the Broad Economic Policy Guidelines (BEPG) are handled by the Council of Economics and Finance Ministers on the basis of Article 99 of the EC Treaty; the Employment guidelines (EGs) are handled by the Social Affairs Ministers on the basis of Article 128 of the EC Treaty. These two political exercises are therefore conducted in parallel, giving credit to the idea that the EGs concern social matters and the BEPGs, the economy: as it happens, the BEPGs and, more precisely, European policies with economic scope can also serve the above-mentioned social dimensions (and likewise, the EGs can have economic goals).

– *Inadequate political communication.* Beyond the Conclusions of successive European Councils – which sometimes do not stress sufficiently that the Lisbon strategy is "a strategy for social cohesion" –, it is up to the national and Community authorities to provide better illustration of the fact that the Strategy's social dimension is, in reality, based on several pillars (promoting employment, preserving purchasing power, equitable tax redistribution, etc.).

2. Guidelines that are sometimes ambiguous from a social perspective

The clear resolve to preserve European social standards has not stopped the European Council from suggesting guidelines that are ambiguous from a social perspective.

Some of its guidelines do seem to express progressive choices. Such is the case for those counting on the dynamism and qualification of European human resources, from a perspective of non-cost competitiveness, which show that the goal of the Lisbon strategy is not to base the competitiveness of EU economies on the lowest social bid. Furthermore, the education and training objectives directly tally with those for social inclusion.

Other guidelines, however, may seem more controversial from a social perspective. Such is the case, for example, of the rise in the effective retirement age by roughly five years recommended by the Barcelona European Council. The aim is certainly to protect growth (with a higher employment rate for elder workers) and the level of retirement benefits, based on the implicit premise that Europeans prefer maintaining their standard of living. However, this guideline prejudges the standard-of-living/leisure trade-off desired by European populations; it also preempts the possible choices for maintaining the viability of pay-as-you-go retirement systems (the duration of contributions being only one of the conceivable adjustment variables).

The European liberalisation dynamics implemented on the basis of the Treaty of Rome and resumed by the Lisbon strategy also seem ambiguous from a social perspective. Though these liberalisations generally contribute to a drop in prices that favours European purchasing power, some of them are contemporaneous with a rise in prices (*e.g.* energy). Above all, the internal and external liberalisations promoted by the EU can be overall positive (in terms of growth, jobs, purchasing power) while penalising this or that sector or territory: these discriminatory effects raise the issue of strengthening the social adjustment and territorial convergence mechanisms implemented at the European level.

IV. A Defective Implementation Method

As explained above, the Lisbon strategy is mainly implemented on the basis of the "open method of coordination" (OMC), a very soft process of intergovernmental coordination. It is not set forth in the European treaties and was "codified" on the occasion of the Lisbon strategy[10]. OMC decisions are taken mostly by consensus. They lead to recommendations for action for Member States and the European Commission that have political significance but no binding legal power.

The OMC gives rise to very mixed opinions. For many observers interviewed by the Mission, there lies the great weakness of the Lisbon strategy: the Lisbon principles are good, but their implementation has been handicapped by OMC deficiencies – no solid legal basis, a weak decision-making capacity because of the requirement of consensus, decisions limited to *soft law* outside the realm of Community *hard law*

---

[10] It was used for the first time in the context of the European Employment Strategy ("Luxembourg Process", 1997).

instruments (directives, Community budget). Thus the difficulties posed by the Lisbon strategy appear to reside, for the most part, in the OMC.

Before looking at these opinions in detail, it is important to stress that *the use of the OMC at Community level expresses the political impossibility of using traditional EU action tools (particularly directives) in areas where Member States (and their citizens) wish to make collective choices autonomously*. The absence of a common public good and the preeminence of national competences for many economic, social and environmental issues constitute an inescapable political fact that it is vital to take into account, at least in the medium term. Let us simply recognize that, at the very least, the introduction of the OMC allowed the EU to handle subjects to which it would not otherwise have had access when this is justified by the interdependence of Member State economies and the existence of many common challenges: the Lisbon strategy should be evaluated in this legal and political context – the advantages and limits of which are recalled below – and which made it a sort of remedial measure to the slowdown of the Internal Market's integration dynamic in the 1990s.

A. The undeniable merits of the OMC

1. A consensus-building method

– This virtue of the OMC can be illustrated in respect of the *employment rate*, for example, or – more recently – *flexicurity*: it was not self-evident that a consensus could exist and spread to the level of national public discourse, as is now the case, ten years after the launch of the European Employment Strategy;

– some of the Lisbon strategy objectives have become symbolic (*3% R&D expenditure*, for example): in a way, criticism that the Strategy has not been correctly implemented is itself proof of the support that the Strategy enjoys;

– *if one thinks in terms of trends*, many of the objectives defined by the European Council have led to efforts and progress for the vast majority of EU Member States (see Annex 1).

2. A method that stimulates the exchange of good practices and the resolve to draw inspiration from successful countries

Regarding the OMC's benchmarking potential, three types of initiative can be pointed out:

– the many workshops held by the European Commission;

– the working groups constituted at national government level in a bilateral or multilateral framework;

– lastly, the many comparisons or rankings produced by think tanks and the European media which also stimulate the resolve to draw inspiration from good national practices.

3. *An evaluation of national performance that is also stimulating*

– the performance evaluation of EU countries in reference to a limited list of 14 structural indicators contributes to producing a synthetic vision of their performances, making them instantly comparable;

– the practice of creating "rolls of honour" is sometimes used by the European Commission, particularly in its 2007 "Strategic report", which – for many major issues – indicates which country group has been successful;

– the annual adoption of "recommendations" and "points to monitor" by countries helps define the nature of the reforms that the Member States need to promote;

– lastly, "peer pressure" is put on EU Member States since the country-specific recommendations proposed by the European Commission are decided on by the Council of Ministers.

B. Deficiencies and negative effects

1. *The problem of the clarity of the Lisbon strategy objectives*

- A constant tension between a broad and a "refocused" approach

Since the Lisbon strategy was launched, it has been through different versions that are in part mutually contradictory and over-ambitious in view of the means allocated to them.

In its initial version (2000), the Strategy sought to make Europe "the most competitive and dynamic knowledge-based economy in the world" by 2010, without doubt an unrealistic objective whose symbolic character has greatly harmed the Strategy's credibility. By emphasising sustainable development in 2001, it tended to target an ideal European economy – at once competitive, social and ecological.

After four years of relative insignificance, and following the 2004 Kok report, the Lisbon strategy was refocused on "growth and jobs" with an improved governance (IGs, NRPs, etc.) in March 2005.

Lastly, in 2007, Lisbon was promoted to the status of being the "European response to globalisation", in particular by adding the energy/ climate agenda and the external dimension.

These variations first raise the issue of coherence: besides the over-ambitious nature of the 2000-2001 objectives, the 2005 refocusing on growth and jobs – which today commands consensus – diverges from the exhaustive version of the Lisbon strategy (competitive, social and environmental). Likewise, there is tension between the 2005 refocusing and the recent promotion of the Lisbon agenda as the "European response to globalisation", a tension which haunts the new 2008-2010 cycle.

Moreover, these different versions of the same strategy produce serious counterproductive effects. First of all, they sustain the confusion over objectives and affect the legibility and credibility of the process.

This failing has not spared the new version of the Lisbon strategy which, by claiming to be a "European response to globalisation", now purports to include fields that fall mainly or even exclusively under Community jurisdiction, without distinguishing in that ensemble between the different types of competences, as the Lisbon Treaty suggests doing.

- Dispersed objectives, without apparent overall coherence

– although the "growth and jobs" slogan adopted for the 2005 relaunch stressed these two priorities, there is no clear distinction between the final and intermediate objectives;

– trend objectives (*e.g.* raising by five years the effective age retirement age) are mixed with level-specific objectives (*e.g.*, a 70% employment rate);

– the figure-based objectives chosen by the European Council are rarely cited in the IG text, with the exception of the 3% GDP objective for R&D expenditure and the 70% overall employment rate objective: the other figure-based objectives laid down by successive European Councils are simply mentioned in the IG "comments" section; as a result, they have less legal power, even though they were adopted at the highest political level;

– in liaison with the Council, the European Commission identified very many "structural indicators" to monitor the implementation of the Lisbon strategy then, in 2005, adopted a "limited list" of 14 indicators. But these indicators only partially tally with the figure-based objectives set by the European Council; moreover, in its "2007 Strategic report", the Commission mentioned a series of objectives (such as high-speed Internet access) that do not coincide with the 14 structural indicators.

As a result, a crucial question arises: what are the objectives that are really identified by the Lisbon strategy, apart from 3% growth, a 70% employment rate and a level of R&D expenditure at 3% of GDP? Though the difficulty of defining clear consensual objectives is partly linked to that of getting Member States to agree, can the European Commission not stick to a limited number of monitoring indicators that are defined once and for all?

2. *The risk of blurring the allocation of competences and weakening European ambition*

In effect, the Lisbon strategy has become identified with a soft intergovernmental coordination in terms of governance. The OMC is legitimate only when it is impossible to make progress otherwise in areas that mainly fall under national jurisdiction: micro-economic structures, employment, social issues, education, research, etc. However unsatisfactory it may be, the OMC thus has the incontestable virtue of helping European coordination make headway where the EC does not have strong legitimacy to intervene.

- Blurring the allocation of competences

However, the blurring of the Lisbon agenda's content with regard to the respective competences of the EU and its Member States – and, more precisely, the tendency of the Commission and Member States to include more and more subjects and policies in this framework, even making it the all inclusive framework of European economic and social policies, without modifying its method of governance – leads to a dispersal of Community competences within a heterogeneous whole that mainly operates as an intergovernmental process.

The criticisms made at the start of the Lisbon strategy (Who does what?), and which the 2004 Kok report repeated, were partly dealt with by the 2005 "relaunch", but uncertainties remain:

– *uncertainties about the method*: the NRP-Community Programme distinction marks real progress, but the Community Programme draws up a list of actions without distinguishing their different natures, whereas the Lisbon treaty signed in December 2007 clearly distinguishes between the exclusive competences of the EU and shared or coordinated competences;

– *substantive uncertainties*, linked to the lingering impression that the EU is venturing into areas where it is scarcely legitimate and poorly equipped to act, and that – consequently – it should refocus on its fundamentals and its added value, *i.e.*, its exclusive competences as identified by the treaties and financial interventions made possible by the

Community budget. Above and beyond this, the EU should change the narrative of its economic and social strategy by placing it explicitly within the framework of globalisation.

- The "check list" syndrome

The Lisbon strategy is not really a growth strategy for the EU that will lead to the coordinated implementation of Community and national policies with adequate means: it looks sometimes more like an OECD-style "check list" from which each State can pick and choose.

Worse still: from being an intelligent remedy for the difficulties of Community deepening, it has gradually become the instrument of a kind of dilution of European ambition. *In effect, the OMC tends to contaminate the whole range of Community processes* through the spread of *soft law* (communications, recommendations, Commission staff papers, etc.), *a-la-carte* directives (Takeover, Working time, Copyright, etc.), resulting is a decline in harmonisation.

C. A deficit in political ownership

Another criticism directed at the implementation of the Lisbon strategy concerns the variable – but, on the whole, limited – political involvement of EU and Member State authorities, who too often turn it into an essentially bureaucratic process, without constraints and clear stakes. Measurements of the degree of political ownership, made in particular by Jean Pisani-Ferry and André Sapir, confirm that *the extent to which the Lisbon strategy is taken into account by the main national stakeholders varies greatly accross the EU.* It is mainly a question of government authorities' "monitoring level" and the involvement of parliaments. This undoubtedly explains the relatively "confidential" character of the Lisbon strategy.

The Lisbon strategy's degree of ownership

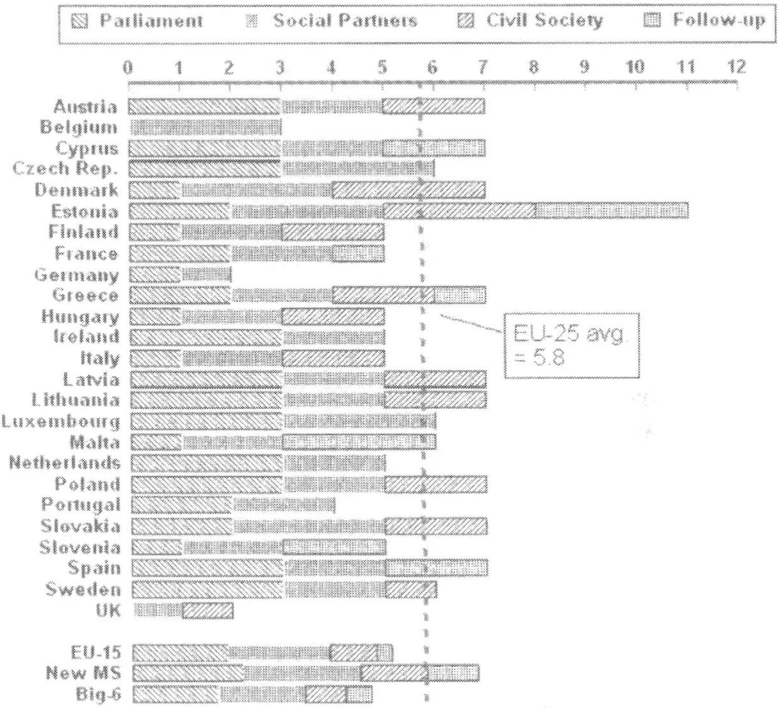

Source: Jean Pisani-Ferry and André Sapir, *Last Exit to Lisbon*, Bruegel, March 2006.

This overall deficiency in political ownership is due to two factors.

1. The OMC's intrinsic inadequacies

In addition to the problems linked to a lack of clear objectives and shared responsibilities between national and Community levels, there are also those connected with *setting general objectives that are not adapted to all countries*. This creates a perspective that is demotivating for countries that are too far from those objectives and unstimulating for those that are already close:

Such is the case with the objectives related to the knowledge-based economy (R&D expenditure equal to 3% of GDP) which concern economically mature countries with many companies close to the "technology frontier"[11] rather than countries in the catching-up phase. Even if

[11] According to Philippe Aghion, in an economic system situated at the technological frontier, most business sectors have reached a maximum level of productivity.

Member States have been invited to define their own objectives, the overall objective of 3% has been laid down and all national efforts are measured by this yardstick.

The same is true of the objectives for the female employment rate (60%) and the percentage of children attending subsidised structures (100% of those between 3 and 6 years of age), which clash with the heterogeneous nature of social and family structures in EU-27 countries.

2. *The more or less receptive character of national politico-administrative systems*

In new Member States, the European framework has positive connotations and is seen as a force for modernisation, whereas it is much more controversial in older Member States (as the results of the 2005 referendums show).

Small countries also tend to be more receptive than large ones to the technical assistance and political pressure provided by the Lisbon strategy.

This ownership deficiency strengthens doubts about how far Europe's good recent economic results can really be attributed to the Lisbon strategy rather than to macro-economic cycles or the determination of certain Member States to reform. After all, the Scandinavian countries, who lead the Lisbon "awards list", began reforming their economies back in the 1990s, before the Lisbon strategy was launched...

CHAPTER II

2000-2008
New Challenges, New Opportunities

The Lisbon strategy's track record with regard to the challenges identified in 2000 is, thus, mixed. The EU's shortfalls in wealth, productivity and innovation when compared with the United States were not reduced in the 2000-2007 period and, though some figure-based objectives have given rise to significant progress, most have not been reached.

A proper assessment of Lisbon's track record should also take account of developments in the European and international context since the strategy was launched. The world and the EU itself have changed considerably, and although the Lisbon strategy too has evolved over the passing years, it has not kept pace with the challenges.

Europe is facing two series of new challenges that should prompt it to upgrade its post-2010 response strategy to globalisation: external challenges arising from changes in its international environment and internal challenges linked to the EU's own development.

Most of these challenges also present opportunities; Europe must also learn how to seize them by better leveraging its assets.

Although it lies in the background of this report, the international impact of the American financial crisis is not specifically dealt with because of remaining uncertainties about its scope, economic repercussions and durability, and the EU economy's resilience as at the date of completion of this report. However, it is clear that the resulting weakening of the international financial system argues in favour of public authorities reinvesting the financial sphere, and Europe's participation in this process. The global financial, food and energy crisis that materialized in 2008 can only reinforce the need for a true external economic strategy for Europe.

I. A Rapidly Changing World

Though the main characteristics of globalisation had already been clearly identified in 2000 (the emergence of new players, the central role of information technology, the establishment of an international division of intra-sectoral and intra-company labour, etc.), *the globalisation process has greatly accelerated since then.* The EU and its Member States are now confronted with an economic game where the speed at which productive systems adapt has become even more critical in maximising gains and reducing losses linked to integration in international trade.

What is more, the acceleration of the globalisation process seems to have led to the emergence of *new challenges and opportunities* which were less sharply apparent in 2000 and, faced with which the EU must adapt its political, economic and social strategy.

A. The "Internal Market": still a relevant horizon?

The data concerning foreign direct investment (FDI) stocks and the average annual trade flows of EU countries show that the Single Market remains, today, the main horizon for European economies, and that the share of third countries (the United States, China, etc.) is for the time being relatively small. Nevertheless, trade flows between the EU and the rest of the world have recently increased more than intra-Community trade flows, and FDI flows out of the EU have also risen markedly.

These recent movements show that the EU and its companies are rightly striving to take advantage of the more dynamic growth of non-European economic areas, particularly Asia. However, they also raise more questions about the relevance of the European Internal Market as a medium-term economic growth horizon, *since gains in growth from pursuing European integration would seem too limited compared to those made through trade and investment with other regions of the world.* Major companies, operating on a worldwide playing field, can be particularly sensitive to questions of this sort, even though they have always supported the creation of the Common Market, followed by the Single Market. The relative erosion of economic elites' support for European unification in the 2000 decade could be partly linked to these diminishing returns.

Average annual GDP growth rate between 1996 and 2005 (in %)

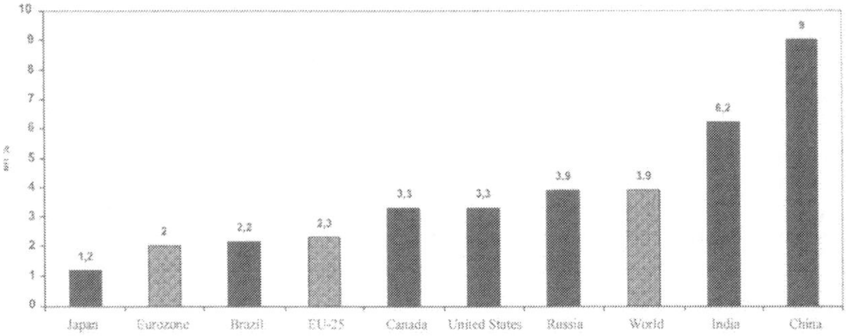

Source: IMF.

The idea that the EU should bank on overseas markets rather than its own "Internal Market" is further fostered by *difficulties encountered in pursuing the European market integration process*:

- the liberalisation of certain network industries (energy) has given rise to many national reservations (blocking some takeover bids under the guise of "economic patriotism", union resistance, etc.), without always producing significant effects in terms of price reduction;
- the liberalisation of the service sector – which has still made little headway in Europe – gave rise to a wide-ranging controversy in 2005 and the adoption of an amended directive whose concrete effects on the sector's liberalisation have yet to be measured;
- tax harmonisation, subject to unanimity rule, has been at a total standstill for a long time.

Thus, the accelerating pace of globalisation and the difficulties encountered in pursuing the European economic integration process are also confronted by a relatively new challenge with regard to the historic dynamic launched by the Treaty of Rome. Faced with this challenge, the admission of new Member States enabled the EU to preserve a stable economic weight in the global economy, even though its performance was not as good as the rest of the world's.

Unlike the integration process, the European consensus in favour of enlargement remains very strong. Following the twelve new Member States who joined in 2004 and 2007, there is the prospect of new admissions in the Balkans. Even though a pause in the process is inevitable, this dynamic should not be allowed to run dry.

Enlargement enables Europe to absorb its margins and integrate geographical areas of the globalisation process that are now becoming a relevant economic horizon. This is clearly the case with the new Member States that offer an intra-European alternative to relocation in Asia and that are poised to become the EU's new engine of economic growth. It would also be the case with Turkey and Ukraine, strategic countries in global geopolitics, even if Turkey's membership continues to raise a considerable number of questions.

B. The rising power of the emerging countries

The rising power of the emerging countries – particularly the "BRIC" (Brazil, Russia, India and China) – was already perceived and forecast in the year 2000. Yet, this phenomenon confronts European economies with a renewed challenge: though they still have to *take advantage of the growth of these countries by competing with their alternative suppliers (particularly the United States and Japan), they also have to confront increasing competition from these rapidly expanding economies* (some of which, like Korea, no longer even belong to the category of emerging countries). This is true in many sectors and is no longer limited to manufactured or low-end products.

In the course of the 2000-2007 period, the (albeit planned) end of the "Multifibre Arrangement" (MFA) in 2005 raised many fears about the life expectancy of a European textile industry and the introduction of transitional protection measures. The latter have mostly been lifted, on the basis of an analysis that is relatively in line with the initial premises of the Lisbon strategy. Sectors such as the textile industry should develop more in emerging countries that produce at lower cost, much to the advantage of European consumers; European countries may retain production that targets top-end products thanks to their added value and their proximity to markets.

Since these controversies about textile competition from emerging countries are mostly behind us, we should now question whether the European approach can be maintained in the face of the rising capacity of these countries in producing goods with high added value. This question concerns the very core of the Lisbon strategy, which was launched in a context of the EU's economic and technological gap with the United States and the advent of the "new economy", based on the observation that the United States (and the other OECD countries) are Europe's main competitors, that their competitiveness is largely based on added value without any marked advantage in terms of labour costs, and that we should therefore count on education and R&D to "catch up" and compete with them.

This European prioritisation of education and R&D is of even greater relevance faced with competition from emerging countries when countries like China or India have already begun major drives to promote higher education, qualifications and R&D, particularly by training engineers and researchers in comparable numbers to the European contingents. But *the lower level of compensation of Asian researchers and engineers is likely to change the premises on which the Lisbon strategy was founded.*

By way of example, between 2004 and 2005 the increase in the number of patents filed in Europe was much lower than in the United States, Korea and China; the last of these countries saw a spectacular increase of over 32%.

Number of patents filed in 2005 and increase compared with 2004 (in %)

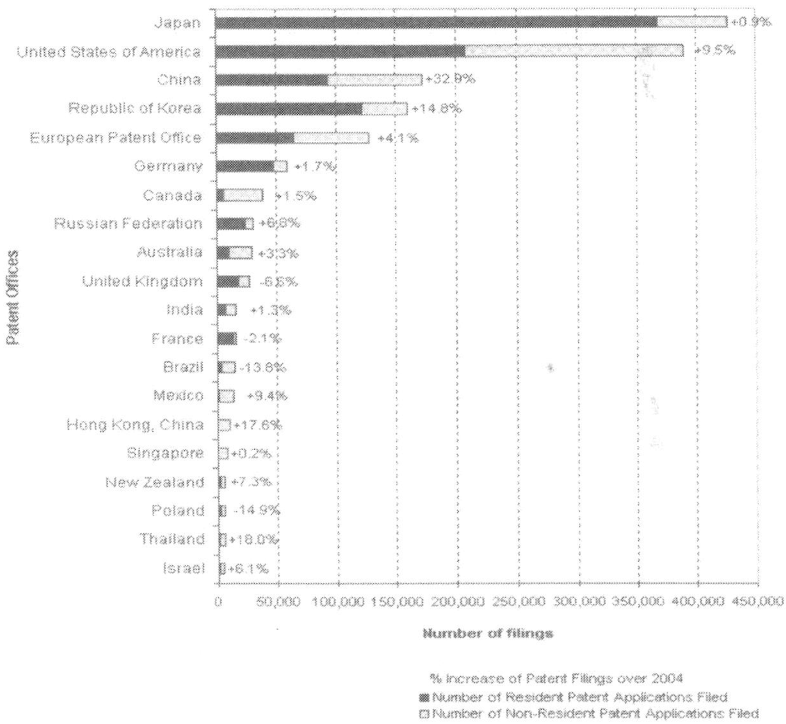

Source: World Intellectual Property Organization, Patent report: Statistics on Worldwide Patent Activity (2007 Edition).

In any event, the EU can no longer base its economic and social strategy on the premise of a clear-cut international division of labour that reserves unfinished or manufactured products and price competition for emerging countries while Europe and developed countries engage in activities with high added value, principally based on innovation and a qualified labour force. This fact constitutes a particularly clear challenge for the EU in general and the Lisbon strategy in particular.

However, the rising power of emerging countries should not solely be presented from the perspective of the competitive threat they pose to Europe. The gradual emergence of 2.4 billion people on the planet from the shadow of poverty can only be welcomed. And it also represents a tremendous economic opportunity for Europe from two points of view.

The production model developed in countries like China is based, above all, on the presence of western companies. It is our companies that ensure China's economic success, and they make part of the profits. Thus, in 2005, EU FDI outflows to the BRIC countries generated revenue of 23 billion euros – 50% of which was for China and 27% for Brazil. Moreover, the return on European investments in the BRIC countries has greatly increased – from a 6% rate of return in 2001 to 11% in 2004.

Rate of return (in %) on EU investments in BRIC countries

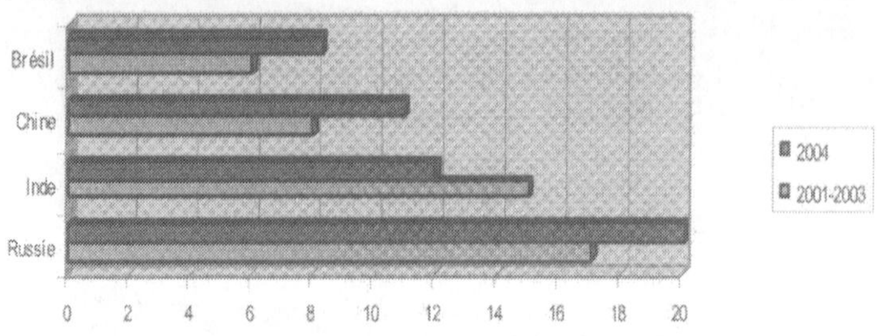

Source: Eurostat.

Above all, these gigantic, rapidly developing countries constitute a huge pool of growth for the industrialised world. The EU-25 FDI inflows from BRIC countries, following a slump in 2003, thus increased.

EU-25 FDI inflows from BRIC countries (in millions of EUR)

	2001	2002	2003	2004	2005
Extra-EU	145,867	126,567	123,541	53,072	94,149
BRIC	11,975	4,240	2,167	8,812	11,287
Brazil	1,023	599	- 878	4,014	5,488
Russia	752	342	704	196	4,107
India	108	133	615	1	220
China	10,092	3,166	1,726	4,601	1,472
Hong Kong *portion*	9,545	2,925	1,436	4,748	1,071

Source: Eurostat.

To be sure, the emerging countries' development model is not based on internal consumption, but on exports. Its tendency, in fact, is to curb wages (and thus consumption) to improve external competitiveness. But the example of South Korea's development shows that gradually, social demands grow stronger for fair distribution of the added value and, today, Korean wages have made up their shortfall; they are at the same level as British wages (outside London). The emerging countries are getting richer and, in the long run, will have consumer markets that are similar to Western markets. What is more, these markets have already started taking off. Thus, between 2006 and 2007, EU exports towards emerging economies greatly increased: +20% for India and China, +13% for Russia.

C. The increasingly geopolitical nature of globalisation

Though globalisation is still driven by the dynamics of economic openness (access to the market economy and trade liberalisation) and even political dynamics (progress towards democracy), it is also characterised by *two striking phenomena, namely the emergence of new major economic and political powers (that are neither European nor Western) and the development of a set of tensions based on issues of identity and geopolitics.*

Energy issues are already among the highest ranking international concerns of our times, mainly because they lie at the juncture of economics and geopolitics.

The fact that most energy resources are located on a geopolitical crescent of crisis (the Persian Gulf, Central Asia, North Africa, the Caucasus, Muslim Africa, etc.) encourages power strategies on the part of the producing countries, which use their resources as a political weapon (Russia, the Gulf States, Iran, Venezuela, etc.), and the deployment of an intense "energy diplomacy" by consumer countries (China, the United States, etc.), which weighs heavily on world prices.

This dramatisation of energy stakes portends the growing politicisation of economic strategies throughout the planet and invests globalisation with a geopolitical dimension that is today much more marked than it was in the year 2000. *With their prestigious national histories and structured by strong traditions of state control, the major emerging countries are using their economic upswing for strategies to win back lost power.* This is notably the case with Vladimir Putin's Russia and, more discreetly, Chinese economic diplomacy in Africa and Central Asia, or the acquisition of major western industrial assets by companies and sovereign wealth funds (SWFs) from emerging countries.

SWF assets growth (2006-2016) (in %)

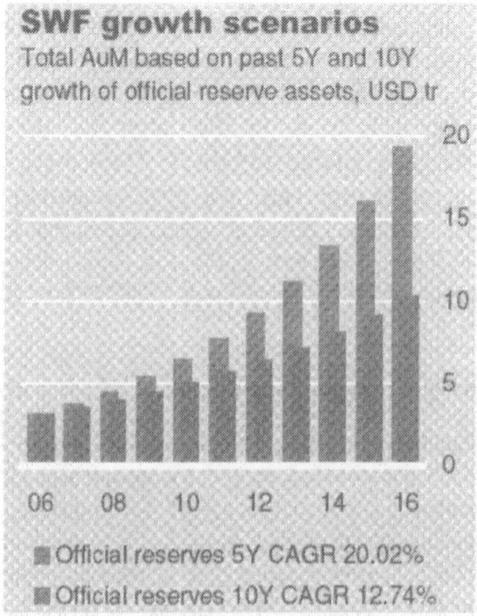

Source: Deutsche Bank Research, Sovereign Wealth Funds, 2007.

That being the case, one may wonder whether the EU is today sufficiently equipped to confront this new situation, since it does not have the same instruments as the continental scale nations that are, at one and the same time, its partners and its competitors:

- European unification has largely been founded on the resolve to control the potentially destructive use of national sovereignty, both politically and economically. It has led to strict limitations on Member States' interventions in sectors that are considered "strategic", without so far clearly defining what the economic "European strategic interests" are (the 2003 adoption of a "European Security Strategy" has not had any visible economic repercussions);
- European unification has largely been based on producing rules of Community law rather than instituting players capable of producing policy choices adapted to a fast-changing environment. Today, the EU only has a few "integrated" action tools (competition policy, trade policy, monetary policy), the use of which is entrusted to bodies whose statutes and missions are defined by the Member States;
- as far as institutions are concerned, European unification has led to the establishment of "shared sovereignty" between Member States on the one hand, and EU institutions on the other, which is much

slower and more complex to exercise than is the case in nation states, and highly centralised (and sometimes authoritarian) countries;

- lastly, on the diplomatic front, Europe continues to project its values of peace and law – and its multilateral credo – onto a world marked by the return of power strategies and realpolitik.

Yet the increasingly geopolitical character of globalisation can open up new opportunities for Europe. In fact, many emerging countries are geographically and historically close, making Europe a favoured strategic partner: Russian and the Caucasian Republics, Mediterranean crescent countries in Africa and the Middle East.

The global economy's swing towards Asia certainly risks undermining the preeminence of the transatlantic economy in favour of an American-Asian duopoly. But the relative decline of American power in the diplomatic and economic spheres offers Europe an opportunity to become a third credible and stabilising force in global geopolitics, if it provides itself with the necessary means.

Whatever the case, these developments constitute a major stake for the EU in the run up to 2010 and beyond.

D. Energy and climate challenges

The previously mentioned fact that energy questions have now risen to the highest rank of international concerns constitutes another challenge that the EU has already partly sized up by announcing the launch of an "integrated European climate and energy policy" at the March 2007 European Council meeting. It now has to give substance to that policy in an international context marked by increasing uncertainty about the security, sustainability and cost of energy supplies against a backdrop of global warming and scarcity. The EU is 56.2% energy dependent, even though the degree of dependence varies greatly among Member States, from -58.8% for Denmark to 105.5% for Cyprus.

The *sharp rise in the cost of raw materials in the 2000-2007 period* indicates, first of all, that globalisation is not only a deflationary supply shock for the EU, but that it can also be an inflationary demand shock. The question of access to raw materials is all the more strategic for EU countries, which are currently 55% dependent on external supplies and are set to be 80% dependent in 2030: this increases the need to adopt joint positions (including with the United States) rather than negotiating with producing countries without a united front.

Commodity prices January 2002 = 100

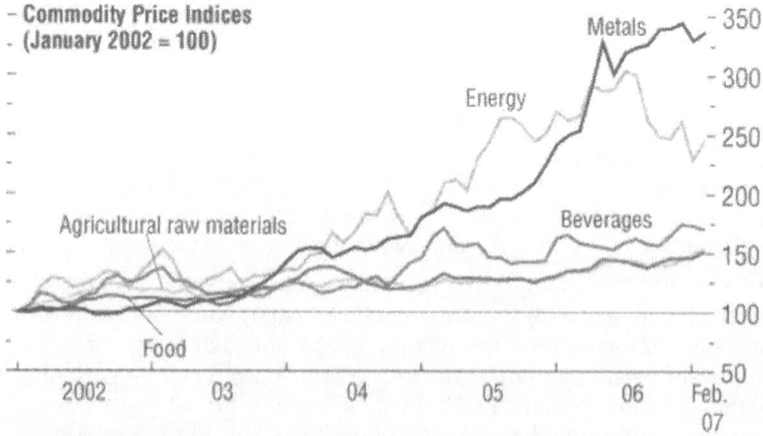

Source: IMF, *World Economic Outlook*, 2007.

The rise in demand for agricultural raw materials can also change the EU's position at the international level. It could allow for a reduction in the level of financial support required by the CAP in favor of other instruments of its globalisation strategy.

As far as climate change is concerned, the EU is expected to respect the commitments it made under the Kyoto Protocol and even to consolidate them further (in the aftermath of the Bali Climate Change Conference), which raises many questions that are more urgent today than they were in 2000:

– should the EU continue to impose environmental constraints on itself that are burdensome to its competitiveness when its main competitors (the United States and China) dispense with them and, in any case, the target objectives will be difficult to achieve (the United States is responsible for a quarter of greenhouse gas emissions)?

Up to 2030, there will be moderate increases in CO_2 emissions in the EU, most of the OECD countries and Russia, but high increases everywhere else:

CO_2 emissions in 2003 and by 2030 (in millions of tons of CO_2)

	2003	*2030*	*Increase in %*
North Africa	295	604	+104%
Brazil	303	626	***+106%***
Sub-Saharan Africa	468	1,031	+120%
Latin America	547	1,153	+110%
Russia	1,515	2,003	+32%
The Middle East	1,102	2,191	+99%
India	1,050	2,283	***+ 117%***
Pacific OECD	2,025	2,319	+14%
Asia	1,291	3,052	***+136%***
EU	3,789	4,219	***+11%***
China	3,760	7,173	***+90.7%***
North America OECD	6,620	8,387	***+26%***

Source: International Energy Agency, *World Energy Outlook*, 2005.

– most of Europe's efforts to reduce greenhouse gas emissions are imposed upon the manufacturing industry, which is only responsible for a quarter of emissions (23% of global greenhouse gas emissions globally after reallocating electricity across sectors[1]) and which, furthermore, is exposed to international competition that is not burdened with the same constraints. If we can find a way out of this paradox, should it not lead to applying the effort to reduce emissions after 2012 to other sectors, namely agriculture (26% of emissions), the residential and service sector (22% of emissions) and road transport (12% of emissions)?

– following the example of the United States, should not the EU and its Member States promote the development of "clean technologies" to a greater extent, encouraging company advances in R&D and innovation (*e.g.* CO_2 capture or progress in producing less polluting motor vehicles). In other words, while the new economy based on ICTs was the major prospect when the Lisbon strategy was launched, should not the "new green economy" referred to in the Stern report establish itself as such in the run up to 2010 and beyond?

Climate change may be a challenge, but it is also in fact an outstanding opportunity, because the "green revolution" will have major consequences for the economy. It will generate a new economic sector. This sector is already significant (1,000 billion euros worldwide). It is expected to show strong growth. It should be one of the driving forces of tomorrow's innovation economy, as much in terms of growth as of employment.

1 IPCC and IEA figures cited in "Changement climatique : le défi majeur", French National Assembly, April 2006

Several recent studies have shown that despite the job losses certain sectors in particular will suffer (notably metallurgy and energy), the overall impact on employment will be largely positive[2]. This is because "green" industries and services are in fact employment-intensive. For example, the Biomass Action Plan[3] could make it possible to create between 250,000 and 300,000 jobs within the EU-25. Wind energy, an expanding sector, already employs 120,000 people in Germany, Denmark and Spain alone. In terms of energy, equipment manufacturing and the building and setting up of electricity generating stations could increase the dynamism of these sectors by 23%. The transport sector also has major growth potential; the number of jobs directly or indirectly linked to rail transport and public transport could quadruple. The extension of the European directive on the energy performance of buildings will make it possible to create between 150,000 and 180,000 jobs. Work on high energy quality could represent the creation of a million jobs[4].

Europe is well-positioned to seize these opportunities. It is the economic leader of the green economy, has a technological advantage in many fields and its standards are likely to be exported throughout the world.

II. The EU Today... and Tomorrow

The EU has itself transformed since the year 2000: some of these changes are immediately perceptible, such as the shift from 15 to 27 Member States or the introduction of the euro. Others should also be underlined because they constitute new political challenges compared to the situation that prevailed when the Lisbon strategy was launched.

A. A heterogeneous Union

First and foremost, the EU is much more heterogeneous than it was in 2000, not only politically, but also economically and socially.

In economic and social matters, the EU is now marked by much more sharply differentiated levels of wealth between its Member States.

---

2 Source: Study produced by a consortium led by the Social Development Agency and the European Trade Union Confederation, Syndex, the Wuppertal Institute and the Istas Institute (2007).

3 Communication from the Commission of 7 December 2005, Biomass action plan, 2005 (COM) 728. Biomass refers to all organic vegetable or animal products used for energy (or agricultural) purposes and currently represents approximately half (44 to 65%) of the renewable energy used in the EU.

4 Source: See above.

This economic and social heterogeneity could require *new social adjustments, since it leads to countries with very low wages being admitted into the EU.* The trend of relocating within the EU that started in the course of 2000-2007 gave rise to a lively controversy when the "Services Directive" was to be voted on, and the freedom to provide services was the subject of two important decisions by the European Court of Justice (the Viking and Laval cases). Discussions relating to the optimum degree of tax differentiation in an area as heterogeneous as the EU have also been relaunched.

More generally speaking, the co-existence within the EU of economies that are "mature", "converging" or "catching up" – or countries close to the technological frontier and others far from it – makes it more difficult to implement the Lisbon strategy on the basis of undifferentiated objectives.

GDP per inhabitant in purchasing power standard in 2006 (Average EU-27 = 100)

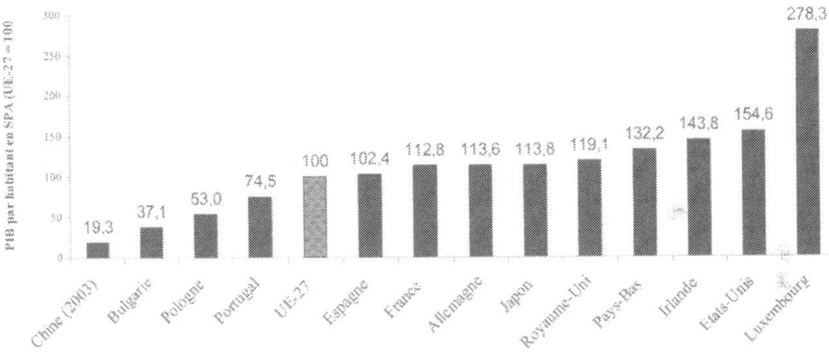

Source: Eurostat.

The EU has also become more heterogeneous in political terms since the Lisbon strategy was launched, not only because it has more members, but also with regard to economic and social topics on which reaching European consensus is a delicate matter due to the diversity of collective preferences and national situations.

Although from the outset the Lisbon strategy has always been a compromise between different approaches (the traditional "liberal" component, the "endogenous growth" component, etc.), it is notable that European countries that are more divided on these issues may be tempted only to opt for what suits them, thereby weakening the coherence of the whole.

In some respects, this heterogeneity can become a source of opportunities. Economically speaking, these opportunities are to be found in terms of the available range of comparative advantages and direct investments (the possibility of investing in very different countries, in Eurozone countries or outside the Eurozone). Unlike the United States, the EU no longer needs to leave its own borders to find low-cost workshops. Thus, Europe has become a "scale model of the global economy" with its drawbacks but also its advantages.

In more global political terms, enlargement also provides opportunities for Europe, helping it become a major player in the globalised economy. First, enlargement brings Europe into contact with the main areas of global geostrategic importance: the Mediterranean, the Middle East, Russia and the Caucasus. Second, enlargement invests Europe with increased economic, diplomatic and demographic influence. In economic terms, particularly, the EU is the world's leading power, with 17% of world trade in 2006 (29%, if one includes intra-Community trade), 26% of world service exports in 2006, 17% of world exports for high-tech products (*i.e.*, first place), and 21% of FDI world flows for 2005[5]. Given their dynamism, the new Member States are also likely to become the enduring engine of European growth, which has so far been lethargic.

B. Growing old

The EU's aging population is now an established fact, as – in most Member States – we observe *waves of people belonging to the huge baby boomer generation reaching retirement age*. Furthermore, these retirements are occurring at a time when the EU is conspicuous as the *area of the world that has the lowest fertility rate* (with the relative exception of France, where the rate is 2 children per woman). The proportion of the working population under 40 years of age will therefore decrease considerably between now and 2025 (see graph below).

These demographic dynamics lead, first of all, to a *very sharp rise in retirement and health expenditures compared to the year 2000* (see Annex 4), which imposes economic adjustments (the senior citizen employment rate) and social adjustments (the financing method for social welfare systems) that are almost as substantial as the adjustments required to adapt to the globalised economy.

Moreover, they would seem to *spur European countries to resort increasingly to an immigrant work force if they wish to maintain their standard of living in the short and medium term* (a hypothetical upturn in the European fertility rate would not produce its effects until 2025).

---

5 Source: Eurostat.

This new factor should incite EU countries to position themselves better on the global qualified labour market, improve their integration policies for immigrant populations and produce co-development strategies that aim to stabilise poor and emerging countries (the European Neighbourhood Policy, a more or less extensive partnership with countries of the southern Mediterranean shore and African countries). *These many challenges, scarcely or never mentioned by the Lisbon strategy, should form a major component of the European strategy for globalisation after 2010.*

Proportion of the active population aged under 40 (2000-2025)
Age pyramid for European active workers (2000)

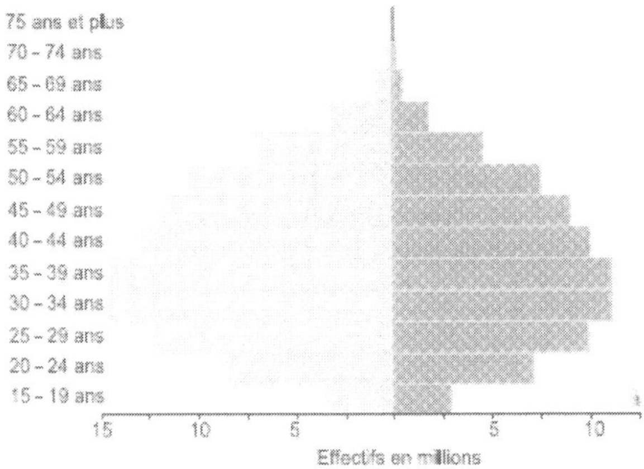

Age pyramid for European active workers (2025)

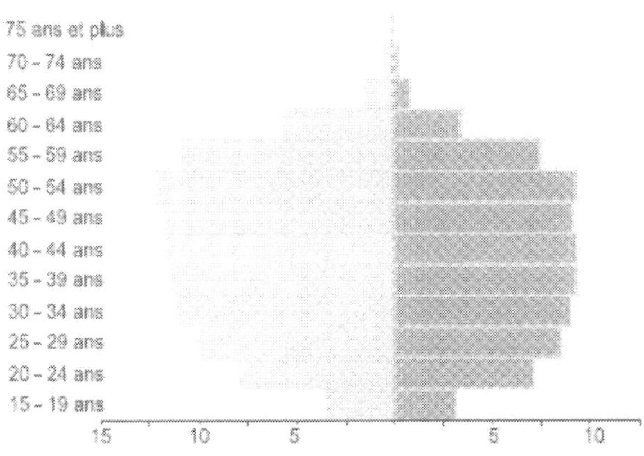

Source: Institut Montaigne, *Compétitivité et vieillissement*, 2003.

The challenge of an aging population has at least one positive side: all regions of the world will end up going in this direction – the western countries, of course, but also (very rapidly), emerging countries like China whose restrictive birth-control policy will soon lead to an aging population within the generation of the present working population, in the next twenty years. Europe (along with Japan) will have been through this experience first and made headway on the "senior citizen economy" experience curve: personal support services, health industries, tourism for the elderly, etc.

C. EMU's unfinished business

The introduction of the euro in 2002 and its use by 15 of the EU-27 countries have encouraged the free movement of capital, goods and services within the Single Market, while protecting many Member States against the currency fluctuations and speculations that used to accompany periods of economic or political crisis.

Real exchange rates of the euro, the dollar and the yen from 2000 to 2007
Real effective exchange rates. Deviation from 1980-2007 average

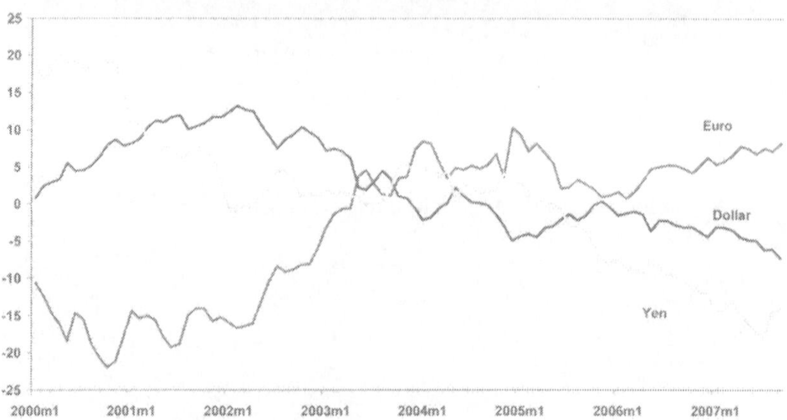

Source: IMF, *World Economic Outlook*, 2007.

Furthermore, the introduction of the euro has been accompanied by two phenomena that did not exist in the early years of the 2000 decade:

- first, *a sharp appreciation in exchange rates between the euro and the dollar and the renminbi*, which has had the advantage of reducing import prices (particularly energy imports) and the disadvantage of handicapping certain European industries' price-competitiveness (*e.g.*, the aeronautics industry);

- second *a mixed effect on the implementation of national economic policies*. Though the introduction of the Stability and Growth Pact resulted in the EU controlling national public accounts fairly strictly, the disappearance of the external currency constraints (risks of devaluation) also seems to have resulted in certain EU countries (Italy, France, etc.) relaxing their efforts for structural reform (in this respect, the creation of the Economic and Monetary Union has acted as a "reform trap").

These two phenomena contribute to a recurrent debate on *the Eurozone's "economic governance"*. The debate is particularly marked in France and less central in many other EU countries, and the way in which it is treated would also seem to represent a major challenge in the run up to 2010 and beyond.

Nevertheless, this reality should not allow us to forget the tremendous opportunity that the euro constitutes[6]. With the plummeting dollar, the euro is set to become the second international reserve currency. The "globalisation" of the euro brings with it considerable advantages for Europe: protection against currency fluctuations, the ability to influence European competitiveness through monetary policy, the constitution of a vast financial market in euros, and potentially making it easier to finance deficits.

What is more, the euro constitutes the Internal Market's monetary superstructure. By creating a vast Single Market and continental scale companies, Europe is leaving behind its historical economic fragmentation and presenting an increasingly unified economy with a critical mass that should help it not only resist, but also influence, globalisation. No economic player in the world can ignore Europe, its currency and its market of 500 million consumers.

D. New forms of euroscepticism

The Lisbon strategy was launched in an economic climate of strong growth within the EU (averaging about 3%) and a context of overall support for European unification. This political context has also changed considerably since then:

- the *rejection by referendum of the proposed "European Constitution" by France and The Netherlands* expressed the relative mistrust

[6] See, for example, European Central Bank, *Review of the International Role of the Euro*, 2007.

of the populations of two founding Member States regarding the European project;

- the previously mentioned *doubts within some economic sectors concerning the Internal Market and the EU's added value* in a context of global competition should also be taken into account. A natural ally of large corporations, the EU is increasingly coming under fire, especially for its propensity to produce economic, health, social and environmental standards that are expensive and/or considered to be unsuited to the current phase of globalisation;
- the European dynamic has largely run dry within national governments. Institutional negotiations – virtually continuous since 1990 (the treaties of Maastricht, Amsterdam, Nice, the European Convention, the Lisbon Treaty, Lisbon implementation negotiations, etc.) – have been a succession of distressing total or partial failures. There is now broad consensus in favour of a long pause, and the required revival of the European project is by no means self-evident.
- in more general terms, European unification is henceforth confronted with the need to provide new evidence of its added value and meaning: what is the purpose of Europe today?

These questions constitute a crucial challenge for Europe, but also a tremendous opportunity to redirect and relaunch the European project. Half a century after the European Coal and Steel Community (ECSC) Treaty and the Treaty of Rome – which initiated a political and economic cycle centred on reconciliation and the construction of an organised Internal Market – *the EU must now rebuild its legitimacy in the eyes of its citizens and its enterprises on the basis of its ability to promote Europe's interests and values in the global economy.*

This vital challenge of the meaning and relevance of European unification in the context of globalisation could be taken up thanks to a profoundly reformed and distinctly more ambitious European strategy for the post-2010 global economy.

Part II

The Short Term (2008-2010)

CHAPTER I

The 2008-2010 Cycle of the Lisbon Strategy: A Temporary Status Quo

The European Council of March 2008 launched the 2008-2010 cycle of the Lisbon strategy (hereinafter, "Lisbon III") by endorsing, for the most part, the December 2007 Commission proposals, marked by strong continuity with the 2005-2008 cycle.

I. The Choice of Status Quo and Implementation

A factual analysis of the Lisbon III package elicits the following summary points.

A. The Commission and the European Council take a favourable view of the implementation of the Lisbon strategy since 2005

Generally speaking, the Council – following the Commission – considers that the Lisbon strategy, in its 2005 relaunched form, works and has produced satisfactory results. The EU's economic growth reached 2.9% in 2007, and 6.5 million jobs have been created in the course of 2006-2007.

Accordingly, structural reform must be pursued and expanded, considering the deterioration in the international economic situation. At the national level, it is noted that certain Member States have reacted better than others, and that a certain fatigue seems to be appearing. R&D investments are tending to decrease, the environment for businesses has yet to be perfected and network industries are still insufficiently open to competition.

At the macro-economic level, it is urgent for Member States to maintain the long-term viability of their public finances, even if public deficits have been cut by over 50% since 2005 and the overall public debt of EU countries has been reduced to under 60%.

The role of the Lisbon strategy in the context of globalisation is reaffirmed: it is intended to help the EU take greater advantage of the assets and opportunities offered by globalisation, while protecting it from negative effects.

The key message of this new cycle is, therefore, to better implement the Lisbon strategy in its present state at both national and Community levels.

B. The Lisbon strategy's steering instruments for the 2008-2010 cycle remain unchanged

1. The Integrated Guidelines (IGs) remain by and large untouched

The Commission and the Council consider that the IGs, as defined in 2005, constitute an appropriate framework for implementing the Lisbon strategy and perform their role to the full. They appear sufficiently broad indeed to remain relevant for the next two years. Their methods of implementation, however, are slightly amended and enhanced with new contextual components, drawing conclusions from recent events without really modifying the substance.

2. A strenghtened Community Lisbon Programme

Ten key priorities are highlighted for the new Community Lisbon Programme, divided into four "priority areas" for action that correspond more or less to those identified by the spring 2006 European Council meeting:

- *investing in human capital and modernising the labour market;*
- *releasing the potential of companies, particularly small and medium-sized enterprises (SMEs);*
- *investing in knowledge and innovation;*
- *energy and climate change.*

In addition to these four areas, there is a set of themes relating to the "external dimension of the renewed Lisbon strategy" that mentions the EU's trade negotiations (particularly at the WTO), but also emphasises the need for the EU to strive to spread its standards throughout the world by increased regulatory convergence and, in certain areas (intellectual property), stricter application of existing rules.

The various actions corresponding to these five priorities are listed by the Commission and divided into three categories, depending on whether they (1) should be adopted by the Commission, (2) should be adopted by other institutions, or (3) require genuine implementation if they have already been adopted. It is a matter of underscoring the responsibility of each institution.

3. Governance status quo

Despite emphasising "implementation", the Commission and the Council did not want to change the governance of the Lisbon strategy. In particular, the "partnership" (*i.e.*, non-constraining) approach toward Member States that has been adopted by the Commission since 2005 remains the rule.

II. The End of a Cycle

This third edition of the Lisbon strategy appears, therefore, more like the end of a cycle than a new departure. *Though the priority given to implementing the existing strategy is relevant for the short term, this new cycle responds neither to the inadequacies highlighted in the first part of this report nor to the challenges and opportunities that Europe confronts in the global economy.* Upon the recommendation of the Mission, the European Council expressly acknowledged this by inviting the Commission, the Council and the "national Lisbon coordinators" to start discussing the future of the strategy beyond 2010 without delay.

A. Substantively, a widening of scope that is more apparent than real

1. Lisbon III widens the scope of the Lisbon strategy anew

Lisbon III endeavours to take better stock of the new challenges generated by the accelerating process of globalisation in the areas of social affairs, energy, climate change and external competitiveness.

On the subject of growth, Lisbon III addresses the need for a Small Business Act (SBA) or the need for the financial services sector to undergo genuine development. Combating climate change and completing the Internal Energy Market are placed at the heart of this new cycle as well. Also referred to are the challenges constituted by the EU's demography and its aging population, in addition to discussions of a common migration policy. Lastly, as mentioned before, Lisbon III has an external component that is intended to respond to the challenges of globalisation, by insisting, for example, on the need to regulate international financial crises, echoing the joint letter from Nicolas Sarkozy and Angela Merkel of the fall of 2007.

All in all, apart from this external component, the Lisbon strategy returns to the fundamentals emphasised in 2000, which referred to the emergence of a genuine "European development model". Following the 2005 refocusing on growth and jobs, Lisbon III seems to be returning to these themes, which are both environmental (via statements devoted to energy and climate) and social (the mid-2008 revision of the Social Agenda is a priority, as is the modification of the Globalisation Adjustment Fund, long statements devoted to flexicurity, etc.).

2. *These changes, however, only respond imperfectly to the challenges identified*

Nothing really concrete is recommended in the social arena, as the content of the Social Agenda remains to be determined. The main themes of this Agenda, referred to in the Community programme (education, migrations and demography), do not cover those linked to the definition of Community standards relating to working time or the secondment of workers.

The new economic and social heterogeneity of an EU of 27 Member States is no more taken into account than in 2000 or 2005 and does not therefore trigger any specific initiative.

The new "external component" is not very substantial. The need to reach an agreement in the context of the Doha Development Round, referred to in the Community Lisbon Programme, was already in the previous programme and is only tenuously connected to the Lisbon strategy. The fact that Europe's unilateral openness has negative consequences in terms of competitiveness seems to be recognised, but the approach consisting of obtaining reciprocity from its partners is challenged. The emphasis is mainly on dialogue with third countries and there is only implicit reference to the issues of markets access – which are nevertheless essential – or regulatory convergence.

3. *In reality, Lisbon III is in line with the 2005 refocusing on growth and jobs*

Despite the return to the broad themes highlighted in 2000 – or a wider range of themes as a response to new challenges – Lisbon III remains very close to the 2005 version of the Lisbon strategy. The fact that the Integrated Guidelines heading and, above all, the method of governance, remain virtually unchanged is, in this respect, revealing.

Furthermore, though the new Community Programme seems more substantial, all Community policies are included in it. As a result, it is difficult to draw precise conclusions from this Programme because its scope of intervention is so wide. Above all, the Commission seems to have wanted to bring a certain number of projects currently under way to a successful conclusion before the end of its mandate, which is understandable.

The inclusion of new themes in the Lisbon strategy may, however, have a further "dilutive" effect. First, on the strategy itself: by widening its scope, it tends to dissipate into an inoperative comprehensive account of policies conducted in Europe. Second, on the new themes: the inclusion within the Lisbon strategy, which is based on *soft law* (OMC), of policies that will become (or are meant to become) Community policies – and thus intended to fall under European *hard law* (directives, budgetary financing) – creates high risks, which have already materialised since 2000, of "downward procedural contamination".

B. On the subject of governance, Lisbon III has little new to contribute

The virtual status quo proposed by the Commission with regard to Lisbon governance doubtless expresses its fear of Member States reacting negatively to any change whatsoever. We can only conclude that this status quo is not up to tackling the widely recognised shortcomings of the present method of implementation.

1. At the Community Lisbon Programme level

The new Community Programme is substantial, but faces the traditional problems of governance, particularly with regard to legal (too frequent recourse to *soft law*) and financial means.

It does not distinguish that which falls under the EU's real competences from that which is more a matter of cooperation between Member States. This omission contradicts the clear resolve expressed in 2005. It is surprising to the extent that the Lisbon Treaty clarifies the allocation of competences.

Nevertheless, one improvement must be pointed out concerning the monitoring of implementation. The proposal is to devote a specific report to this subject, which the Commission will address to the European Parliament and Member States. It will be incorporated into its annual report on the implementation of the strategy.

2. At the national reform programmes implementation level

The multilateral surveillance system for the strategy, as introduced in March 2005, remains unchanged, even though the national implementation of Lisbon is undermined by an absence of ownership in many Member States. In the context of multilateral surveillance, the European Council invites the Commission and Member States to increase the exchange of good practices by taking full advantage of the OMC and through improved coordination within the Eurozone.

One welcome innovation is the Commission's December proposal that the European Council debate Member States' responses to the recommendations that are addressed to them in order to reinforce the multilateral surveillance mechanisms and Member States' compliance.

In its March 2005 Conclusions, the European Council had already referred to the need to appropriate the Lisbon strategy: "*Alongside the governments, all the other players concerned – parliaments, regional and local bodies, social partners and civil society – should be stakeholders in the Strategy and take an active part in attaining its objectives*". This resolve was reaffirmed by the Council in its March 2008 Conclusions, but no concrete way forward was indicated.

C. A consensus by default

The Member States may be divided into three major categories depending on how they perceive the Lisbon strategy:

- those (particularly the new Member States) for which it is a useful reference framework for implementing national reforms and for whom the partnership with the Commission constitues welcome technical assistance;
- those that carry out their reform programmes in a relatively autonomous fashion, often in conformity with the main approaches of the Lisbon strategy, and do not want greater interference by the Commission (Germany, the United Kingdom, the Scandinavian countries…);
- lastly, those that have faced difficulty reforming but do not always want a reinforced multilateral surveillance system that would point a finger at them (France, Italy…).

This conjunction produces a sort of "weak consensus" around the 2005 version of Lisbon. Its objectives are unanimously considered valid, but the implementation conditions suffer shortcomings that nobody bothers to remedy. In more general terms, the desire for stronger European intervention in areas that are central to the strategy appeared to be limited as of the end of 2007.

* *
*

The Mission acknowledges the consensus choice in favour of the status quo and implementation for 2008-2010 and supports it inasmuch as the Lisbon strategy is approaching its 2010 horizon and given the forthcoming renewal of European institutions. At the same time, we take satisfaction in that the European Council has heard our recommendations as to the necessarily temporary nature of such a choice and the need for immediate fresh thinking for a renewed strategy beyond 2010.

In the meantime, the Member States must step up their efforts to implement Lisbon III, France in the lead.

CHAPTER II

Recommendations For the French EU Presidency

Since July 1, 2008, France holds the presidency of the Council of the European Union. The agenda for this presidency is very full. Among the official priorities, some – like energy and combating climate change – are dictated by the European agenda. Others reflect French concerns: a European immigration policy, progress in European defence, a complete overhaul of the Common Agricultural Policy (CAP).

But this presidency should also be *an opportunity to express a French vision of Europe's role in the global economy. There are several reasons for this.*

First, this issue – and the economic and social stakes linked to it – was at the core of the 2005 French referendum debate and will shape the European project's return to favour in the hearts of many European citizens.

Second, France has often spoken out on the social aspects and external dimension of European competitiveness and its partners are expecting it to address these subjects.

Last but not least, the French presidency must *seize the invitation of the spring European Council meeting to launch post-Lisbon discussions, and seek to influence the definition of a post-2010 European strategy for globalisation.* The attention paid by Community institutions and several of our European partners to the Mission's work has created specific expectations from France on this subject, which the deteriorating international economic situation has only served to reinforce. The vigorous structural reform agenda it is presently implementing at the national level gives France increased legitimacy to do so (see Preface).

For other matters relating to the Lisbon strategy, the 2008-2010 cycle has just been adopted by the European Council, but the French presidency has room for manoeuvre to influence the content of the Community Lisbon Programme which, at the moment, is still at the planning stage. Above all, the French presidency must focus all its efforts on those measures already within the scope of Lisbon III that it considers to be priorities. We also suggest a few *new concrete initiatives – limited, in order to remain realistic – to be achieved within the 2008-2010 time frame. If these initiatives cannot be realised within this period, they should be part of the post-2010 agenda.*

Besides the energy-climate package, which is already among the priorities of Lisbon III, *the Mission recommends that the French presidency commit itself thoroughly to four areas: the knowledge-based economy (research and higher education), establishing an integrated European financial market, strengthening the social dimension of the European project, and shaping the post-Lisbon strategy for globalisation.*

I. Enhancing Europe's Knowledge Economy

A. Prioritising research

Research is the major, worrying paradox of the Lisbon strategy. R&D is Lisbon's key policy for the knowledge-based economy, yet Europe seems to have been falling behind in this area since 2000, as much in terms of the financial means available as in results (see Annex 1). The emerging countries are fast catching up; China, with 136 billion dollars of investment in 2006, has become (in financial volume) the second largest R&D investor in the world[1]. At this rate, it is set to overtake Europe's consolidated investment (presently 230 billion dollars) by 2010.

Under its presidency, France must revitalise research in Europe. It could stress the importance of *effectively creating the European Research Area (ERA).* This ambition dates from 2000 and was taken up again in Lisbon III, which proposes the creation of a "Fifth Freedom" of movement – that of knowledge. The ERA's objective must be to improve opportunities for our researchers, via pan-European careers, and to create better working conditions (pooling knowledge, creating pan-European research structures, etc.).

Beyond this, the French presidency could take a further initiative by proposing to *complete the reform of the governance of the Community research budget.* The management of the Framework Programme for Research and Development (FPRD) has come under severe criticism in the past for its administrative allocation criteria and its heavy, bureaucratic procedures. FPRD reforms implemented by the Commission are heading in the right direction. Above all, the creation of the European Research Council (ERC) marks an important breakthrough. This is an

1 Behind the United States (220 billion dollars), but ahead of Japan (130 billion dollars).

independent agency run on the model of the American National Science Foundation[2]. It is composed of renowned scientists and is responsible for allocating Community funds to fundamental research, *i.e.*, 1 billion euros of the FPRD's annual 7 billion euros, in accordance with criteria for scientific excellence. It has just handled its first applications. Based on an assessment of the ERC's operation – and, of course, if that assessment is positive – the French presidency could propose extending the scope of its jurisdiction to the whole FPRD. The ERC would thereby become a genuine European Science and Research Agency with jurisdiction over the entire European "research" budget.

However, it will be necessary to go further to revitalise European research on a long-term basis by increasing the European research budget, curbing the decline in national government research and stimulating private research (see Part III, Chapter II in this volume).

B. Launching an initiative to bring European universities up to standard

Although human capital is the main asset of a knowledge-based economy, in Europe the higher education system, and students themselves, lack adequate resources. We are falling critically behind the university systems of our major American and – in the near future – Asian competitors.

In this area, Lisbon III does not provide an agenda for progress and the Mission suggests that this should be a major post-2010 priority. However, France can try to mobilise its presidency to start making headway.

Higher education presently falls under national jurisdiction and it is therefore at the national level that action must be taken. But budgetary constraints limit the Member States' capacity to inject the funds required to raise the standards of our university systems. Part of the solution lies in increasing private financing for higher education: chairs financed by companies, raising tuition fees. Tuition fees pose an equality problem; to avoid ending up with a situation in which students with modest means are ousted (resulting in a worse situation, in this respect, than is currently the case), fee increases must be accompanied by corresponding increases in grants and student loans. In the United States, the most advanced knowledge-based economy, the State guarantees student loans in the event of repayment default, among other methods of financial aid. This system means that any student wishing to follow a course

2 Or, indeed, research councils in Scandinavian countries and the United Kingdom.

of studies may do so. It has a limited cost, with only 1% repayment defaults and 10% repayment incidents.

This scheme could be transposed to Europe to good advantage. Member States could, of course, implement it at the national level. But it could be even more effective if operated at the EU level within the framework of an "all students" initiative. In particular, it would serve to pool efforts that certain European countries presently in transition do not have the financial means to prioritise. The European Investment Bank (EIB) could guarantee bank loans and, if need be, guarantee portfolios of student loans granted by European banks. If a horizontal guarantee open to all European students (40 million) profoundly changed the financial balances and the EIB's business purpose, a more targeted initiative – linked to the knowledge-based economy and the EIB's new innovation-centred undertakings – would appear feasible.

A Community initiative of this kind would facilitate higher education financing by raising tuition fees while guaranteeing – or even enhancing – equal access to higher education. Indeed, the obstacles to pursuing university courses encountered by students of modest means are not restricted to tuition fees, but also include the cost of student life – a cost that guaranteed student loans could also cover.

II. Progressing Towards an Integrated European Financial Market

The establishment of a Europe-wide integrated financial market would contribute triple added value to growth. First, there would be economic gains linked to the Single Market's economies of scale; the liquidity of a major integrated financial market would enable a financing of the economy and companies that is both broader (development of venture capital, pension funds – highly underdeveloped sectors in Europe compared to the United States) and less costly. Second, there would be increased legal certainty; today, there is an awkward imbalance between prudential rules and national supervision authorities faced with the increasing number of transnational players and risks. Third, there would be the development of new services; these services are not profitable in narrow national markets, but they would become so with a deeply integrated European market.

Thanks to the euro, we now have the opportunity to create this large market. The euro market has developed considerably and now constitutes – for companies and governments throughout the world – a reliable source of liquidity that is now greater in size than that of the dollar. In the framework of this new monetary area, European financial markets have made progress, with the implementation of the Financial Services

Action Plan (FSAP) and the "Lamfalussy Process". European capital markets have developed considerably and market capitalisation has virtually tripled. In 2005, the value of initial public offerings was higher than that of the United States and the euro interest-rate swap market leads the world. Bond issues have more than doubled and, since 2004, the euro has ousted the dollar as the leading currency for international bond issues.

But this progress remains limited considering the potential the European currency has to offer. Financial institutions must still be established under the laws of a Member State to access its market, which deprives these institutions and their clients of the simplifications and economies of scale that could be offered by an integrated market with, in particular, common infrastructures and standards for payments, securities and Undertakings for Collective Investment in Transferable Securities (UCITS). In fact, as they have observed, it is scarcely any easier to develop in another European country than it is elsewhere in the world.

Furthermore, the fragmentation of prudential regulation and supervisory practices does not provide the different supervisors with a global overview of the real risks taken by each cross-border financial group. It leads to overlapping prudential requirements that increase the cost of services offered to European citizens and, as a result, impair financial institutions' competitiveness.

The diversity of the national implementations of these European laws, the many national options authorised by the legislation and the European legislative framework's failure to respond to market innovation are behind these inadequacies.

Decisive progress may now be made. It is widely known what reforms are required. They could be accomplished under Lisbon III and the French presidency could instigate them.

A. Common standards and infrastructures to benefit from the Internal Market's economies of scale

1. Speeding up European regulatory harmonisation

For the most part, regulatory standards are still national. Where European laws exist, they leave the door open to numerous national exceptions, thereby limiting real harmonisation (the most spectacular case being the EU Takeover Directive, the exceptions to which enabled the survival of inconsistent national systems). The French presidency will have the task of ensuring the successful adoption of European laws that are on the agenda for the second half of 2008 (the "Solvency II" directive, the revision of the EU UCITS directives). The French presidency should also launch discussions to limit the scope of national exceptions; for example, it could propose a horizontal *de minimis* rule stipulating that national players may use national exceptions, but not European-scale players.

2. Promoting infrastructures for unified Delivery versus Payment (DVP)

At the national level, these infrastructures are presently fragmented, which greatly increases European transaction costs. They also raise a question of principle; these are networks that constitute natural monopolies, but they are private and mixed with competitive services. In other networked sectors, the EU has implemented a policy that separates service providers (who are thrown into competition) and the infrastructure administrator, a government monopoly. Why should we not also apply to financial services what has already been applied to gas, electricity and rail transport? In the United States, for example, DVP infrastructures constitute a national public service. In this respect, the ECB's initiative to develop by 2013 a joint DVP platform in the Eurozone (known as "Target 2 Securities") responds to these questions. The French presidency should give it strong political impetus.

B. Integrated prudential supervision to guarantee financial security

This is a complex technical question, but it is vitally important. The national fragmentation of prudential rules comes with a high price tag: financial institutions must conduct different expert evaluations and procedures in each Member State. The absence of integrated supervision is dangerous because national controls are ineffective when faced with cross-border operators. The French presidency could speed up work in progress that should lead to integrated prudential supervision.

C. The development of micro-credit as a new financial service

Micro-credit represents an instrument of social cohesion because it helps transform outcasts into wealth creators. It is also an economic niche that creates growth and jobs. It offers bank-type financing for projects that previously did not have access to this. At present, it is underdeveloped in Europe. In November 2007, the European Commission released a communication on a "European initiative for the development of micro-credit". This communication is included in the Community component of Lisbon III. The French presidency could make this one of its political priorities at a time when the government is adopting it as part of the drive to revive national growth (see the recommendations of the Attali Commission and the Hurel report on self-employment).

III. Strengthening Europe's Social Dimension

France is not necessarily the best-qualified Member State to encourage the new EU to act more on social issues.

Its shortcomings in this realm stem, on the one hand, from its traditional historical references to the theme of "social Europe", which tend to generate a certain fatigue in Community institutions and other Member States and, on the other, its uneven national performance in social matters (demographic success, but high unemployment), with the result that France is neither exemplary nor in a strong position to address these challenges.

At the same time, the French authorities could quite justifiably base their "social Europe" demands on two realities. The political distrust created by an EU perceived as "not social enough" contributed, in particular, to the French rejection of the European constitutional treaty. However, this does not only concern France; the series of economic and social reforms begun in spring 2007 should bolster the government's claim that it is vigorously tackling the main social problems that fall under its authority, even while France asks the EU for intervention for those who depend on it.

Though France's room for manoeuvre on social affairs is limited, using it requires that it specifically identifies the issues on which it desires stronger EU action in the course of the next two years and beyond. The fact that the new Social Agenda referred to in the Community Lisbon Programme is in the planning stage provides France with an opportunity that it may use by concentrating its efforts on three areas[3].

A. Strengthening the European Globalisation Adjustment Fund (EGAF)

The EGAF was created on 1 January 2007. It aims to provide financial assistance for workers who lose their jobs because of globalisation, especially by financing pro-active policies in the labour market. In October 2007, it was used in France in cases of lay-offs by Peugeot and Renault suppliers in the automobile sector.

---

3 Entrusted to Mr. Bernard Brunhes by French Labour Minister Xavier Bertrand, the mission on the European Social Agenda provides further recommendations on these issues.

A review is scheduled for the second half of 2008. The French presidency could seize this opportunity to extend the system on three aspects:

- *Scope*: since the Fund is limited to redundancy plans for more than 1,000 employees, this threshold could be lowered because small to medium-sized enterprises (SMEs) are also very vulnerable to globalisation;
- *Triggering conditions*: these are limited to downstream intervention, when employees have been made redundant. They could be extended to create a preventive system on the model of the American Trade Adjustment Act (TAA) to provide help upstream for companies subjected to particularly intense international competition;
- *Financial endowment*: the EGAF is allocated 500 million euros. Initially, its budget could be doubled without renegotiating the financial perspectives in order to cover the proposed extension of its scope.

B. Developing the emerging European labour market

In Europe, there is an internal goods market that is already sturdy and an internal services market that is presently taking shape. However, there is no internal workers' market. Professional mobility in Europe is still low; less than 2% of European workers work in another EU State.

The main obstacle to mobility is the portability of social rights (health, retirement). This is a long-term task. We shall return to it in Part III.

In the short term, however, progress can be made by providing the political impetus required to *finalise current negotiations* that are very much bogged down in important issues concerning the European labour market (temporary work, working hours, secondment).

We would like to stress the issue of secondment. *Many secondments are presently illegal and hard to regulate because of the difficulties involved in setting up innumerable bilateral cooperation initiatives between national labour inspectorates.* That is why the French presidency could propose strengthening cooperation between labour inspection bodies with improved resources and creating a centralised system of secondment notification, opening the way to the creation of a European supervisory authority for secondments.

France would increase its influence in this domain if it completely lifted the worker mobility restrictions it imposes on citizens from new Member States before the planned date[4]. Symbolically, to leave behind

---

4 France has announced its decision to do so in June 2008.

the unfortunate "Polish plumber syndrome", it should also strive to implement the Services Directive before the end of its presidency.

C. Developing the Internal Market's international dimension in terms of social standards

To maintain high social standards in Europe, it is also necessary to raise international social standards. This is the logic of the "level playing field" that has long been championed by France and is now gradually beginning to get a hearing.

After evaluating their potential economic impact, the French presidency could propose two initiatives along these lines.

1. Incorporating Core Labour Standards into bilateral agreement negotiations conducted by the EU

The "internationally recognised human and labour rights" (International Labour Organisation, ILO) could be more actively promoted in the context of European trade negotiations.

The EU already subjects some of its trade concessions to Core Labour Standards. This is the case with GSP+ agreements that grant broader preferential access to European markets for countries that implement the main ILO conventions[5].

The EU is having difficulty making progress on this point in multilateral negotiations (WTO). But Lisbon III provides for increased recourse to bilateral agreements to circumvent the blockage in WTO negotiations. The EU could therefore incorporate this cross-compliance into its future bilateral and regional trade agreements either by renewing an incentive policy based on positive GSP+-type measures or by adopting a more binding approach on the model used by the United States in NAFTA (cooperation agreement in the field of labour, with mutual surveillance and sanctions).

The Commission has made commitments along these lines through many declarations of intent. The French presidency could propose making it a requirement for the signature of future agreements negotiated by the EU.

---

[5] The EU has suspended the GSP+ agreement with Belarus for failure to respect these Core Standards, following condemnation by the ILO.

2. *Incorporating the theme of "corporate social responsibility"*[6] *into international negotiations conducted by the EU*

This would be a step forward beyond the Core Labour Standards. On this subject, the EU plays an exemplary role within its borders; it is in the EU's best interest to promote its standards internationally.

France achieved a breakthrough in this direction at the G8, in the framework of the Heiligendamm process. In particular, it obtained a commitment from its G8 partners to invite their companies listed on the stock exchange to publish a "corporate social responsibility" section in their annual reports.

The EU must make the same breakthrough in the international negotiations it conducts. It is an opportune time to do so; corporate social responsibility is a subject that is generating increasing international interest as illustrated by the UN report entrusted to John Ruggi.

IV. Paving the Way For a Post-Lisbon Globalisation Strategy

Lastly, the French presidency provides France with *an opportunity to structure an in-depth discussion on the future of Europe's strategy in the global economy for the next decade*. The period is particularly auspicious since it will precede the entry into force of a new treaty, the election of a new European Parliament and the appointment of a new Commission.

A. A European strategy for globalisation

It is perhaps *in the economic and social arenas that the French presidency is likely to make its most important and most useful contribution, which could be based on three initiatives*.

By way of introduction, the first initiative would serve to hail France's reinvestment in the Lisbon strategy and would consist of *organising, under the French presidency, a "forum of best Lisbon practices" gathering delegations from all EU Member States*. The 27 Member States would each be invited to present two or three policies or practices that have succeeded at national level in the course of a two or three-day multilateral "benchmarking" event. For its part, France could promote the research and development tax credit, competitive

---

6 Corporate social responsibility is "a concept whereby companies integrate social and environmental concerns in their business operations and in their interaction with their stakeholders on a voluntary basis" (European Commission definition).

clusters and its day care policy for young children within subsidised structures.

The two other initiatives ensue from the European Council's invitation (March 2008) to start discussions relating to a post-2010 strategy. As the first Member State to hold the EU presidency following this Council meeting, France should pursue this subject in the course of its presidency, not only procedurally, but also substantively.

This initiative could include *setting up an operational working party composed of representatives from the Commission and the national Lisbon coordinators*, in accordance with the European Council's recommendation. It could also form the subject of *an ad hoc debate at an informal European Council meeting.*

With this in mind, Part III of this report outlines an overall European strategy for globalisation beyond 2010 that could serve as a reference for the presidency's initiatives and EU-wide discussion.

B. Opening the debate on the review of the EU's financial framework

It is, moreover, in France's interest to launch the debate concerning the EU budget review that was scheduled for "2008-2009" in the Conclusions of the December 2005 European Council meeting.

It is somewhat unrealistic to think that these negotiations could make it possible to finance the initiatives of Lisbon III; indeed, the 2007-2013 financial perspectives will be very difficult to reopen. Nevertheless, recent decisions concerning Galileo have shown that it was possible on a very small scale. Be that as it may, these negotiations will concern the next financial perspectives (2014-2019) and, as such, will form an essential part of elaborating the "post-2010" agenda. In reality, the two exercises should be carried out in parallel. If the shift to a knowledge-based economy and the socio-environmental development model envisaged by the Lisbon strategy genuinely constitute the political priority at the EU level, they should be fully reflected in the future Community budget.

France's decision on this subject is eagerly anticipated. The negotiations that led to the December 2005 adoption of a "financial framework of the European Union for the period 2007-2013" had already demonstrated the resolve to make greater use of the Community budget to further Lisbon strategy objectives. But they were marked by apparent opposition from France, anxious to prioritise preserving the level of appropriations granted to agriculture.

It is in France's best interest to embrace, rather than defer, the 2008-2009 meeting. In fact, this meeting is the opportunity to tackle interdependent subjects in a coordinated fashion: the EU budget, the evolution of the Lisbon strategy and the CAP (which is also due to be reviewed on the occasion of the CAP "Health Check", scheduled for the same period). Such a general negotiation would enable global compromises of a kind that negotiations sequenced "in instalments" preclude.

The meeting would also be an opportunity to shake off the defensive posture that France too often adopts on European budgetary matters and influence debates in a positive manner. As to substance, for example, France could promote a vision of European public expenditures that is no longer institutional (EU budget and national budgets) but consolidated (covering all Community and national expenditures). An aggregated vision of this sort would put criticism of the agricultural policy into perspective, highlighting the fact that European governments spend no more on their agriculture than the United States or Japan (on the order of 0.5% of GDP) and that they spend less on agriculture than on education (5.2% of GDP) or R&D (0.7% of GDP). It would make it possible to make policy decisions based on financial realities, over and above questions of jurisdiction or "Who does what?"

The period is also favourable for appeasement on the agricultural question. The rise in world prices for agricultural raw materials tends to justify both maintaining a strong European agriculture and reducing the financial assistance it requires.

Part III

EuroWorld 2015: A European Strategy For Globalisation

CHAPTER I

Heading For Globalisation

I. Thinking Beyond 2010

Why think beyond 2010, when the European Council has only just ratified the Commission's proposals for the 2008-2010 cycle of the Lisbon strategy, centred on improved implementation of what already exists at the national and European levels?

There is no shortage of reasons for anticipating the initial deadline of the strategy launched in March 2000:

- 2010 is less than two years away and much of 2009 will be taken up with the election of the new European Parliament, the subsequent renewal of the Commission and the possible implementation of the Lisbon Treaty;
- the Lisbon strategy risks appearing to have failed in 2010 as far as its symbolic objectives are concerned. This negative perception will be diminished if new prospects going beyond that date are already outlined;
- a number of processes that are more or less linked to Lisbon (the "energy/climate" integrated policy, the European Social Agenda, the revision of the financial framework) already take us well beyond 2010;
- lastly and most importantly, in itself and in its present configuration the Lisbon strategy no longer seems to live up to the challenges. When it was launched in March 2000, it was visionary and gave Europe a head start over the rest of the world (other than the United States). Eight years on, because of implementation failings, Europe is once again behind in a world that is moving at unprecedented speed. The desired short-term continuity is, therefore, only justified if it is accompanied by anticipating the next step.

At the initiative of France and with the support of the Slovenian presidency and other Member States, the European Council has itself adopted this analysis by launching the reflection on a post-2010 strategy without delay.

The first question to be settled concerns the very fate of the Lisbon strategy beyond 2010: should we prolong its existence or move on to something else? The assessment in the first part of this report makes it possible to answer this question clearly: *the agenda defined in Lisbon in March 2000 (and subsequently supplemented) remains valid because its objectives are still relevant and will not have been achieved by 2010.* Furthermore, the Lisbon strategy has aroused a certain form of appropriation by governments, the social partners and civil society, and generated positive effects. *However, we should clearly quicken the pace and adopt a global viewpoint, failing which the European Union will be out of the race by 2020.*

In effect, the Lisbon strategy has not enabled Europe to reduce the gap with the United States that appeared in the 1990s. In the course of the next decade, maintaining the status quo will also lead to Europe being overtaken in certain sectors by the major emerging countries, many of which (China, Brazil, etc.) have implemented similar strategies with the determination and effectiveness that their national unity and the sometimes authoritarian nature of their political regimes make possible. Lisbon has its emulators – and they are about to catch up with us.

Doubtless, the aim of turning Europe into "the most competitive and dynamic knowledge-driven economy by 2010" has never been a realistic objective. *The real global challenge with which Europe is now confronted is to stay in the race, in terms of prosperity and international influence, in a world that is bound to be dominated by an American/Asian duopoly.*

The following chapters assume that Europeans (and their political leaders) wish to meet this challenge and consider the European Union to be the appropriate frameword for doing so. Accordingly, they describe the policies and other instruments that Europe needs to meet the challenge, by reference in particular to those of its main partners and competitors. They identify the obstacles, without, however, succumbing to a suicidal immobility.

II. A Copernican Revolution

"Succeeding in the age of globalisation" – to use an expression that the Commission has recently and rightly identified as being in "the European interest"[1] – calls for an urgent, vigorous reaction both internally and externally. The internal component has been clearly identified. It involves adapting to globalisation to make the most of it

---

1 European Commission Communication (3 October 2007): "The European interest: Succeeding in the age of globalisation", COM (2007) 581.

and limit negative effects, while respecting our values: that is the Lisbon strategy, which will need tighter content and stronger implementation. But even if it is strengthened, this internal component will not suffice to meet the challenge without an external dimension that seeks to consolidate its results.

This external component was not present in 2000. It appeared recently on the fringes of the Lisbon strategy under the shy designation of "the external dimension of competitiveness". In reality, it consists of nothing less than constructing an external economic strategy for the European Union by first identifying its own interests – not just a matter of finding the lowest common denominator of the national interests that it comprises – with a view to governing the EU's relations with the other major players of globalisation and helping shape globalisation in accordance with our own interests and values.

This approach is relatively new in the recent history of European unification, which partly explains the misunderstandings it sometimes gives rise to. Indeed, in the past ten years, the accelerating pace of globalisation has presented Europe with a challenge that has not been sufficiently explored and that is not unconnected with the crisis it is presently undergoing. That challenge is the need to shift the centre of the EU's preoccupations away from itself and towards its relationship with the rest of the world.

Over the first five decades of its existence, the European project's main goal was, by definition, the elimination of national barriers and the construction of a framework for peace, an economic community, and an integrated internal market and legal system. All its founding concepts, its ideological and legal "software", was designed to attain this end. Today, even if the Single Market still needs to be perfected, this objective is in the process of being achieved and the framework required to preserve it is in place. At the same time, a new and noticeably different imperative is making itself felt: the need for the European Union, thus constituted, to play a full role in a globalised economy whose main players are continental scale nations and whose centre of gravity is shifting rapidly towards Asia and the emerging world.

Certainly, the creation of a critical mass to face global competition has always been in the background of the European enterprise, yet another testimony to the visionary capacity of its founders. But for a long time this has remained a virtual aim. Now, however, Europe exists and globalisation is here to stay. Europe is the leading trade power in the world and depends on external trade for supplies, particularly of energy. As such, of all players, Europe is the least capable of cutting itself off from the constraints and opportunities of globalisation. To defend its interests and competitiveness – the precondition for preserving its social model and values – Europe must become a global economic and, indeed, political player.

This challenge is something quite different from the construction of an internal economic, legal and political framework, it obeys a different logic and requires different instruments. Of course, it is still necessary to establish common *rules* at the international level and ensure that they are respected by members of the international community, but this requires a parallel definition and defence of common *interests*, the development of *strategies* and *policies*, and *decision-making*. To date, the European Union is very ill-equipped – intellectually, politically, institutionally and financially – for this new role that is gaining the upper hand over the previous role without, however, replacing it[2].

This inadequacy is at least partly behind the feeling in public opinion that Europe, as such, is ineffective in the global economy, and the resulting disaffection in certain Member States. National political leaders have too often allowed globalisation to become, in the eyes of their citizens, "the problem" of European unification, whereas the latter could well constitute the solution to the challenges of globalisation if the European Union decides to find the ways and means of becoming a global player.

III. EuroWorld 2015: A New Ambition for Europe

The Lisbon strategy, even if it had been more successful, could never have constituted "Europe's response to globalisation" on its own. It is just one of the two components to that response. Though essential, through a well-targeted set of *internal structural reforms*, the Lisbon strategy's role is to help the economies and societies of the European Union *adapt to globalisation in order to get the most out of it.* But this internal adaptation, which is far from having been achieved, leaves intact the need for a European *external economic and political strategy* like those established by all the great powers, aiming to consolidate the benefits of and *shape globalisation.* This second goal should not be confused with the Lisbon strategy, either in spirit or (and above all) in method.

Defining a European strategy for globalisation beyond 2010 thus involves making a clear distinction between:

---

2 See Sapir A. *et al.*, *Fragmented Power: Europe and the Global Economy*, Bruegel, 2007.

- an *internal component* – that we shall call "*Lisbon Plus*" – involving a structural reform process, the content of which is to be recentred on the challenge of competitiveness via innovation and its social and environmental accompaniment, and strengthened by improved governance and the mobilisation of all Community instruments, and
- an *external component*, based mainly on a panoply of integrated common policies, implemented coherently by institutions with real decision-making ability in the framework of a global strategic vision.

We suggest naming this global strategy "*EuroWorld 2015*", a brand name that has the virtue of being easy to translate into the different languages of the EU (EuroMonde, EuroWelt, EuroMundo, etc.). The "Lisbon brand", already weak and now strongly challenged in the public mind by the treaty of the same name, would only survive as its internal component ("Lisbon Plus"). The time frame for this new strategic vision would be reduced from ten to five years – 2015 – to reflect accelerating changes in the world and to correspond to the next European term of office.

Let it be clearly understood: this is in no way about inventing yet another "strategy" to add to the myriad "processes", "agendas" and other "programmes" that sustain daily life in Brussels, but it is about *constructing a coherent, overall strategic European vision for the global economy from what already exists – the Lisbon strategy on the one hand, and the common external policies on the other.*

Another potential misunderstanding needs to be dispelled. The internal and external components of any single common policy – energy or the environment, for example – should naturally remain closely interwoven and managed by the same people, as is particularly the case for agricultural policy. But this necessary continuity does not in any way reduce the need to distinguish the internal and external components of the overall strategy for globalisation, insofar as they obey different contraints and function according to different political logics and institutional mechanisms.

The conviction that the European Union's external economic strategy – unlike the Lisbon strategy – cannot rest upon the open method of coordination or other intergovernmental process, but rather requires common policies, is not the result of any ideological preconception but of an observation of fact. Europe only truly counts within the globalised economy in the few realms that are governed by common policies and institutions and integrated decision-making processes: the common trade policy, the Internal Market (notably competition policy), the Common

Agricultural Policy and monetary policy. The European Union is, as such, a major player in WTO negotiations; it can block a merger of American companies authorised by the US antitrust authorities; Community law applies to multinational companies that wish to benefit from the Internal Market; and ECB decisions have a major impact on the world's financial and currency markets.

It is only when Europe speaks with one voice – in terms of content and institutionally – and with genuine decision-making power, that it is a true player in the global economy. Conversely, the intergovernmental method (or the relative absence of cooperation), which continues to govern too many areas of economic life, does not give Europe sufficient strength to influence its external environment, except (to a limited extent) in matters of foreign policy and common security. Herein lies the main explanation for the forementioned gap between the EU's global economic and trade stature and its poor ability to exert a normative influence internationally.

* *
*

IV. Reaching Consensus on the External Dimension

The following chapters, therefore, outline the content of an overall strategy for Europe in the global economy. Its internal dimension, embodied by the Internal Market and the Lisbon strategy, benefits from cumulative experience over the previous decades and a wide European (and international) consensus on the objectives to be attained, the EU Member States differing only from each other – as we have seen – in their implementational ability or will and in their results.

Such is not the case with the external dimension, which (with the exception of the Common Trade Policy, one of the oldest EEC policies) is, on the contrary – in addition to the aforementioned institutional and decision-making deficiencies – characterised by a lack of consensus and, *a fortiori*, common doctrine within the European Union. This lack is the result of the relative novelty of the external perspective (apart from purely trade issues) in the history of European unification, as well as the diversity of national attitudes, interests and ideological positions towards globalisation in general or one or another of its different aspects. The situation is all the more harmful that these issues are now critical for preserving Europe's competitiveness and social model and, as a result, lie at the heart of its citizens' concerns.

The most obvious illustration of this lack of consensus is the opposition between partisans of unrestricted free trade and open markets

– now in the majority – and defenders of negotiated (or, failing that, unilateral) international regulation. A debate of this kind is absolutely legitimate and necessary, but unfortunately it is contaminated by excesses on both sides: the advocates of the free market stick to a dogmatic and unconditional vision of competition and free trade, caricaturing upholders of regulated globalisation as "protectionists". As for the latter, with the French leading the field, they often provide grist to their opponents' mills by confusing international regulation and national protectionism, European ambition and sovereignist rhetoric.

These false debates serve only to blind us to the real issues. Protectionism has long ceased to be an option for Europe, even more so than for any other player in world trade, *a fortiori* its Member States. On a planetary scale, the European Union is a medium-sized player, highly dependent on external trade. Likewise, economic nationalism contradicts the whole European project and leads to a dead end, even when Europe fails to deliver. What is more, contrary to the relentless propaganda machines of certain Anglo-American media, Europe is one of the world's most open economic areas to trade and international investment[3]. Protectionist temptations resurface periodically, of course, but this phenomenon is by no means specific to Europe and does not presently constitute in itself the cardinal threat brandished by advocates of full-scale free trade.

However, such a threat could become a reality under pressure from public opinion if the principles of free movement that govern the European Union were transposed as they stand into a global economy that still lacks a coherent system of rules to ensure fair and balanced competition and a minimum of social cohesion and solidarity within a global political and economic community. The multipolar world that is now coming into being will, on the contrary, be characterized by increasing heterogeneousness and rivalry among different economic and social systems.

Free trade advocates sweep this objection aside, arguing that the opening up of borders will, in due course, benefit countries that practise it, even in the absence of reciprocity: hence the exclusive emphasis on

---

[3] The European Union's stature in global trade is considerable: in 2006, excluding intra-Community trade, the EU represented 18% of world trade or 28% if one includes intra-Community trade. For exports, the figures for 2006 come to 16.2% and 30%, respectively. The flow of direct extra-Community foreign investment into the European Union was 145 billion euros in 2006. Furthermore, foreign investors loom large in the capital of European companies: in France, in November 2007, nearly 47% of CAC 40 company capital was held by foreign investors, whereas in Germany the 50% threshold was crossed in December 2007 for the capital of companies listed on the Frankfurt DAX index (the level was 10% ten years ago).

internal strategies of adjustment to global competition such as the Lisbon strategy. This argument finds an objective ally in a certain European idealism that maintains that Europe should appear "exemplary" in all respects in the eyes of the world, in conformity with its "values". The alliance of free trade doctrinaires and idealists thus produces a European consensus in favour of "a policy of exemplary conduct", which is now the EU's substitute for an external economic strategy: "let's impose upon ourselves the constraints that seem right to us and strive to convince our partners and competitors to do the same".

V. The Key Challenge of the Emerging Countries

This policy – which is sometimes dubbed "positive reciprocity" – is progressive in principle. However, it runs the risk of naivety if it does not anticipate the consequences of its own failure. What is to be done if your partners do not play the game *and, in any case, during the long transitional period required for that purpose*? The most important economic and social challenge of the 21st century is the rising power of the major emerging countries – China, India, Russia, Brazil, South Korea and many others – which raises four kinds of questions that can be answered in different ways:

- the question of the price competition these countries wage – and will wage – with Western economies in every sector, including the most technologically advanced;
- the question of the respect paid by these new players to existing rules of international trade and the market economy, such as openness to investment, access to markets, competition and intellectual property law. The massive presence of the State in emerging economies is, in this respect, problematic;
- the question of their adherence to the new norms and obligations required by climate change, the scarcity of natural resources, social progress and development;
- and, lastly, the question of using their increasing economic and financial power to geopolitical ends, as is already obviously the case in contemporary Russia and China.

Faith in the virtues of openness and competition and the rejection of protectionism legitimately lead Western economies to respond to the first of these issues which, in Europe, is what the Lisbon strategy aims to accomplish. But, as we have seen, the process of internal adjustment is slow and difficult, and the corollary should be *the adherence of emerging countries to the fundamental rules of the market economy* at a sufficiently rapid pace. Since we are talking about economies that are broadly state-controlled and have a poor rule-of-law tradition, the process will nonetheless take time. As a result, it is absurd to oppose the policy of openness and the quest for reciprocity, or even the threat of sanctions: the two should go hand in hand, though in varying proportions depending on the situations and how they develop.

The question of *sharing the burden of new obligations* with emerging countries is much more complex, both for reasons of equity and feasibility. The acceptance of a gradual, differentiated upgrading of emerging economies in terms of environmental and social norms is inevitable over a long transitional period. That being the case, it is the responsibility of the developed economies to reflect carefully on the competitiveness handicap they impose on themselves in the name of the common good, along with the industrial and social consequences that are likely to result from it in the long term, and to provide the necessary internal compensations in favour of economic activities and social groups suffering from this situation.

As regards the new *geopolitical dimension of globalisation* resulting, in particular, from the rising power of emerging countries, it remains largely ignored in Brussels, which continues to operate as if the world economy were still reduced to competition between market economies and liberal democracies – that are, moreover, militarily allied – in other words, to a rivalry between Europe and the United States. This is obviously no longer the case with the emergence of new major economic and political powers which, for the most part, are neither market economies nor liberal democracies, nor natural allies of the West, and which have no qualms about using economic weapons to achieve politico-strategic ends, and vice versa. Whether we like it or not, the liberal dogma of economic and political disconnection that marked the last two decades of the 20th century has had its day.

VI. Difficult New Issues For the EU

All these developments pose many new and difficult questions for Western leaders and the European Union, which transcend the opposition between free trade and protectionism and make the implicit projection of European rules and values onto the rest of the world even more difficult than it was in the recent past. The revolution in the emerging world is a major and many-sided historical consequence of globalisation. It calls, therefore, for a well thought-out re-examination – free of preconceptions – of the Community doctrine as it applies to the EU's external relations.

Lastly, with globalisation the European Union is faced with an ultimate challenge: *that of the speed at which the world's economic hierarchies are being redefined and of its own capacity to react.* The emerging countries are often authoritarian, centralised regimes that are capable of conducting massive transformations with great rapidity. The United States, for its part, enjoys strong national unity, dynamic financial markets and an unparalleled capacity for innovation, in addition to an effective linkage between public and private sector policies. These advantages enable it to react quickly. In contrast, Europe took over ten years to reach agreement on a new treaty that strengthens its institutions minimally, and it continues to drag its feet on the path to economic and political integration.

The recommendations that follow should be evaluated in the light of this assessment. *In this respect, we suggest that the Commission resulting from the June 2009 European elections launch the EuroWorld 2015 Strategy at the Spring 2010 European Council, making it the priority of its mandate.*

CHAPTER II

"Lisbon Plus"
Adapting More Effectively to Globalisation

Though the 2010 deadline has been useful in mobilising European and national public institutions and civil societies, it cannot constitute a point of conclusion for the EU, all the more so because the results obtained to date by the Lisbon strategy are mixed. In the current context of the global economy, it is unlikely that Lisbon III (2008-2010) will provide more convincing results. This being the case, staying on course beyond 2010, while quickening the pace, would seem to be an urgent necessity: that, indeed, is the aim of Lisbon Plus.

I. Lisbon Plus: Why? How?

A. European competitiveness has not been sufficiently strengthened since 2000

The assessment contained in the first part of this report demonstrates that the Lisbon strategy has not enabled Europe to strengthen its competitiveness to a sufficient degree. The EU has not fully implemented the shift towards a knowledge-based economy. According to certain key indicators, no progress has been made at all; this is true for higher education and innovation. The results are spectacularly grim for research: European research has been on the decline since 2000.

Overall, Europe's economic performances remain disappointing. Admittedly, the new Member States are carrying out a vigorous catching up. But the advanced European countries are not getting off the ground in terms of growth: for the 1980-2007 period, the European Union was the area of the world with the weakest growth. Over the last twenty years, growth in the EU-15 was each year weaker than the United States, creating a considerable wealth deficit that is symbolic of Europe's economic decline. In this respect, the relatively good results for 2007 (2.7% growth for the EU-15 compared to 2.3% for the United States) would seem to signal not so much a break in the trend as an exception linked to the American economy's doubtless temporary difficulties. The forecasts for 2008 reverse back once again (2% growth for the EU, 2.4%

for the United States). In reality, only the Nordic countries have crossed the technological frontier that separated them from a knowledge-based economy and are now enjoying a high growth rate.

B. Global competition has intensified

Over the last few years, we have gradually entered a world of "total" globalisation, characterised by intense competition in all fields, including areas that, traditionally, were the most protected: education, research, public services, etc. Global trade has increased spectacularly, not only in volume but also in terms of area of activity; from agricultural and industrial goods, it has extended to services, which constitute 70% of the economic activity of the most developed countries. And going beyond goods and services, capital, companies – industrial sites, and now head offices and research centres – and human resources have become nomadic. A predominant share of our economy and our companies, and also our territories, is now subject to global competition.

In this new context, the EU runs a greater risk of losing status. In 2000, it ran the risk of falling behind the most advanced countries: the United States, Japan, Korea. Today, it is exposed to the risk of the emerging countries catching up (China and India, but also Brazil, Russia, South Africa, etc.). The EU was regressing in the first division of the global economy; it is now threatened with demotion to the second division.

The Lisbon strategy defined precisely a path of "exit from above" centred on supply policies around the notion of quality-competitiveness. Our calling is to take part in added value competition with the most advanced countries, led by the United States and Japan. The aim is to break through the technological frontier that separates us from tomorrow's knowledge-based economy rather than fight it out in yesterday's industrial sectors with emerging countries.

In a European and international context marked by new challenges and new opportunities, the Lisbon strategy may remain a very useful conceptual matrix for the EU, provided that its content is refocused on essentials and its governance reinforced.

* *
*

As far as post-2010 developments in the scope of the Lisbon strategy are concerned, two major options are conceivable, reflecting conceptions that have been confronting each other ever since the strategy was launched. Each has its advantages and its shortcomings.

• *In the first, broad approach, Lisbon reflects the model of European development.* This model has three pillars: economic, social and environmental. Lisbon must consequently encompass all public policies involved in the European model.

This concept has the advantage of reflecting a global vision, incorporating all policies and thereby providing a certain intellectual satisfaction. It limits the risks of bureaucratic fragmentation; in effect, it tends to help the countless existing European coordination processes converge towards a "single strategy": processes such as the "Cardiff process" on structural reform, the Broad Economic Policy Guidelines, the Employment guidelines, the "Social Agenda" for employment law and social protection, the "Sustainable Development Strategy" for the environmental pillar, etc.

However, a shortcoming of this broad conception is that it is not focused enough and, as such, is a source of inefficiency and irresponsibility. Different Councils of Ministers have jurisdiction over different fragments of the strategy, administrative coordination is difficult and, in reality, only the European Council can ensure synthesis and trade-offs, which it only does imperfectly. This administrative scattering often goes hand in hand with bureaucratic complexity. The enlargement of the Lisbon strategy brings into play a growing number of committees and Commission directorates, encouraging the production of an ever-increasing number of documents, rapidly sinking into nominalism.

This approach also runs the risk of increasing dilution. On each reassessment of the strategy, new policies are added. Today, the temptation concerns energy policy and "the external dimension of the Lisbon agenda". Little by little, the strategy tends to transform itself into a hotchpotch that claims to integrate all the policies conducted by the EU and its Member States.

• *The second more restrictive, approach is that Lisbon is above all a growth and competitiveness programme for Europe,* centred on policies that are capable of increasing Europe's growth potential and economic competitiveness, the condition for preserving its advanced social model.

This second approach makes it possible to assert priorities. It ensures that Lisbon specialises in its "core competencies". It emphasises the "knowledge triangle" (higher education, research, innovation) and structural reforms. Naturally, it does not consider that social and environmental issues in the broader sense deserve less political attention, but that many of them should be treated distinctly and be subject to equally explicit and autonomous strategies.

The disadvantage of this approach is essentially political: the narrow content risks offending those who defend a strict balance among the economic, social and environmental components of the Lisbon strategy.

From the outset, Lisbon has been wavering between these two conceptions. It was the broad concept that prevailed in 2000-2001. In reaction, the 2004 Kok report on the evaluation of the Lisbon process favoured the strict approach and it led to the 2005 refocusing. *Lisbon III hesitates between the two concepts*. On paper, the Commission seems to have opened the door to integrating new subjects once again – in particular, the external economic component. But when one looks into the detail, things are much less clear; the courses of action that are brought up have hardly any concrete content in terms of public policy requirements.

Against that background, what should be the right scope for Lisbon Plus?

The approach chosen by this report incorporates the internal structural reform process that is characteristic of the Lisbon strategy into a more comprehensive strategy for globalisation, aiming to strengthen European competitiveness on the world stage. This strategy has two distinct but interlinked parts: internal competitiveness, focused on innovation (Lisbon Plus), and external competitiveness, relying on common external policies.

Lisbon Plus should, therefore, be an internal structural reform programme that aims to make Europe an effective innovation economy that is socially advanced and "clean" in the global economy. It is not intended to become a conceptual synthesis of all the policies undertaken by the EU and, on the contrary, should devote itself to a central task: adapting the European economy to globalisation, *i.e.*, implementing the structural reforms required to make the European economy more effective in the sphere of international competition.

European competitiveness is no longer about catching up. Europe's most advanced Member States have reached the technological frontier, while others will be converging there sooner or later. Innovation alone can push forward the technological frontier and bring about further progress in terms of productivity. So Europe must invest in the innovation economy and Lisbon Plus must focus on internal policies that have a direct impact on innovation ("quality competitiveness") – on these policies *alone*, but on *all* these policies.

This focus on competitiveness and innovation does not mean that Lisbon Plus should be redefined purely in terms of the "economic pillar", leaving aside the "social" and "environmental" pillars. The social and environmental policies that contribute to European innovation should be an integral part of Lisbon Plus; we will touch on them later. However, overall social security or environmental protection policies should not be part of it. A corollary of this is maintaining and restarting different existing processes, particularly the Social Agenda and the Sustainable Development Strategy. Their task is to coordinate policies undertaken in the social and environmental fields that are, for the most part, only remotely linked to competitiveness.

Likewise, not all European economic policies should be incorporated into Lisbon Plus but only the structural policies that seek to make Europe an innovation economy. In effect, the objective of economic growth and the objective of shifting to an innovation economy are not identical. In the modern globalised economy, breaking through the technological frontier into an innovation economy is the key growth factor, but other factors also contribute. There are short-term macroeconomic policies, even though they have lost their effectiveness and are difficult to mobilise in a European context; and there are certain structural reforms that are useful for European growth but not directly related to the innovation economy.

The Lisbon agenda has encouraged confusion. Its objective was clearly focused on quality-competitiveness, but its recommendations were broader in scope and incorporated all growth factors. This report proposes that Lisbon Plus concentrate clearly on quality-competitiveness factors alone.

Lastly, *the distinctions among economic, social and environmental pillars are instructive but fairly artificial: in reality, economic, social and environmental challenges are often deeply interwoven.* This interweaving produces a number of positive synergies: the promotion of education and training, which pursues both economic and social objectives; "flexicurity", which also aims to combine economic flexibility and social protection; and the development of the "green economy", which promotes economic, social and environmental progress.

In other cases, the interweaving can appear to produce contradictions; this is true of respecting the rules of the Stability Pact, raising the age of leaving the employment market and the ambivalent effect of environmental norms on economic competitiveness. But these contradictions also emphasise that economic, social and environmental issues are inextricable, that they cannot be artificially separated, and that refocusing Lisbon Plus on a central objective of competitiveness and innovation is not tantamount to expressing a predilection for one or another of these "pillars".

What is more, *this choice is in no way prejudicial to the need for serious thinking about ways and means of strengthening the social dimen-*

sion of European unification in response to the expectations of many citizens in the EU. However, a prerequisite for such thinking should be an open and honest debate by political leaders and European unions on the legal, socio-cultural and practical limits of a "social Europe" that most Member States (each for its own good reasons) seek to define narrowly.

Strengthening the *governance* of the Lisbon strategy does not raise dilemmas of this sort. We will go into more specific detail on this matter once we have outlined the *scope* of Lisbon Plus.

II. Refocusing on Innovation

Refocusing on competitiveness through innovation is this report's first recommendation for Lisbon Plus. The aim is to prioritise reforms that are absolutely necessary in order to break through the technological frontier. If we do not achieve this, that frontier will continue to act as a glass ceiling to European growth, and Europe will fall behind.

Accepting the urgent necessity of quality-competitiveness and innovation is a move that is all the more strategic given that these two themes would seem to have both a rallying and mobilising effect at the European level.

With regard to their international competitors, *one thing all EU countries have in common is their reliance on a diminished work force due to a structurally weaker demography and shorter working time* (annually, and over the whole life-span). If these countries wish to maintain their standard of living and high social standards, it is vital for them to offset these handicaps in qualitative terms by increasing productivity and backing innovation (even if this does not exclude increasing the working time over a lifetime and resorting to immigration).

Innovation would also seem crucial to enable EU countries to respond to the new planetary challenges caused by global warming, the structural rise in the cost of raw materials and the increasing economic power of countries with low-paid workers.

The EU has major tools available to encourage innovation: the stimulation of competition by applying Community rules and strengthening the Internal Market; the promotion of joint R&D projects; increasing the mobility of human resources; the exchange of good practices, and comparison and emulation among Member States.

All in all, innovation must be the vital, central area of a competitiveness strategy that allows all EU States to make up in part for lost time with regard to the United States and maintain their head start over emerging countries.

So what, in concrete terms, should a strategy that is refocused on internal competitiveness and innovation comprise? The innovation economy has two main engines: today, the knowledge-based economy (which was at the heart of Lisbon) and, in the longer run, the new green industry revolution. *The sphere of Lisbon Plus should, therefore, include three elements to drive these competitiveness engines*:

- a first element focused on research, quality-competitiveness factors in the Internal Market (in particular, financial services), industrial innovation (strategy for growth markets, competitive clusters, information and communication technologies (ICTs), small and medium-sized enterprises (SMEs), etc.);
- a second element centred mainly on policies to reinforce human capital. These policies concern education; the priority is higher education – the key to the innovation economy – but also educational policies that lead in this direction (particularly in early childhood), and those that maintain it, such as lifelong training. They also concern the employment market, with the main reform of flexicurity and the creation of a "European mobility area" to enhance the value of European human capital. Lastly, they concern policies facilitating adjustment to globalisation;
- a third element focused on the environment as an engine of growth and competitiveness: the development of green industries as well as the ambivalent question of environmental norms, a source of both losses and gains in economic competitiveness.

A. An economic strategy to serve innovation

1. Making research a real priority

Research is the linchpin of an innovation-based economy. Hence, one of the main objectives that the EU set itself in Lisbon in 2000 concerned research. If the EU proves unable to reverse the current trend in this critical area, it will decline rapidly and lose its footing in global competition. The objective is still to haul ourselves up to the level of the best in global performance. As a result, the target of 3% remains highly relevant. It should be a global objective for the EU, adapted to each country depending on how close it is to the technological frontier. But all Member States, whatever their level of economic development, should converge on this objective as they approach that frontier.

What policies should be followed to attain this? Developing private or public, national or European, fundamental or applied research? Favouring budgetary investments or structural reform? Taking into account the disappointing results since 2000, it is no longer a question of which means to select, but of how to combine them. To prioritise research and make it a reality, all the levers need to be pulled, including qualitative and quantitative improvement, private and public research, each at the Community and national levels.

- Strengthening the development of national public research

The EU is behind in public research, which is 20% lower than in the United States and 40% below the Lisbon objective, and the financial effort is on the decline in many countries. Public research provides an impetus to private research. And that is where the main point of leverage is to be found today.

National public research represents more than 95% of overall European public research and nearly half the total research. Here the authorities can take immediate, direct action, which is not the case with private research; it is "sufficient" to increase public budgets. For example, Lisbon Plus could require Member States to increase their annual public research budget by 10% until Lisbon's overall objective has been attained. To lighten the budgetary constraint, Lisbon Plus should also insist on the dynamic application of the Stability and Growth Pact, in its revised 2005 form, making it possible to fulfil the following European Council proposal: "Only major reforms which have direct long-term cost-saving effects, including by raising potential growth, and therefore a verifiable positive impact on the long-term sustainability of public finances, will be taken into account".

- Making R&D a budgetary priority at the European level

Quite the opposite is true today, with no more than a residual Community contribution to R&D (5% of the budget, 0.04% of European GDP). If research is truly at the heart of European economic strategy, this should be reflected more clearly in the Community budget. Critical mass phenomena in research justify pooling means. Member States that are at the catching-up stage do not have the financial means to conduct an ambitious policy of public research. European support would be doubly welcome. When the forthcoming financial perspectives are negotiated, research should become one of the EU's top policies[1]. It is also necessary to develop major joint research initiatives – whether managed by the EU ("joint initiatives") or not ("Eureka") – which would constitute further useful and strengthened cooperative R&D ventures.

---

[1] The "Sapir Report and the report on the future of Europe prepared by Dominique Strauss-Kahn and submitted to the President of the European Commission in June 2004 proposed a level of Community research of up to 0.25% of GDP.

- Stimulating private research in Europe

One cannot compel companies to invest in research, but the authorities can create a framework that provides greater incentives. The most advanced countries have achieved this. The United States has successfully increased private research by 0.2 points of GDP in ten years and Japan by 0.7 points to reach 2.6% of GDP today. Many EU Member States use a traditional support instrument: the research tax credit. But the EU has still not managed to create a unified European space for innovation. The Community patent is a recurrent, well-worn issue that remains unresolved, such that patentability is still in a fragmentary state. Despite the existence of a European Patent Office, all patents must be registered, translated, examined and implemented in each national patent office. As a result, the cost of registering a patent in Europe is eleven times higher than in the United States and fourteen times higher than in Japan.

Over and above these players, studies show that, in order to stimulate private research, the social and economic environment is of fundamental importance: industrial specialisation, the absence of barriers to market entry, a vigorous financial market, first-rate higher education, excellent infrastructures, quality of life, etc. Other factors which promote innovation generally will also contribute to the development of private research.

2. Directing the Internal Market towards innovation

The strengthening of the Internal Market should, of course, be pursued with vigour. It has constituted one of the most important engines of European growth over the last twenty years, stimulating competition between European companies and lowering prices for consumers. But, historically, the Internal Market has been based on a logic of economies of scale and price competitiveness and not always on innovation and quality-competitiveness. This does not mean that there is no link with innovation, quite the contrary.

First of all, intensifying competition within the Internal Market indirectly constitutes a factor that promotes innovation; increased competition means increased innovation. Strengthening the Internal Market generates an environment conducive to innovation. That is why liberalising services, network industries and the "Better Regulation" initiative are important reforms. But certain dimensions of the Internal Market contribute directly to the shift towards an innovation-based economy: as a matter of priority, Lisbon Plus must put the emphasis on these dimensions.

• *As a general rule, the EU must take on more clearly its implicit change of strategy for the Internal Market with enlargement to the east.* This no longer means creating a vast homogeneous market (at least in the short term), which was the EU-15 objective. It means, on the contrary, integrating an EU-27 European market that is intentionally heterogeneous, based on the comparative advantages of its constituent Member States.

The EU must affirm that its economic, social and even monetary heterogeneousness constitutes a major competitive asset, making it possible to refine its trade and industrial specialisations. At the same time, it should do a better job of offsetting the adjustment costs linked to operating the European market by strengthening its policy of social and territorial cohesion, the legitimacy and effectiveness of which must be reinforced.

• *The EU should also direct its tax strategy in aid of innovation.* The persistence of different national tax systems is not a problem in itself, so long as it stimulates Member States' productivity initiatives. A certain heterogeneousness in tax policies is natural, allowing peripheral areas, for example, to offset their economic handicaps with lower rates of taxation. However, wholesale fiscal competition leads Member States into a downward race that is counterproductive and in conflict with the public investments required by Lisbon Plus. Tax policy cannot be overlooked in the context of a European strategy for globalisation.

• *From a sectoral standpoint, significant gains in terms of innovation can be made in government contracts.* Given their volume, government contracts are likely to have a considerable impact on the promotion of innovation. Indeed, they represent 16% of European GDP, 40% of construction expenses and nearly 100% of defence and security expenditures. The use of public authorities, via government contracts, as "vanguard clients" to support innovation is a significant lever. For example, imposing High Quality Environmental standards (HQE) in public authority invitations to tender promotes the development of innovative green industries.

To give another example, it is a known fact that innovative small and medium-sized enterprises (SMEs) are excluded from government contracts; public authorities favour the reliability of major groups and invitations to tender often require accounting figures for three or even five years which, by definition, start-ups cannot present. In this respect, the Small Business Act proposed by the European Commission significantly paves the way for improving the economic environment for innovative SMEs.

3. *A dynamic financial market to serve innovative SMEs*

Financial services have not been at the heart of the Lisbon strategy[2]. As such, credit market reform has always been considered secondary to the Lisbon objectives as other issues were thought more urgent – reducing the rigidities of the employment market, for example – and because the development of European financial markets around the euro was generally deemed satisfactory. Recent studies[3] and the American example refute this opinion: an effective financial services market is a priority for the innovation economy.

Certainly European financial markets have achieved satisfactory depth, and this is as true of equity markets as it is of debt markets. But these markets are only accessible to major companies. Innovative start-ups have either limited access or none whatsoever. These companies have very high investment requirements. They are experiencing rapid growth and, as a result, generate strong demands for working capital. For the most part, they invest in intangible assets that, unlike tangible assets, are difficult to use to secure bank financing.

Faced with these investment needs, the credit market adapted to start-ups has remained very narrow in Europe, unlike its counterpart in the United States. Indeed, the American financial system has evolved very rapidly to develop specific markets (seed capital, business angels, venture capital) and suitable solutions (high yield bonds, mezzanine debt, private equity). Nothing of the sort has happened in Europe, with the noteworthy exceptions of the United Kingdom and Sweden. As a result, *European innovative start-ups have difficulty finding the capital structures required for their development.* A European start-up company grows, on average, six-fold over its first seven years, as opposed to sixty-fold in the United States.

One influential school of thought plays down the impact of this reality on innovation. According to its advocates, though the American Silicon Valley model is indeed based on the success of innovative SMEs on Schumpeterian principles, the European innovation model – following the Japanese model – should, on the contrary, be based on the investment of major industrial groups: these groups can carry out risk

---

[2] No guideline is devoted to financial services even though four out of 24 concern them more or less directly.

[3] See the recent Bruegel policy papers: "A Primer on Innovation and Growth" (Philippe Aghion, October 2006); "Financing Europe's Fast Movers" (Nicolas Véron and Thomas Philippon, January 2008).

arbitrage internally and operate cross-subsidies using surplus from mature divisions to finance investment in innovative sectors. The European financial markets would be well-adapted to this model precisely because they provide broad financing, both in debt and capital, for major groups listed on the stock exchange.

However, economic studies tend to demonstrate that the Schumpeterian innovative start-up model is more effective for an economy that is close to the technological frontier. Innovation is more often breakthrough than incremental and it calls into question the existing economic models that the established players, who benefit from it, do not want to upset. In any case, whatever the innovation mix between major groups and start-ups, it is patently obvious that the latter have inadequate access to financing.

Suitable financial services must be developed for these small innovative companies. Lisbon Plus should devote itself to this task. We know what instruments are required. Public financing is one: public capital equity, "funds of funds", guaranteed loans, etc. But, in a number of Member States, these means are limited by public budgetary constraints. For this reason, indirect interventions should also be considered to allow better allocation of private capital (which exists in abundance) towards innovative SMEs. Some of the possible reforms include relaxing prudential rules to enable financial players from outside the banking sector to offer financial services[4]; developing financial markets with simplified regulations to enable start-ups to be listed on the stock exchange more rapidly; adapting insolvency legislation[5]; reforming the tax system to make it easier to direct savings towards these financings[6].

Lisbon Plus could also make the most of the reorientation presently under way at the European Investment Bank (EIB). The EIB's historic missions concentrated on the objectives of cohesion and convergence, particularly in the area of Trans-European Transport Networks. But the EIB is reorienting gradually towards innovation. It first launched the "Innovation 2010" (i2i) initiative in the context of the Lisbon strategy. Nearly 50 billion euros in loans were granted to finance the knowledge-based economy for research, financing innovative SMEs (debt and risk capital), investments in education, information technology and tele-

---

4 For example, banks always have a monopoly over leasing and factoring in France, Austria, Italy and Portugal.

5 Start-ups are all the more illiquid because they are experiencing rapid growth: in other words, because they are doing well.

6 Even today, in France the tax system favours rent over risk, investments in bonds rather than investments in capital, the short term over the long term, public financing over private financing.

communications. Among the projects financed by the i2i initiative, for example, were research infrastructures (the CERN particle accelerator), support for developing technopoles and industrial R&D programmes in the field of aeronautics. The EIB has set a financing objective of 65 billion euros between now and 2013 in the context of i2i. More recently, it developed a research facility (the Risk Sharing Finance Facility (RSFF)) intended to provide joint financing for research projects that are eligible for the 7th Framework Programme for Research and Technological Development (FP7) in the context of a global budget of 10 billion euros in loans.

It is desirable to strengthen the EIB's role with regard to innovative industries. Countries that are in the catching-up phase are presently hostile to this reorientation, which benefits first and foremost the most advanced European countries. But this hostility should diminish as these countries converge towards the technological frontier. A "Lisbon Plus Innovation" initiative on the part of the EIB could be the crowning achievement of this evolution.

4. Restoring industry to its right place

The Lisbon strategy rightly emphasised services, which constitute both the main sector in the EU (approximately 70% of its GDP) and the basis of its economic future. Lisbon Plus should continue down this path, while laying particular stress on the need for innovation to spread through the services sector. However, Lisbon Plus should also initiate a return to industrial activities.

Industry's weight in the economy has certainly decreased (to 16% as against 30% at its European peak), but statistics clearly underestimate its real influence. The outsourcing of support functions in industry leads to activities that used to be listed as industrial when they were still carried out within the industrial company (computer services, accounting, catering, cleaning, etc.) being categorized as services activities. The European economy has not desindustrialised itself; it has not become a service economy. In many of its strategic industrial sectors it leads the world with technological flagships: aeronautics and space, transport, nuclear power, energy and the environment, industrial tools, agribusiness, and so on.

Industry provides structure to general economic activity. It creates clusters attracting universities, research centres and services activities (in this respect, the case of Airbus in Toulouse is emblematic). Above all, industry remains the predominant source of private research and innovation. New technologies invented by industry generate productivity gains throughout the economy. Thus, the spread of information and communication technologies has enabled productivity gains in all sectors (services, industry, agriculture) and boosted growth. This is particularly true in the United States.

This does not only concern high-tech. Agronomic research spearheaded by agribusiness has led to innovations in the agricultural sector, and in the future this will be even more evident. In addition to progress in production techniques, research is now being undertaken to create an agriculture that is "sustainable" and no longer has a negative impact on the environment[7].

Various initiatives launched by the European Commission and other Community institutions in recent times show increased mobilisation on behalf of industry[8]. Moreover, most of the components of an industrial innovation strategy seem to exist at the European level: the reorientation of industrial specialisation towards the most innovative sectors (Lead Markets, "Sustainable Industrial Policy"); strengthening innovation capacity in these sectors (industrial research, joint technological initiatives, competitive clusters); and the protection of their competitiveness (impact studies). More indirectly, one could add flexicurity and higher education. An active university policy should lead to the supply of human capital required by the innovation economy. Flexicurity should contribute the flexibility needed to manage human resources during the very marked economic cycles that characterise industry. This being the case, it will be important to consolidate these as yet scattered components within a more coherent industrial strategy.

If industry is at the heart of the innovation economy, a European industrial strategy should be at the heart of Lisbon Plus. Of course, this is not a question of establishing an old-style, defensive or protectionist "industrial policy" that seeks, for example, to provide financial support for this or that company, or a particular sector, but rather a cross-sectoral strategy that aims to promote innovation.

The first objective of such an approach should be *to direct Europe's industrial specialisation towards innovative sectors*. Europe must shift more rapidly from the more mature sectors of yesterday's industrial economy towards the growth-promoting sectors of the innovation

---

7 It is worth noting that innovation will also be necessary to avoid the reverse negative impacts of climate change on agriculture. For example, global warming has caused the destruction of the pedunculate oak, an important forestry resource in France, by promoting the development of its parasite, the Oidium, a microscopic fungus that proliferates in mild winters.

8 Particularly "A Policy Framework to Strengthen EU Manufacturing – towards a more integrated approach for industrial policy" (October 2005); "Mid Term Review of Industrial Policy – a contribution to the EU's Growth and Jobs Strategy" (July 2007).

economy – information and communications technologies (ICT), biotechnologies, energy, "green" technologies[9], etc. Pouring research subsidies into sectors with little innovation potential and low-level R&D has considerably less impact than directing aid towards innovative sectors.

The second objective is to strengthen Europe's competitive position in these innovative sectors. Besides instituting a favourable environment for industry and sectoral strategies that already exist at the European level (the Competitive Automotive Regulatory System for the 21st century (CARS 21), textiles, etc.), an industrial strategy for innovation should rely on the following instruments.

- Regulation and industrial standards

In principle, adopting regulations and demanding standards in the European market works in favour of innovative industries. In waste management, for example, the obligation to put an end to waste collection sites has promoted the development of household waste incineration plants and ceramic furnaces with high added value.

However, regulatory constraints generate rises in industrial production costs. Excessively demanding regulations risk penalising European industries when faced with foreign competitors who are not subject to such additional expenditure. In reality, we must distinguish between different types of regulation.

Regulations that concern the "industrial process" increase production costs for European manufacturers alone. They burden production costs for all products, including those intended for export. On the other hand, these regulations are not applicable to imported products; the World Trade Organisation (WTO) prohibits it. Such is the case for Regulation, Evaluation and Authorisation of Chemicals (REACH) directive obligations in the chemical sector or the CO_2 emission permits (Emission Trading Scheme, ETS) that are under discussion to apply the Kyoto obligations. For this kind of regulation, the industrial impact studies planned for in the above-mentioned integrated competitiveness strategy will play an important role.

Conversely, industrial standards concerning the technical characteristics of products apply as much to imports as to European products. One of the problems is how far imported products actually respect these

[9] Six high-potential niche markets have been identified by the Commission's Lead Market Initiative, through economic studies and wide-ranging consultations with professionals: renewable energy, sustainable building, the recycling industry, biological industrial products, e-health and protective textiles. The development of these six markets could lead to the creation of a million jobs in Europe by 2020.

standards. The controversy over the Chinese-made dolls contaminated with lead provides an illustration: using lead-based paints for toys is banned by EC standards, but the imported toys were not subject to adequate inspection. Better still, these industrial standards could give European manufacturers a decisive edge in international competition, if Europe is capable of exporting these standards throughout the world.

Lastly, in new sectors where several standards are in competition, the size of the European market can also make a difference. Here the oft-cited example is that of mobile telephony where the European GSM standard has become the global standard. More recently, in the high-definition DVD sector, the presence of European manufacturers alongside Sony is not totally unrelated to the victory of Blue Ray technology over Toshiba's HD-DVD.

We shall return later to the importance of a genuine normative strategy for the EU at the international level.

- Support for major European projects

Joint Technology Initiatives (JTIs) represent an important tool for a European industrial strategy. These are joint undertakings that bring together the Commission, Member States and the private sector. They concern research projects with high capital intensity (requiring the presence of the public authorities) and potentially profitable commercial application. Four JTIs are in the process of being adopted: they concern innovative medicines (Innovative Medicines Initiative (IMI)), sustainable air transport (Clean Sky), onboard aviation systems (Advanced Research and Technology for Embedded Intelligence and Systems, ARTEMIS) and nanoelectronics (European Nanoelectronics Initiative Advisory Council, ENIAC).

In the same spirit, a joint undertaking is behind the European GPS project, Galileo. Europe is supporting the development of its space industry with the Ariane launcher, and Airbus continues to benefit from Community financial support through the refundable advance system. So Europe also knows how to develop major structuring industrial projects in a pragmatic fashion. Lisbon Plus should promote and strengthen this approach.

Lastly, *Lisbon Plus should set up more substantial financing initiatives for infrastructure investments*, particularly for European transport and energy networks (Trans-European Networks, TEN). These networks seemed less important than ICTs when the Lisbon strategy was initiated, whereas in fact they are essential. Since then, they have been the subject of broadly consensual forward-looking plans and deserve at least twice the Community investment they are currently receiving. They promote innovation directly (the TGV, buried very high-voltage electricity lines, etc.) and indirectly in a EU whose economy has not "dematerialised" and in which goods, services and human capital should be able to circulate with much greater ease.

- Information and Communication Technologies (ICTs)

It is thanks to ICTs that the most advanced countries, notably the United States, have been able to push back the technological frontier and provide high-level sustainable growth through the 1990s and the 2000 decade. Europe had fallen behind in this field, which was the very justification for launching the Lisbon strategy.

Today, Europe has partly, but not completely, made up for lost time as far as ICTs are concerned. The Member States that are in the convergence phase are, of course, still under-equipped. In the more advanced Member States, there are still areas that lack equipment: SMEs, public administrations and rural territories. "E-government" Community initiatives for the public services and the Small Business Act for SMEs are heading in the right direction. They should be strengthened within the framework of Lisbon Plus.

B. Mobilising human capital, a key resource for the EU

Human capital is the key to a successful innovation economy. From now on, Europe must train not just the foremen of yesterday's factories, but also scientists, engineers, creators, designers, experts in synthesising ideas, executives and technicians for the innovation economy. Investing in human capital requires, above all, higher education, but also educational policies that pave the way there for one and all, particularly in early childhood, and policies to keep that education alive, with provisions for lifelong training. Investing in human capital also concerns the employment market, with the principal reform of flexicurity and measures for addressing the social costs of adjusting to globalisation, as well as the creation of an appropriate "European mobility area" to enhance the value of European human capital. These different directions converge in giving content to the "active social State", already mentioned at Lisbon in 2000, which combines a genuinely protective dimension with a dynamic environment conducive to innovation and competitiveness.

1. Investing in education

- Higher education

In the "knowledge triangle" (research, innovation and higher education), higher education has always been looked on as the poor relation. Yet it is a crucial challenge for the innovation economy in which Europe is falling critically behind. It is not only a question of promoting the competitiveness of the European economies, but also of ensuring the sustainable preservation of centres of decision-making, research and expertise within EU territory.

The present performance gaps between the EU and the other OECD countries have a twofold explanation. The main explanation is budgetary; the United States invests 3.3% of its national wealth in its universities, compared to 1.3% in Europe – nearly three times more, with a staggering gap of two points in GDP. It is generally observed that the difference mainly concerns private investment. Private investment is certainly marginal in Europe (0.2% of GDP, compared to 0.6% in Japan and 1.8% in the United States). But even public investment is considerably higher in the United States: 1.5% compared to 1.1% of GDP. As a result, the American academic system helps more students succeed and devotes more resources to them (36,500 euros per student compared to 8,700 euros in Europe) in all areas – teachers' pay, teacher-student ratio, the excellence of the university libraries, computer equipment, the quality of campuses and student accommodation, and so on.

The second explanation concerns governance. All the studies show that the quality of universities is correlated with their autonomy – in particular, budgetary autonomy, freedom in taking on staff and freedom in setting salaries. European universities, on the other hand, are still run in a highly centralised manner by the State in the majority of Member States.

The EU should make higher education its top post-2010 priority. Lisbon Plus should set clear objectives, like those that exist in other fields: 50% of each age group with a higher education qualification, a given number of European universities ranked in the Shanghai Top 100 list[10], 3% of national wealth devoted to higher education.

There is a lively political debate about how to achieve this additional investment in Europe: public or private financing? This debate would seem secondary. The real issue is about increasing investment in higher education and, with this objective in view, all available means should be combined.

One could decide to make public investment bear the burden. That is what the more advanced European countries in this field do – namely the Nordic countries, where universities are almost 100% state-funded.

---

10 The European performance in the Top 500 is more acceptable: it has 55% of the United States' level. This corresponds to a reality. Europe has many good-quality middle-range universities, whereas the standard deviation is more marked in the United States between excellent world-class universities and regional universities.

This is first and foremost a challenge for the Member States, for they have exclusive jurisdiction over higher education. But it would not be unjustified for the EU to provide financial support by investing, for example, in networks of academic centres of excellence labelled "European universities" and required to rank among the best in the world. In this respect, it would seem reasonable to include a "higher education" heading when the financial perspectives of the European budget are revised.

One could also make the students themselves bear part of the burden by charging higher enrolment fees, as the United Kingdom has chosen to do. This is a legitimate option in terms of equity: it is known that using general taxation to pay for the higher education of a few students who, statistically, come from privileged social backgrounds, amounts to back-to-front social redistribution. Naturally, charging higher enrolment fees should be accompanied by increased financial aid for students from modest backgrounds. There is a more general justification for such increased support because the effort of making higher education available to one and all is hindered by social inequalities. Young adults who lack resources abandon the idea of higher education because they do not have the financial means to live as students. As a result, they begin their working lives immediately. This is why we suggest coupling the charging of higher enrolment fees with an initiative that aims to make student loans widely available through a guarantee from the European Investment Bank (EIB) or Member States[11].

Lastly, large companies should play a role in this investment, which concerns them to a considerable degree. In particular, they can do this via the system of company-sponsored university chairs, as is now the case in the French *Grandes Écoles*. To avoid "privatising" qualifications and ensure that the universities' total independence is preserved, company financing could be mediated by foundation-type structures operating in the public interest. These university foundations, endowed by companies, would specialise in the joint financing of higher education courses. They would make it possible to forge public/private partnerships in the context of an innovative means of governance in the public interest.

Beyond the critical issue of financing, Lisbon Plus should also promote the autonomy of universities and the distribution of best European and international practices in this field.

---

[11] See above – Chapter IV-2.

- School teaching and early childhood

To enter higher education, it is first necessary to have successfully completed one's schooling.

The general availability of secondary education has been achieved, or is being achieved, in almost all of the EU's Member States. Furthermore, the EU would have difficulty getting involved in this, because it is a period of schooling that is closely linked to culture and national identity. Early childhood, on the other hand, deserves to be addressed within Lisbon Plus.

Indeed, the knowledge-based economy rests on the ability to learn – at university, then in professional life through training. The sociologist Gøsta Esping-Andersen has shown that this ability to learn requires a "cognitive capital" that is mainly acquired in early childhood, up to the age of six. It so happens that inequalities between children are enormous at that age, ranging from those who receive active intellectual stimulation from their parents to others who are abandoned in front of television channels (public or private) for which "promoting the knowledge-based economy" is the least of their worries. Thus, social inheritance plays a key role in the early years of life and has a decisive influence on individuals' cognitive capital.

This is why one must "invest in babies" by making day nurseries and public services for early childhood generally available. One such model has been successfully established in Denmark. France also has very sound resources in this respect. It is important to help such facilities become widespread in Europe. This was one of the Lisbon objectives and Lisbon Plus should push it even further, also taking into account the European demographic deficit. Investing in early childhood is largely the responsibility of local authorities, but the EU could serve as a facilitator by ensuring joint investment through a *specific "Early Childhood" fund*. Community intervention would also make it possible to get around the shortcomings of certain new members which, like Poland, have done away with public day nurseries and do not as yet have sufficient financial means to replace them.

- Integrating all population groups

A large share of European human capital is today unexploited because our economies leave too many constituent parts of the active population on the fringes of the employment market. The employment rate for the older and young workers is inadequate in many Member States. Women are in the process of being integrated but some countries still lag far behind. Above all, the employment situation for immigrant populations, or populations stemming from immigration, remains problematic throughout Europe.

It is crucial for the future of Europe – and not only its economic future – for investment in human capital to include all constituent parts of its population. Given the accumulated delays and discriminatory practices, this requires policies that are specifically targeted to benefit these disadvantaged populations. It means "giving more to those who have less" – more public capital for those who have less individual capital.

2. *European "flexicurity", between common principles and social adjustment*

Mobility is vital to distribute innovation throughout the economy, from one company or sector to another. It can benefit from the existence of high levels of social protection in EU countries, which must make it possible to take charge of transition periods between two jobs. Though the EU has recently adopted "common principles" on flexicurity – and it is important to remember their strategic character and ensure their implementation –, it could do more in the future to take responsibility for transition periods in the lives of European workers.

- Essential "common principles"

As far as "flexibility" is concerned, the recommendations are simple: employment law relating to hiring and firing must be made more flexible. As regards "security", however, a major change is required. In effect, this involves *ensuring that the community takes full responsibility for the transition period between one job and another* – what economists call organising "transitional markets":

- *establishing active policies for a return to employment.* National employment agencies are struggling to provide workers with the permanent logistical support they require. "Transition agencies" must be invented, drawing inspiration from the "outplacement" missions that companies sometimes offer their executives who are on the point of leaving: skills assessment, practical support, personalised follow-up and psychological support, until a new position has been secured;
- *validation of knowledge gained through experience.* Unskilled, or relatively unskilled, workers have no qualifications to show in the employment market. Their skills were recognised through the work they did within the company. It is necessary to make skills acquired within a particular company "transferable": this involves recognising these skills in the *curriculum vitae* by certifying them in a way that is equivalent to a diploma;

- *a high replacement rate*. Unemployed workers in Denmark receive 90% of their previous salary, compared to 55% in France for example;
- *a huge effort to provide continuing education*. Many European salaried employees now have to change companies and professions several times in the course of their professional careers. As such, they have to acquire new skills throughout their lives, hence the increased importance of continuing education. This is not a question of providing employees with additional marginal knowledge in order to make progress within their companies, but of teaching them a new profession to enable them to change company or business sector.

- An increased financial contribution from the EU for adjustment expenses

A genuine flexicurity policy is very expensive. Its cost may reach up to at least 2 points of GDP per year. This is a matter of national responsibility and it is known that Member States have varying difficulties in producing budgetary room for manoeuvre. If the EU really seeks to place flexicurity at the heart of a social policy to enhance the value of human capital, it has a duty to mobilise an increased share of its budget to support policies conducted by Member States.

Increased financial intervention by the EU is particularly justified for all adjustment and training expenses linked to restructuring. *Since the EU is invested by its Member States with the responsibility for liberalisation processes both internally (Internal Market and enlargement) and externally (trade policy), it must take on even greater responsibility for compensating their adverse social consequences.* The latter are certainly marginal compared to their positive effects, but nevertheless affect the lives of thousands of Europeans.

This compensatory intervention by the EU should be an important component of the *EuroWorld 2015 Strategy*, covering both the internal and external dimensions. It could take effect within the framework of a strong build-up in the Globalisation Adjustment Fund that should be devoted not only to globalisation, but (as is already partly the case) to all restructurings and relocations, including those within the EU. A much more active and direct mobilisation of the European Social Fund (ESF) should also be organised on the pattern of the Globalisation Adjustment Fund (constituting dossiers to benefit workers who are made redundant and granting direct investment from the ESF). This would strengthen citizens' support for Europe.

3. Creating a "European socio-professional mobility area"

Human capital feeds on mobility. It is enriched by the exchange of experience and cross-fertilisation. Given its diversity, Europe has a considerable potential asset in this respect. However, it still needs to make the most of it by ensuring genuine internal mobility.

We, therefore, propose the creation of an overall plan for a European mobility area within the framework of Lisbon Plus. This would include three components.

- *Student mobility*, with the increasing importance of Erasmus. The Mission suggests that, in the long run, university master's degrees include a compulsory term in another European State. This obligation has already been successfully introduced in Luxembourg and in French *Grandes Écoles*. Making this practice more widespread will naturally take time: 2020 could be established as the deadline, with a resulting gradual increase in application and budgetary provision – multiplying Erasmus financing by four for the next financial period, and by ten for the following periods. Budgets for the other current exchange programmes (Leonardo for apprentices and Grundtig for teachers, etc.) would also double. This increase in Community financing would serve to stimulate additional financing by States and local authorities, who already play a major role in supporting student mobility.
- *Mobility of salaried employees*. This is presently very limited and involves an average of 2% of the active population in countries of the EU. Several avenues may be explored to remedy this situation:
  - first, creating an assistance programme for mobile Europeans, a "Workers' Erasmus", which would include language learning, help with job-seeking in an unfamiliar employment market, the treatment of problems arising from a lack of harmonisation between diplomas and financial help with costs linked to mobility (*e.g.* moving expenses). Though implemented locally, this investment would come under the Community budget because the action would cover the whole of the EU;
  - next, guaranteeing effective, widespread equivalence between diplomas and qualifications within the EU. Though the recognition of diplomas is under way and certain regulated professions are now open to citizens of all Member States (doctors, lawyers), this process is only in its early days and needs to be brought to a successful conclusion;
  - lastly, ensuring that workers' social rights are respected. This presupposes reducing all the obstacles to making social rights (health, retirement, unemployment) totally transferable between countries

and establishing more effective control over workers' secondment on the basis of a European agency that regroups European civil servants and national employment inspectors.

To tackle these issues, the introduction of "European local delegations" to oversee the effective application of Community law for citizens and workers throughout the EU would be a welcome initiative.

- *Finally, any ambitious mobility strategy should seek to improve the learning of European languages, since shortcomings in this field constitute one of the main obstacles to mobility.* In this respect, it is advisable for the EU to make a much higher financial contribution than is presently the case to Member States so as to guarantee that each and every one of them can provide early education in two living European languages.

C. The "new green economy"

Thirdly, Lisbon Plus must concentrate on *the environment* as an engine of growth and innovation. Post-2010, the environment should be granted the same status as ICTs when the Lisbon strategy was launched in 2000 because environmental industries are being required to expand rapidly (particularly as a result of Kyoto) and they bring with them technological innovations. They should, therefore, have a strong impact on economic competitiveness as the driving force behind innovation. However, unlike ICTs, they also have a negative effect by increasing production costs. The objective of Lisbon Plus should be to maximise gains and minimise costs.

1. Enhancing the value of environmental policies as an engine of growth

The environment is an essential market for the future with a global turnover already in excess of 1,000 billion euros (the equivalent of the aeronautics or the pharmaceutical industry), a high rate of growth (6% a year) and major development prospects with the fight against climate change.

Europe is very well positioned in this market. It is the world leader, has major global companies (*e.g.* in the water and energy sectors), is developing cutting-edge projects (the GMES project for satellite observation of land and deforestation, the ITER nuclear fusion project, etc.) and innovative standards (CO_2 standards for cars), and it is deploying a very active environmental diplomacy (Kyoto, the first international treaty for the protection of coasts in the context of the "coastal zone" protocol of the Barcelona Convention, a biodiversity convention, the convention for humid zones, debt-for-nature swaps, etc.).

Europe should take advantage of its lead in a high-potential market to foster its growth and competitiveness. Lisbon Plus can contribute to this by developing a three-part action plan.

- Innovative environmental technologies

At the March 2007 European Council, the EU set itself ambitious objectives for the fight against climate change: a 20% reduction in greenhouse gas emissions; a 20% share of renewable energy sources in the European energy mix; a planned 20% reduction in global primary energy consumption by 2020.

These objectives cannot be achieved with the current state of technology. Europe needs a specific policy to accelerate the development and deployment of low-cost, low carbon technologies.

This will not be easy because Europe has fallen behind, albeit less than the rest of the world. With oil and gas, we have benefited from abundant, inexpensive energy supplies. Apart from the brief period of the oil crisis in the 1970s, chronic public and private underinvestment in new energy technologies has prevailed.

Above all, the innovation process in the environmental and energy field suffers from structural handicaps. It is characterised by lengthy waiting periods – often amounting to decades – before innovations come onto the market, and very large-scale investments are required. Even though the rising cost of hydrocarbons is opening up opportunities, new technologies are facing initial costs that are generally higher than those they replace, with a long experience curve. They sometimes come up against problems of social acceptance (nuclear energy, wind energy) and often against main players who want to preserve their income from high carbon technology.

In short, *innovative environmental technologies are not naturally upheld by the market.* This gap between supply and demand is often called the "Valley of Death" for low carbon energy technologies.

For this reason, public intervention must help ensure the initial development of these technologies until they themselves make money available as an effect of lowering production costs as the experience curve proceeds. The main technological challenges have been identified.

In the medium-term (2020): the development of second-generation biofuels, the commercial use of CO_2 capture technologies, doubling the production capacity of large wind turbines, setting up wind turbines at sea, large-scale development of photovoltaic energy and concentrated solar energy, establishing long-term solutions for managing nuclear waste.

In the long term (2050): marketing vehicles with hydrogen fuel cells, the arrival of fourth-general nuclear fission plants, the bringing into service of the ITER fusion reactor, etc.

The ground was prepared in November 2007 by the Commission's communication "Towards a European Strategic Energy Technology Plan" (SET-Plan). The effective deployment of this plan should be at the heart of the Lisbon Plus agenda. It should both coordinate national action and mobilise all Community instruments: regulations, research programmes, innovation financing (EIB, budgetary line in the context of the new financial perspectives).

- Energy efficiency

Lisbon Plus should make a particular effort to improve energy efficiency for several reasons. First, energy efficiency has a twofold economic impact; it is a direct source of technological innovation and an indirect source of increased competitiveness for the whole European economy via the savings it generates. According to the Green Paper published by the Commission in 2005, a 20% reduction in consumption by 2020 would have a considerable impact: savings of 60 billion euros a year (between 200 and 1,000 euros a year for an average household), a 50% reduction in CO_2 emissions and the creation of a million jobs.

Second, Europe has fallen far behind in this respect (energy consumption continues to rise in Europe by about 2% a year) and there is much more room for progress in energy demand than in supply.

In the field of transport (30% of European energy consumption), incentives to use more economical cars, traffic management and, most of all, the development of public transport and restrictions on car use in urban areas (half the fuel used by road transport is consumed in town) are promising avenues to explore.

As far as buildings and households are concerned (40% of energy consumption), waste is still high: poor insulation, high-energy lighting and domestic appliances, poorly calibrated air conditioning, etc. The "sleep mode" for domestic appliances alone represents 7% of total electricity consumption!

Lastly, in industry (30%), there are also many sources for improved energy efficiency. In particular, there would seem to be significant room for improvement in the electricity sector. Two thirds of the electrical energy produced is consumed in the production and transport process, before it even reaches the user.

- Environmental standards

Given the size of its internal market, the EU is able to impose its standards on the world market. This globalisation of standards gives a strong competitive advantage to European manufacturers who, by definition, are the first to adapt their production and, as a result, benefit from a head start in terms of the experience effect. Regulatory standardisation (and its equivalent in soft law) and product certification will find a vast field of application in the environmental area.

2. *Limiting economic surcharges linked to environmental policies*

Environmental constraints are expensive. Their costs are variable and should be weighed against the above-mentioned gains to assess the net effects, but they certainly exist. As far as European climate change counter-measures are concerned, they are estimated at 0.5 point of GDP by 2020.

These costs are not equally distributed. They can put great pressure on certain sectors. In the climate change context, the *weakened sectors are energy-intensive industries*: aluminium, steel, paper, inorganic chemistry, cement, ceramic glass, electro-intensive industries, etc. The Emission Trading Scheme (ETS) regulations for carbon dioxide emissions set a CO_2 emission price of between 32 and 40 euros a ton. This is a heavy burden for these industries. It corresponds, for example, to a 60% tax on the price of coal. If nothing is done, the competitiveness of these sectors will suffer and the risk of environmental relocation ("carbon leak") is serious. Europe could lose entire parts of its heavy industry. The electro-intensive industries should be given even more sustained attention because the liberalisation of European energy markets often leads to upward renegotiation of their electricity supply contracts.

A first solution is to grant special dispensations to these energy-intensive industries (*e.g.*, in the form of free permit allocations). This solution would certainly resolve the problem of economic competitiveness in these sectors, but it would challenge the environmental objectives pursued. It could also entail pernicious effects, such as a "bonus" for polluting industries. The latter could sell their rights to pollute (received free of charge) and relocate at the same time.

The other solution would involve equalising conditions of international competition (the "level playing field") – preferably by negotiation, so that the rest of the world applies equivalent counter-measures to climate change. If need be, an adjustment mechanism could be set up at borders (import levy and export refund). But such a mechanism is far from commanding consensus approval in Europe; we shall return to it later.

In any case, Europe is sure to suffer a loss in competitiveness as a result of the policy to fight climate change. This is a rarely mentioned fact, highlighted by the Stern report. National economies are affected differently by the same environmental measures, depending on their industrial specialisation. European exports are more specialised in capital-intensive, high carbon products, whereas American and Japanese exports are specialised in products involving intensive research and intangible innovation (producing lower carbon levels), and Asian export products are manpower-intensive (with low carbon levels).

As a result – and contrary to popular opinion – Europe's international competitiveness is more sensitive to CO_2 *tariff-setting than that of its rivals. This is an additional advantage to be gained from Europe shifting towards an innovation economy: developing an industrial specialisation in products with high intangible content will make Europe less vulnerable.*

III. A Stronger Governance Structure

The governance of the Lisbon strategy has been steadily improving over the years (see Annex 3), particularly within the framework of the relaunch of 2005. Though largely based on the open method of coordination (OMC), it also relies on more traditional Community tools (directives). In reality, the EU has developed different types of OMCs depending on sector. The Lisbon strategy's OMC is characterised by not insignificant political monitoring (*e.g.* multilateral surveillance and country-specific recommendations) and cannot be likened to the much softer intergovernmental coordination that prevails for social issues.

In any case, the OMC constitutes "the worst system, except for all the others" for organising EU intervention into the many economic and social matters that are mainly the responsibility of Member States, are destined to remain so, and through which the OMC has made it possible to introduce the beginnings of European coordination.

These reminders do not exclude the need for a clear reinforcement of the implementation of Lisbon Plus compared to the current operation of the Lisbon strategy. Our proposals for improvement, which ensue directly from the assessment set forth in the first part of this volume, concern mainly:

- establishing better-targeted, better-differentiated and better-evaluated objectives;
- strengthening the Community dimension of Lisbon Plus;

- enhancing the incentives for Member States to act;
- increasing the involvement of political authorities and social and economic stakeholders.

A. Better-targeted, better-differentiated and better-evaluated objectives

1. Better-targeted overall objectives for the EU

First and foremost, Lisbon Plus should be based on a *single, limited and homogeneous list of objectives expressed in figures* that could be selected from those identified by the European Council (see Part I of this volume for the 2000-2007 period) and the 14 "structural indicators" chosen by the European Commission. These overall objectives should be selected for their political legibility (*e.g.* the investment objective of 3% of GDP in R&D), but also for their social and economic scope. They will then serve as a central reference point for all stakeholders in the implementation of Lisbon Plus.

Among the ranges from which the new strategic objectives should be identified, it seems relevant to select productivity per working person, the level of expenditure on education (or higher education) and the ratio of those of non-working age to those of working age (*i.e.*, the dependency ratio). Conversely, it is inadvisable to incorporate into the Lisbon Plus objectives the rules set by the Stability Pact (which fall within the macro-economic sphere) or CO_2 emission reductions (which come under the Sustainable Development Strategy).

2. Differentiated objectives, by category of Member States

In addition, Lisbon Plus should take account of the social, economic and political heterogeneousness of the EU-27 and use differentiated objectives depending on Member States (or groups of Member States in a comparable situation) – objectives that are thus capable of attracting support. In fact, setting single objectives appears increasingly ill-suited to an EU comprising countries that are catching up and still far from the technological frontier together with others that are close to it, countries with very different development levels and sociological structures, etc.

When these objectives are set as absolute values (*e.g.* 3% of GDP for R&D expenditure), they can be psychologically counter-productive; countries that are very far from the target will tend to "throw in the towel" and stop investing in the area concerned. When they are set in the form of trends (*e.g.* the gradual increase of 5 years in retirement age), they may appear out of step with the efforts that Member States must agree upon. This rise does not make much sense in countries where the retirement age is already over 65, nor does it necessarily make sense for countries where the retirement age is much lower than 60.

This being the case, the most appropriate option may consist of *differentiating global European objectives by country or group of countries, as is already the case, for example, for greenhouse gas emissions.* As for the 3% R&D objective, it will be important to state much more clearly (and not only in the national reform programmes presented by the Member States) that this objective assumes that certain Member States will exceed it while others will make progress and remain below it, but the goal is an overall total of 3% for the EU as a whole.

3. Better-evaluated objectives

Performance evaluation by the EU and its Member States should be based on figures that are as reliable and comparable as possible, ensuring coherent monitoring of the implementation of Lisbon Plus while stimulating national performance. These conditions are not always satisfied. Employment rates, for example, are not easy to compare because the selected criteria (the number of hours worked per month, etc.) for the definition of an employed person varies among Member States. It is up to the European Commission, and particularly Eurostat, to strive to reduce existing disparities in order to produce data expressed in figures that are strictly comparable such that imperfections cannot be cited by Member States as a pretext for inaction.

Moreover, the performances of Member States should be more systematically evaluated in comparison with those of their international competitors, *i.e.*, not only OECD countries (notably the United States and Japan) but also emerging countries (particularly Brazil, India, China and Russia). From this perspective, it is also up to the Commission and Eurostat to supply comparable international data for all economic and social objectives and issues relating to the European strategy for globalisation.

B. A strengthened Community dimension

Though Lisbon Plus will continue to be implemented largely on the basis of the OMC, it is nevertheless vital to strengthen its Community dimension, which requires the following.

1. Clearer identification of Community action tools

The implementation of a "Community Lisbon Programme" since 2005 constitutes a step forward that needs to be consolidated by clearly distinguishing within it between Community processes and the OMC. This is not the case for the 2008-2010 programme.

As the Lisbon Treaty has invited us to do, the measures contemplated should be distinguished as to whether they involve the exclusive competence of the EU (trade policy), shared competences (Internal Market) or support and coordination action (education). This distinction ought to enable us to identify clearly the nature of Europe's added value, while placing each level in front of its responsibilities. It should aim to safeguard Community policies and instruments from a "coordination drift" that sometimes tends to distort them.

2. A resolute mobilisation of Community instruments

Community intervention complements national interventions for reasons that are both legal (treaties) and political (critical mass, economies of scale, a manifold lever effect, etc.). Such intervention employs regulatory and financial tools that need to be put to full use. First and foremost, it involves "better regulation" at the European level, for which the Commission should also be the guardian and Member States the promoters: *a-la-carte* directives do not help Europe progress, quite the contrary.

EU interventions should be focused in fields where the EU has clear jurisdiction and an unquestionable capacity to produce added value (see Chapter IV below). The subsidiarity principle should not only work one-way.

3. A timetable based on that of the next European legislature

Like the entire *EuroWorld 2015 Strategy*, Lisbon Plus, which is its internal component, must be carried out in step with the pace of Community political life, which depends closely on the renewal of the European Parliament and Commission.

Increasing Community political mobilisation to serve Lisbon Plus should consequently lead to *implementing that strategy for the 2010-2015 period, which is tighter than a decade-long timeframe*, and at the end of which an assessment may be made for which European leaders would be accountable.

This tighter timetable is all the more desirable given the topicality of the issues at stake and the risk of Europe's marginalisation in the global economy. It could enable Europe's positioning in the global economy to become a central political issue in the June 2009 parliamentary elections and allow the new European Commission to be politically "mandated" and technically prepared from the moment of its investiture. The new strategy could then be formally launched by the European Council and applied from spring 2010 in the framework of a programme for the Commission's next mandate.

C. A firmer constraint for Member States

Since 2004, the Commission has been developing a soft "partnership approach" with Member States for implementing the Lisbon strategy. This has led the latter to draft more or less artificial "national reform programmes" and negotiate bitterly over the recommendations that are made to them. One of the major issues of Lisbon Plus will continue to be the effective involvement of Member States – which will still be solicited mainly through incentives – but this should be strengthened on the basis of the following considerations.

1. Giving substantive technical content to the "partnership" approach

First of all, the European Commission could strengthen its "partnership" role with Member States, over and above simply controlling the implementation of national reform programmes. In this way, Commission teams could undertake technical reform assistance missions and help willing national authorities to put Lisbon Plus into effect (legally, financially, technically, etc.). It could also make its databases available and increase the number of European meetings on good practices for putting Lisbon Plus into effect.

Beyond these bilateral Commission-Member State relations, it would also be desirable to develop discussions within the Council on spreading good practices, inviting each representative to describe how his or her country has successfully pursued a particular reform (these contacts between Member States exist today, but in a non-Community context).

2. Strengthening the impact of "country-specific recommendations"

Country-specific recommendations have been used since 2006 and are a useful reminder of the main orientations recommended by the EU for each Member State, especially given the excessive number of orientations and recommendations produced by the EU. Their impact could, however, be strengthened in two ways:

- first, by applying these recommendations not only to the ability of Member States to meet the objectives they set for themselves in the context of their national reform programmes, but also to all the orientations of the Integrated Guidelines, which they do not necessarily cover, and which, in reality, constitute the common strategic framework for all EU countries;

- second, by holding a genuine European debate about country-specific recommendations (which are formally approved by the Council) rather than a mere succession of bilateral dialogues between the Commission and Member States, in which the latter expend considerable energy trying to limit the scope of the recommendations and, sometimes, empty them of their substance.

3. Developing peer pressure and "naming and shaming"

Decisions relating to NRPs carried out by Member States proceed mainly not from legal commitments (with the notable exception of directive implementation) but from political commitments. Whether they are successful or not, it would seem logical for their implementation to give rise to "rewards" or sanctions of the same kind. In this area, the "naming and shaming" practice has proved effective. It is clear, for example, that despite its limitations, the Shanghai ranking of world universities has had greater political impact than Lisbon's monitoring indicators for higher education. *It would therefore seem desirable to create a similar "scoreboards" for Lisbon Plus, based on a single, limited list of objectives expressed in figures.* These scoreboards are already published by different European think tanks and are based on variable global indicators that are not officially validated. It would be desirable for them to be drawn up by the European Commission, thereby strengthening their political and media impact.

4. Using the Eurozone as an area of reinforced coordination

The Eurozone should become a special area of coordination for Lisbon Plus national policies. The fact of sharing a common currency and being more integrated in terms of trade and FDIs promotes greater involvement for States who are members of the zone. The latter often appear to fall behind in relation to the current target figures. *The Eurogroup should take on a horizontal supervisory role in the implementation of Lisbon Plus.* This supervisory role should also be provided by the other councils that represent the Eurozone, particularly the "Competitiveness" and "Employment and Social Affairs" councils.

D. Greater involvement of political, economic and social stakeholders

To avoid a situation in which work relating to Lisbon Plus remains at a purely administrative level – mobilising energy and means that are out of proportion to their actual impact, there should first be a greater involvement of political leaders at the European level and within each Member State.

1. *Quarterly meetings of the European Council*

The European Council must devote more than one annual meeting (the spring meeting) to economic and social issues: *it should meet* formally once a quarter and *tackle these issues on each occasion.* Appointing a permanent President to the European Council as provided by the Lisbon Treaty should help ensure better structuring and improved monitoring of progress. This mobilisation of the European Council is vital in providing overall coherence since neither the "General Affairs" Council nor the High Representative for the CFSP has sufficient legitimacy to conduct the required economic and social trade-offs.

2. *A "Lisbon Plus" Council of Ministers*

No Council of Ministers presently has jurisdiction over the whole Lisbon strategy, which covers a wide range of subjects. Centralising this responsibility within the "Ecofin" Council would not be very effective as Ministers for the Economy and Finance, who are certainly the most concerned, would not be able to commit their governments on the many subjects that do not fall under their jurisdiction.

The Mission suggests creating a "Lisbon Plus Council" modelled on the "Internal Market Council" that was set up to implement the Single European Act. The Council would bring together "national Lisbon coordinators" (see below) and provide the Lisbon process with political unity of place. Failing that, the "Competitiveness Council" created in the context of the Lisbon strategy should play a leading role in piloting a Lisbon Plus that is refocused on the challenges of competitiveness and innovation.

3. *A responsible and homogeneous college of national Lisbon coordinators*

Today, the "national Lisbon coordinators" form a disparate assembly of ministers and civil servants of various ranks who do not really work together as a group. Their involvement in the national implementation of the Lisbon strategy is also very variable – often weak, or even non-existent.

The Mission proposes standardising the profile of these national coordinators to allow them to collaborate more effectively. The effective implementation of the Lisbon agenda needs political impetus and the ability to coordinate and arbitrate among ministries and cross-disciplinary subjects (the economy, social affairs, higher education and research, the environment...). *The "Lisbon coordinators" should therefore be government officials dedicated to this task and directly attached to the heads of state and government of Member States.* They would be authorised to decide on the subjects concerned and would represent their countries on the Lisbon Plus Council.

4. Quarterly meetings for ministers most concerned by Lisbon Plus at the national level

Ministers for the Economy, Finance, Social Affairs, Education, Research, Environment all need to be involved in implementing Lisbon Plus. Their involvement should be coordinated by the national Lisbon coordinator on the basis of regular meetings that could, for example, precede and prepare the regular European Council meetings and contribute to a genuine political monitoring of the implementation of Lisbon Plus.

5. Engaging the social partners and local authorities

The Lisbon strategy has had difficulty emerging from its administrative spheres to win over economic and social players.

This is true at the European level, where *social dialogue is now at a standstill. Lisbon Plus could be the opportunity to restart it.* As a matter of fact, some of the key themes of Lisbon Plus are at the heart of the dialogue between social partners: adapting working relations (flexibility and security), improved access to professional training, investment in human capital.

The European social dialogue could be revived at a centralised level, between European social partners (the European Trade Union Confederation and Business Europe), but also within companies, in European Works Councils (EWCs), as the Commission proposed in its 2004 communication on enhancing the contribution of the European social dialogue in an enlarged Europe. The European social dialogue could serve as a reference-point for national social dialogues in certain new Member States where social partners' technical capacity is still under construction.

This is also true at the national level. The involvement of social partners and local authorities could be significantly improved. This is particularly necessary for the regional and local authorities. Since enlargement, the EU comprises approximately 250 regions and 1,000 regional and local authorities. These authorities have many competences relevant to Lisbon. For example, in France, the regions have broad jurisdiction for industrial development, research, professional training, etc.

Their involvement should be enhanced through improved association of the European Committee of the Regions (CoR). In effect, the CoR is the appropriate intermediary to help the European Commission build up effective dialogue with local authorities who have jurisdiction over relevant themes and identify the European and national associations capable of representing them. This attempt to raise public awareness at the European level should be accompanied by national awareness-raising. It is up to national governments to guarantee the participation of local authorities in the national administrative coordination of Lisbon Plus. It is also their responsibility to spread appropriate information through forums, debates and other exchanges.

CHAPTER III

Common External Policies To Help Shape Globalisation

This chapter outlines the external component of the *EuroWorld 2015 Strategy*, which is based on the coherent structuring of a range of common policies.

Beyond the objective of establishing lasting peace between European nations, European unification has from the outset aimed at creating a critical mass that would enable its Member States to wield greater influence in the context of what was to become known as globalisation. This aim is now destined to govern future advances in the European project. However, Europe should already be promoting its assets on the international scene – it is the leading economic power in the world, an integrated market of 500 million inhabitants, an unrivalled trade power and has the world's second international currency. The first goal of an external economic strategy should be to bridge the existing gap between Europe's economic stature and its still weak international influence.

The EU can also take on new meaning in the eyes of its Member States and citizens if it improves the effectiveness of its action in the global economy, *not only to adapt to globalisation, but also to help shape it and defend its own interests and values, as it has the means to do*. To achieve this, the EU must supplement the "inward-looking" economic vision of the Treaty of Rome (centred on constructing a Single Market) with an economic and social vision that has global scope and is supported by corresponding external policies. This is all the more necessary given the fact that the EU is much more dependent on external trade than other economic powers (for example, it imports 72% of its energy, compared to 42% for the United States).

This common approach has already been at work for a long time in the field of trade policy, but it is still at an embryonic stage in other fields such as energy, and non-existent elsewhere. It is important to take a common approach further in relation to the *new economic and strategic challenges* that were not sufficiently identified at Lisbon in 2000, and by extending European action to all economic and social spheres with regard to which the 27 would be well advised to act together. To do this, an overall political vision of the European strategy for globalisation needs to be adopted. Such a vision would in particular include two new types of objectives:

• *First, consolidating or reinforcing access to vital resources for European economies and societies – resources that the EU does not always possess in sufficient quantities on its own territory:*

- energy resources: the need for a common political and industrial vision that goes beyond simply liberalising European markets;
- human resources: following the Lisbon undertaking to increase employment rates, the need to resort to external immigration, particularly of highly qualified people;
- agricultural and food resources: the need to preserve an industry that has become of strategic importance with the prospect of increased food scarcity and price rises throughout the world;
- financial resources: taking into account global competition to attract capital;
- technological and industrial resources: defining and defending a core of "strategic European interests" in the economic field.

Faced with this first type of challenge, it is particularly important to add an economic dimension to the European Security Strategy established by the EU in December 2003, which has hitherto remained largely confined to political and military dimensions.

• *Second, going beyond simply managing the flow of products, capital and workers, to developing cross-sectoral external strategies aimed, in particular, at:*

- strengthening Europe's assets as an "international normative power" by developing a strategic vision of normative activity;
- defining a global approach to developing countries that combines public aid measures, openness to trade and the management of migratory flows;
- taking into account geopolitical factors in external economic policies (for example, maximising European consumers' welfare provided a significant justification to openness towards Asian textile markets, although this openness has nonetheless been destabilising for areas near the EU (in particular, North Africa)).

For these two types of challenge – as for more traditional challenges with which the growth and competitiveness of European economies and societies are confronted – more effective EU action presupposes:

- better identification of strategic interests that are common to EU countries and capable of justifying the reinforcement of the EU's *competences*;

- setting up the organisation and tools required to serve those interests best, *i.e.*, better *governance* of the EU and its policies;
- carrying out the political trade-offs that are best suited to the interests of the EU and its Member States, one consequence of which may be the need to review the *substance* or orientations of certain common policies.

From this perspective, we will distinguish below between:

- policies for which the EU already has exclusive or principal jurisdiction as established by treaty and for which, therefore, it is essentially a question of reviewing their governance and content to evaluate their appropriateness in the new context;
- common policies that are in construction and particularly necessary for our times, the implementation of which may require an adjustment of the current political, legal and institutional framework to equip the EU with suitable instruments for the global economy.

I. Revisiting Existing Policies

With the Common Trade Policy and the international dimension of the Competition Policy, the Internal Market, the Economic and Monetary Union and the Common Agricultural Policy, the EU already has significant jurisdiction in external economic matters.

It is up to it to make better use of this asset than it has so far done, by adapting these policies to the new challenges with which it will be confronted in the next decade, to enable Member States to make better use of the opportunities of globalisation while protecting themselves against the risks it generates.

A. New stakes for the Common Trade Policy

Today, the EU is the world's leading economic power (with a GDP of slightly less than 30% of world GDP). It is also the leading trade power at the international level, being both the leading exporter of goods and services and the leading importer.

As the world's leading trade power, the priority of Europe's trade policy should be the opening of foreign markets.

Prior to undertaking an offensive strategy of opening external markets, the terms of the European trade debate need to be explained clearly. Europe must leave behind the simplistic debate between "free traders" and "protectionists" and commit itself to the advancement of its commercial and economic interests, free of inhibiting complexes. Beyond this, an offensive strategy poses two strategic questions. Faced with the paralysis of the Doha round of multilateral trade negotiations, should we continue to focus all our diplomatic efforts on this or redirect our priorities? What can be done when countries refuse to open up their markets, discriminating against European trade and investment?

1. Going beyond the simplistic debate between "free traders" and "protectionists"

The system of governance adopted to implement the Common Trade Policy often makes it possible for the different positions of Member States concerning openness to international trade to converge. But this process of convergence frequently generates significant political and social tension around a debate that is polarised between supposedly radical "free-traders" and reputedly inveterate "protectionists". It sometimes ends up creating "qualified minorities" who block and damage the effectiveness and legitimacy of European trade policy.

Debates concerning this policy could doubtless be more constructive if the EU and its Member States accepted more clearly two kinds of political reality:

• First of all, it should be recognised that EU Member States have *different commercial interests*. For example, small countries are more commercially (and financially) outward-looking and, among them, some do more overseas business than others for both historical and industrial reasons.

It would be preferable if trade debates explicited these factual differences more systematically to avoid allegedly "ideological" antagonisms that are more difficult to resolve.

It would also be desirable for Member States to adopt a new and more offensive operating principle: that of defending the interests of the countries most concerned. Today, the structural trend is quite the opposite: Member States who are not concerned by a particular dossier strive not to defend the interests of the concerned Member States, either through inertia or in an active fashion, in favour of preserving the quality of their diplomatic relations with certain partners.

• Secondly, it is advisable *to include all dimensions in the debate on European trade policy* rather than reduce it simply to considerations based on mercantilism or a policy of strong state intervention in the economy:

- the economic dimension: above all, it is a question of preserving EU States' capacity to import certain indispensable products into their economies (the primary aim of international trade) while endeavouring to increase European market shares at home and abroad;

- the social dimension: this involves measuring the employment content of European trade flows, both in negative terms (relocation, market losses) and in positive terms (job creation linked to export), and evaluating more precisely the impact of international trade on European purchasing power while striving to ensure that products bought by Europeans are produced in conformity with core labour standards;
- the geopolitical dimension: this will involve carrying out European trade-offs in commercial matters that include not only economic but political considerations regarding our main traditional partners (the USA and OECD countries) and emerging partners (notably China), with better measurement of the consequences of these choices on the growth and stability of developing countries adjoining the EU (in this respect, the liberalisation of the textile industry could be seen as a counter-example).

The conclusion of current discussions on trade defence mechanisms practised by the EU could be a good test of the possibility of leaving behind the simplistic debate between "liberals" and "protectionists". In effect, we ought to be able to reach consensus regarding the need to apply these rules to all companies located outside EU territory, even when they are subsidiaries of European companies. At the same time, it should be reaffirmed that the notion of "dumping" should not be used in social or environmental areas, as long as the countries concerned sell their products above their production costs, even if they are lower than European costs because of a different local and historical context.

2. *Reconciling multilateralism and bilateralism*

Faithful to its vision of international relations, which reflects its own experience, the EU has always been trade multilateralism's main supporter.

With the European Community project, European nations started a revolution in international relations. Rejecting the power politics behind the two world wars, they turned away from the balance of power and applied a new approach to regulate their mutual relations – that of the rule of law. Relations between States have become peaceful and cooperative, war is no longer an option, conflicts are resolved by negotiation, compromise and, in the event of failure, arbitration by a "trustworthy third party" (the Commission, or the Court of Justice).

Europe is now trying to export this model internationally. It is fighting to ensure the primacy of international law and defend the priority given to the peaceful settlement of differences in the framework of the United Nations. It promotes regulation of the international financial system through institutions like the G8, the G10, the G20 and the IMF for the architecture of the international monetary and financial system, the Paris Club to handle the public debt of developing countries, the Financial Action Task Force (FATF) in the fight against money laundering and the OECD in the fight against international corruption and tax havens. It is seeking to strengthen institutions like the International Labour Organisation (ILO) and the International Maritime Organisation (IMO) and to create a World Environmental Organisation to ensure the effective implementation of international environmental agreements. In accordance with these principles it presided, with Canada, over the creation of the WTO to provide a normative framework for international trade and avoid trade wars, unilateral sanctions and the law of the jungle.

Europe's support for trade multilateralism also arises from its feeling of inferiority when faced with the American giant. Multilateralism was the instrument for avoiding bilateral confrontations where Europe felt it was "the weak against the strong", thereby "tying Gulliver down" with a collective net.

The EU should, of course, continue supporting trade multilateralism. But should it go on investing most of its diplomatic efforts on the success of the Doha round? Let us recall the bargain at the heart of the Doha round from a European point of view:

- a quest for more open access to third-party markets, both for European industry and services;
- in return, relaxing European trade positions on agriculture, partly begun in Hong Kong with the announcement of a possible removal of export subsidies.

The negotiations now appear to be deeply bogged down. Sometimes the media blame Europe for defending its agricultural interests too rigidly. In reality, the blame is shared equally between North and South. The problem lies elsewhere; one can go on incriminating this or that country or group of countries, but the fundamental question concerns the nature of the WTO as it stands.

Initially, the WTO and its forerunner – the General Agreement on Tariffs and Trade (GATT) – were regulatory authorities for trade conflicts between developed countries, essentially Japan, the United States and Europe. The enlargement of the WTO to some 150 members in the 1990s had the effect of applying conventional measures aimed at regulating relations between developed countries to developing countries, or even the least advanced countries. These measures included the widest possible opening up of economies, the removal of barriers, national treatment of foreign companies, etc. The application of these measures, which were created for rich countries, was not adapted to poor countries. The poor countries realised this and blocked the trade negotiations at Seattle. Against this backdrop, the round was redirected to become, at Doha, the "Development Round"; many unilateral concessions in favour of developing countries were introduced. But this redirection raised the questions of how to treat emerging countries such as China and where the interests of Western countries lay. The WTO must decide which path to take: a regulatory organisation for developed countries or a development organisation for emerging and excluded countries?

Some countries have drawn the consequences from this crisis of multilateralism and adopted an alternative strategy of reinvigorating their bilateral agreements. This is particularly the case for the United States and Japan.

Europe should follow the same path. Through bilateralism, the United States has obtained advantages that are not pooled within the WTO and hurt European companies. For example, a few years ago a bilateral agreement with Thailand opened insurance and banking sectors up to American investors. Fifty per cent of the market is now held by American companies, which are the only ones present on this market. A bilateral approach is also in our interest in relations with the major emerging countries. Bilateral negotiations favour strong states that use the leverage conferred by their economic weight to obtain concessions. Europe is a trade power and, since it has the same offensive interests as the United States, it should have the same preference for bilateral agreements.

The European Commission recently moved towards restarting bilateral agreements[1]. The Mission believes that this reorientation should be pursued while awaiting more favourable prospects at the WTO, with a view to defending European economic interests without inhibitions.

In accordance with this principle, *the new European policy of trade bilateralism should range as widely as possible, in keeping with Europe's strategic interests*. In particular, it should include public tenders; here, European companies are discriminated against by most of our partners, including the most developed. It should also include non-tariff barriers to trade, intellectual property law (the key to the innovation economy), investment and competition law.

1 See the "Global Europe" report by the European Commissioner for External Trade, Peter Mandelson, 2006.

This new policy should be aimed at priority target countries. So far, bilateral and regional agreements concerned partner developing countries, particularly the ACP countries. The European Commission rightly proposes reorienting country targeting and suggests "trade potential" as a common selection criterion, combining growth rate and market size. This is a good approach for our strategic economic interests. The Commission identified the Association of Southeast Asian Nations (ASEAN), Korea, Mercosur, India, Russia and the member countries of the Gulf Cooperation Council (GCC) as priority targets. It advises caution with regard to China which, despite its WTO membership, is not as yet fully integrated with regard to international trade rules and in relation to which we have important defensive interests.

The Mission only partly shares this order of priority. *China should be a major European priority*. With China, we have major offensive interests (counterfeiting, intellectual property rights, access to a very rapidly growing market) and the existence of defensive interests provides, on the contrary, significant room for manoeuvre in negotiations.

Furthermore, Western countries are excluded from the targets identified by the Commission although the United States, Japan and Canada are ranked 1st, 3rd and 8th in the world, respectively, in terms of "trade potential". They remain, for the time being, our priority partners. And their degree of openness is still limited for highly developed countries. This is especially the case for the United States. There are many discriminatory practices. A few examples will bear this out. R&D subsidies are reserved for US-owned companies and must even be returned if those companies come under foreign control; in government contracting, the "Buy American Act" stipulates that an American offer can be selected on grounds of national discrimination if the offer is up to 50% higher than the foreign offer; when constructing incineration plants, American-made ceramic furnaces must be used; in many States, agricultural land can only be held by American citizens, etc. *Broadening the "transatlantic agenda" should help further integrate economies on both sides of the Atlantic.*

3. Being realistic about the "reciprocity principle"

Whether it is multilateral or bilateral, the European trade strategy may not produce results. In this case, what attitude should be adopted when faced with countries that refuse to open up their markets and discriminate against European trade and investments? Should Europe maintain an open attitude or, on the contrary, retaliate by closing its own markets? In other words, what should the role of the reciprocity principle be in conducting a common trade policy and, more broadly speaking, in economic negotiations led by the EU?

From a legal point of view, the WTO statutes define reciprocity as the basic principle for international trade negotiations from which stem the most favoured nation clause and the national treatment clause. But these statutes also specify that there are two exceptions to the application of this principle:

- the first one concerns countries that decide to form a regional EEC-type customs union, granting themselves advantages that third countries do not benefit from; today, such customs unions concern more than half of international trade flows (intra-zone trade);
- the second exception benefits "developing countries", which can obtain trade advantages without offering compensation because of their intrinsic weaknesses and the asymmetric character of the trade relations they have with developed countries. These legal measures have not been reviewed and may still be applied to emerging countries whose trade stature is ever-increasing.

In this context, *it hardly seems realistic to make the application of the reciprocity principle the cornerstone of European trade policy since its economic and legal bearing is relatively limited.*

When agreements providing for a reciprocal opening of markets are concluded by the EU, the latter naturally has a duty to ensure that they are applied. This is the case with the 1994 multilateral Agreement on Government Procurement (AGP), the imperfect application of which in Canada and Asia is hindering the access of European companies (particularly in the sectors of transport and other utilities), while the European market is open. In cases such as this, the EU has so far favoured the concept of "positive reciprocity", which consists in seeking greater openness in foreign markets. Since the EU's economic development is largely based on access to the resources and markets of its trade partners, it is legitimate for it to continue favouring such an approach on condition that it does so more effectively in the future. But it also has to equip itself with the legal means to limit access to its public procurement, if necessary, for companies from recalcitrant countries by revising directive 2004/17/EC coordinating procurement procedures to this effect.

A similar demand for reciprocity can also be made in the area of foreign investment which falls outside the strict range of trade, but for which no multilateral agreement exists. In such a field, the EU must negotiate on a case-by-case basis with its trade partners to obtain greater openness and transparency in their markets.

Except in those cases provided for by trade agreements that have already been signed by the EU, invoking the reciprocity principle in international negotiations that are in progress is likely to spark off fairly legitimate tension from emerging countries. With good reason, the latter may consider that this principle does not concern them directly, either from a legal or economic point of view, since the fact that they are either fragile or trying to get off the ground partly justifies the protection of their "fledgling industries". In this context, the promotion of certain standards – particularly social and environmental standards – that is sometimes made part of trade policy should fall under a much broader "normative strategy" of which the trade dimension is only one component (see below). As far as the environment is concerned, the main international agreements – in particular the United Nations Framework Convention on Climate Change – also grant differentiated status to developing countries, since they are considered to have fewer responsibilities and less ability to reform their economies.

There is certainly room for discussion between the EU and the main "developing countries", which the WTO statutes do not define and which can choose whether or not they consider themselves as such. In particular, *one may well wonder whether China, which commits more and more money to official development assistance, or Brazil, which is now an international creditor, still fall into the "developing countries" category, with all the corresponding legal and trade advantages that it brings.* But this discussion can only be held on the basis of a global, open political dialogue between the EU and these countries, and invoking the reciprocity principle would be a difficult point of departure. Though it is perfectly fair to emphasise that emerging countries cannot claim rights without accepting certain duties, the possible change in current political balances of power cannot be imagined without offsetting increased duties and responsibilities – at the same time, or beforehand – by new rights (such as better representation for emerging countries in multilateral institutions).

It is natural for the EU to be tempted to link greater access to its huge market to increased trade concessions from the main emerging countries for which it constitutes an important outlet (this access having already been broadly granted to the Least Advanced Countries (LACs) in the framework of the "Everything But Arms" initiative). However, it should do so while assessing the advantages and limits of a strict application of the reciprocity principle in trade negotiations and in pursuing political trade-offs that factor in all relevant considerations, such as the risk of complicating access of one's own products to these emerging countries which, moreover, trade with other major developed areas (the USA, Japan, other OECD countries) in a context of fierce international competition, the possibility of accessing resources and outlets in third-country markets, the prospect of importing products at more reduced prices, etc.

B. Increasing the international stature of Europe as an economic and financial actor

Internationally, the EU has considerable monetary, financial and economic stature (nearly 25% of global GDP). Since 2004, for example, the euro has been the leading world currency on the bond markets, it has become the second international reserve currency (with more than 25% of official reserves), and this rise should continue in the next decade.

However, the EU's lack of external unity prevents it from making the most of these strengths just as the US financial crisis and its international repercussions call for a stronger contribution from Europe to help stabilise global financial and monetary markets. The conventional idea that Europe is "an economic giant but a political dwarf" has been partly confirmed, in the economic and financial sphere as well. Here, the EU should organise itself better in the future, along two main lines.

1. Consolidating its external representation in multilateral institutions

- *at the Eurozone level*: joint diplomatic missions involving the President of the Eurogroup and the European Commissioner for Economic and Monetary Affairs, accompanied by the President of the ECB, should become regular practice for everything concerning international monetary questions. The fall 2007 trip of this trio to meet the Chinese authorities is a propitious precedent and should lead to establishing regular international dialogue concerning developments in exchange rates between the EU and its main partners; a vision of common positions on the international strategy for the euro also needs to be developed, and the Eurogroup is the right forum for doing this;
- *at the EU level*: it is important to identify more clearly a limited group of European commissioners responsible for managing all the EU's external economic policies (trade policy, development policy, migratory policy, the external aspects of competition policy and the Internal Market, energy diplomacy, etc.) that can give the EU a "collective face" in the international economic sphere, in liaison with the High Representative for the Common Foreign and Security Policy (CFSP);
- *at the multilateral level* (Bretton Woods, G8): since the prospect of a unified EU representation does not seem the most realistic option in the short term, EU Member States could form more coherent and influential "geographical groupings" within the Bretton Woods institutions. It would also be in their interest to coordinate their positions more system-

atically before all important IMF, World Bank and G8 meetings, as they are formally obliged to do within the framework of the WTO, in order to maximise their impact. Preliminary consultation with the United States and Japan on subjects of common interest would further increase this influence.

2. *Strengthening Europe as a financial entity and in terms of regulation*

The EU would be more influential on the international financial scene, particularly in the current crisis, if it could rely on three levers that remain to be developed:

- a *sufficiently unified and deep European financial market* to diminish the cost of capital invested in Europe and strengthen the EU's "external strike force". This requires a vigorous strengthening of the financial market integration process (which the Lamfalussy Process is meant to favour) and the development of European pension and investment funds that are robust enough to carry weight in international financial transactions;
- creating *European supervisory bodies* capable of intervening effectively in the event of an international financial crisis, going even further than the effective ECB interventions in the banking sector alone (but not, for example, in the financial or insurance markets). The advent of such supervisory bodies would ensue from progress in European financial market integration made possible by the Lamfalussy Process and rely on mechanisms for high-level coordination between national supervisors;
- more coherent involvement in *international forums for financial regulation* with frequent informal meetings of groups of regulators and national supervisors (the International Organisation of Securities Commissions (IOSCO) for financial markets, the International Association of Insurance Supervisors (IAIS) for insurance, the Basel Committee (BC) for banking and the IMF's Financial Stability Forum (FSF)). This move for greater coherence assumes a clarified allocation of competences between national and European levels and systematic coordination of European positions prior to each international meeting.

By developing its own market, the EU would intervene more effectively to improve the regulation and transparency of international capital movements, as advocated by Germany and France upon the burst of the US subprime crisis.

C. A fresh look at European Competition Policy

Competition policy has long been one of the EU's most powerful instruments on the international economic scene, enabling it to impose its decisions far beyond its own territory, as illustrated by the recent Microsoft case as well as the attempted GE/ Honeywell merger earlier on. Nevertheless, this policy has long given rise to criticism, particularly in France, arguing that it impedes the emergence of national or European "champions" of critical mass on the global stage. Some critics also seek to introduce "industrial policy" criteria into competition law.

Where does this old debate now stand in the context of intensified globalisation?

1. There is generally satisfactory monitoring of mergers and abuses of dominant positions

The EU's competition policy gives rise to a greatly disproportionate degree of criticism. In the course of the last 20 years, the EU has hindered only approximately 30 European mergers or acquisitions (out of 3,000 notifications), while it has allowed the creation of a large number of European and national "champions".

When assessing the impact of the mergers, acquisitions and abuses of dominant position that are submitted to it, the Commission relies on a definition of relevant markets that includes their geographical dimension and the context of globalisation.

Some of the controversies caused by certain prohibitions have resulted in very useful Commission reforms: the appointment of a chief economist to the Competition Directorate-General substantively, and of auditors on procedural issues.

Recent reversals of European Commission decisions by the Court of Justice are resulting in an even more rigorous analysis of a few problematic cases.

2. Do "industrial policy" considerations have their place in competition law?

The European Commission monitors State aid in accordance with sectoral guidelines (*e.g.* for innovation aid) that allow its analysis to include considerations of economic policy other than those relating to the protection of consumers and taxpayers. It is sometimes suggested that it adopt a similar approach to monitor concentrations and abuses of dominant positions using, for example, the European Council and Parliament's identification of a list of critical technologies and business sectors for which there exist risks of loss in terms of international competitiveness (mainly linked to loss of independence in certain sectors or of control of certain processes).

The Mission believes that these "industrial policy" considerations would only have their place in competition policy if they aimed at authorising otherwise anti-competitive transactions or conduct in the Internal Market in the name of higher strategic interests. A volte-face of this kind is unlikely to muster European consensus in the foreseeable future given that competition law already makes it possible to adjust prescribed remedies to the scope of competition infringement. Thus, a local or even regional anti-competitive situation in the Internal Market is generally subject to specific remedies that do not hinder the overall achievement of a transaction.

3. *The challenge of the emerging economies*

The rising power of emerging and largely state-controlled economies on the Western market for corporate takeovers confronts competition policy with a new challenge. Faced with this challenge:

- in the first place, the EU should strive vigorously to promote the international convergence of competition regulation. This is difficult to do within the framework of the WTO, but easier in that of the OECD or the International Competition Network (ICN) and in a bilateral context. Also in a bilateral context, and in liaison with the United States and Japan, it should encourage emerging countries to equip themselves with clear and transparent competition regulation;
- alongside this long-term process, the EU should define a specific doctrine for the acquisition of European companies by foreign companies benefiting from massive state aid, a phenomenon that could well increase over the coming years given the economic development of countries in which companies are largely state-owned or strictly subject to governmental decisions.

Since this twofold approach also comes under the Common Trade Policy, close coordination between the two domains is essential.

D. Reforming the Common Agricultural Policy

Although the Common Agricultural Policy (CAP) is an "internal" policy, from the beginning it has also had a strong external dimension because it was established alongside the European customs union with the particular objective of offsetting the differential between European agricultural prices and corresponding world prices. It allowed Europe to regain food supply independence from the 1970s and become a major agricultural exporter, which is a genuine asset internationally.

At the same time, the CAP's mode of implementation gives rise to many tensions, both internationally (at the WTO) and internally, when the European trade and budgetary negotiations take place. The reform agreed upon in 2003 made it possible to continue the level of agricultural financing in the long term but, by making it depend mainly on the level practised over a reference period or the volume of land cultivated (whatever the production concerned), it also weakened the CAP's policy foundations.

As the main CAP beneficiary, *France is at the heart of these tensions and uncertainties*; it must play an essential role in the necessary refoundation of this policy. *It is by softening its traditional stances regarding the CAP that France will be able to better influence this reform, which will involve rebuilding an "agricultural consensus" and implementing new strategic orientations.*

1. Building a new consensus on European agriculture

Is agriculture a thing of the past or does it represent a strategic asset for the EU in the early 21st century? In attempting to answer this question, one must first tackle the CAP debate, based on the following considerations:

- the fact of having significant agricultural and food resources is *a strategic asset for the EU* in an international context marked by a structural rise in global agricultural prices and demand tensions for essential products like wheat and rice. In this respect, the CAP can be thought of as a "European food policy" that can command wide support from all EU countries;
- with its production methods that meet important health and environmental requirements, European agriculture helps supply safe and varied food to 450 million consumers; faced with increasing worldwide food demand and a rise in health risks, the EU needs measures that guarantee respect for these standards;
- besides its essential economic functions, which enable the EU to show appreciable trade surpluses, European agricultural production carries important social functions (the use of European land, a large share of which it occupies), environmental functions and even energy-related functions (biofuels, etc.). These multiple functions justify a high level of public support which can, of course, come through different channels (Community preference, agricultural economic policy, land-use policy, etc.);
- the European agribusiness sector generates a limited and highly variable share of the wealth produced by the Member States; it mobilises a limited proportion of the EU's active population; *in the eyes of*

many Member States, it does not always represent a strategic national interest. Thus, from a political and diplomatic viewpoint, it is difficult to subject the agribusiness sector to European choices (budgetary) that put other more important sectors of the population and economy at an excessive disadvantage;

- *the current methods of implementation of the CAP give rise to major criticism* from economic and political observers: technical criticisms concern the content of the support measures from which it benefits (export subsidies that distort competition, aid distribution according to occupied land area rather than economic objectives, a concentration of aid for the most prosperous farmers, despite recent progress). Criticisms of a more political nature question, if not the level of European public support for agriculture (which does not exceed that practised in the United States or Japan), then at least the way in which it is distributed between Community and national levels.

Since France has chosen to make the refoundation of the "CAP" one of the priorities of its European presidency in the second half of 2008, it must take into account all these factors if it wants its partners to heed its promotion of agriculture's strategic character and diminish the tension and resentment provoked by previous European negotiations on this subject. By abandoning the primarily defensive stance it took in the past, France would be able to take a "leap forward" with the CAP and help put it back in the centre of the European political agenda, reinforcing its influence on the definition of the major EU trade (and budgetary) choices. In return, France's partners should adopt a more constructive attitude toward European agriculture, which cannot be reduced to a relic of the past, either in international trade negotiations or in the context of the forthcoming discussions of the EU's financial framework.

2. *The bases for CAP reform*

The new political consensus on European agriculture will be all the more solid if it succeeds in reforming EU agricultural strategy along the following lines:

- first and foremost, the EU has to *increase the efforts it has already agreed to, not only regarding the least advanced countries, but also its main WTO partners*: decreasing public support measures with the strongest impact on international trade negotiations (2003 reform), proposing the effective abolition of export subsidies (yet to be confirmed in fact) and substantially reducing customs duties to obtain real returns from other parties to the negotiation. If only for symbolic reasons, a reduction in some tariff quotas and tariff peaks practised for certain agricultural yields should be envisaged if the main trade partners offer effective compensation for other agricultural products or other economic sectors;

• next, we must *preserve a European policy of direct aid to farmers*, targeting the economic needs of agricultural firms and individuals and not allocated according to occupied land area or previous levels of aid. Establishing this kind of aid policy will lead to a substantial reduction in expenditure on production that benefits from structurally well-directed prices (cereals) and an increase for those with more fragile production (animal rearing, organic farming, mountain agriculture);

• given the fragmentation of agricultural companies, the aim of the farming aid policy should be to consolidate the organisation of different channels by giving them instruments to structure the agricultural supply so as to anticipate and, if necessary, manage crises and stabilise farmers' income. The goal of crisis management mechanisms based on insurance systems (climate, health and market risks) would be to support not agricultural prices but farmer's profit margins to guarantee their stability;

• lastly, we have to *implement a genuine European policy for rural development*, founded on the need to preserve the cohesion of certain European territories and the quality of the environment. This policy is very similar to a structural and cohesion policy and should be put into effect with comparable mechanisms (in particular, the choice of zones and EU-Member State co-financing);

• in any case, *a decrease in Community support for agriculture, be it trade or budgetary support, should be compensated* both at the European level (through the Globalisation Adjustment Fund, structural funds and rural development policy) and, at least partially, at the national level (since each Member State is required to give public support to agriculture to a degree that best corresponds to the collective preferences of its citizens).

II. Developing New External Policies For the 21st Century

To implement a comprehensive strategy for globalisation, the EU must also develop new common policies. Such policies were embryonic, if not totally absent, when the Lisbon strategy was launched. For some, these new policies respond to challenges of which public awareness is recent. They should allow EU Member States to achieve with greater ease objectives that are now largely shared:

- strengthening and securing EU access to the energy and migratory resources it needs in a context of increased global competition;

- exercising influence internationally in negotiations regarding the preservation of the environment and, more generally, the implementation of industrial and social standards that best serve European interests;
- protecting its strategic assets against possible attempts at predation to geopolitical ends.

A. A European energy diplomacy: a strategic necessity

Most of the major powers have put energy matters at the center of their foreign and security policy. This is as true of energy-producing countries (the Gulf states, Russia, Iran, Latin America) as it is of the major energy-consuming countries (the United States, China, India). The launch of the integrated "Energy-Climate" policy by the European Council in March 2007 is evidence of a new awareness that could give rise to a genuine European energy diplomacy if the Member States and the EU make far-reaching changes to their present approach. *For the EU, this is the most important challenge and, given the divergences among national interests, the most difficult to meet.*

1. Reducing together the risks associated with external energy dependence

To establish a genuine, long-term energy diplomacy, Member States must clearly identify and accept its main political objective, namely:

- not to strengthen the national energy independence of each State, which in fact none is capable of doing (with the exception of Denmark, whose oil reserves are nevertheless depleting) and will be even less capable of doing in the future;
- *but to reduce the risks linked to the increasing energy dependence of the entire EU (56% in 2006, 80% in 2030). This requires collective action, which is more effective than separate actions on the part of individual Member States or their energy companies.* This objective means making choices going far beyond preserving national industrial and administrative positions.

Having failed to accept such a change in perspective clearly, the Member States are today still confined to autonomous strategies that may be justified from a national point of view (with each country adopting the "energy mix" that best suits its situation and collective preferences) but which, taken together, are harmful: bilateral negotiations from a position of weakness with energy-supplying countries (whereas a common front would put the enormous consumption potential that the

EU represents to better use), the construction of three rival gas pipelines between Russia and Europe, etc.

2. From liberalising energy markets to an integrated approach

Such a change in perspective for Member States must be accompanied by a change in the approach adopted by the EU towards the energy sector:

- Europe can no longer base its energy policy solely on a logic of market liberalisation which, though useful in itself, cannot respond to all European energy challenges;
- its decisions must also take on board other considerations, particularly from an external viewpoint: combating climate change (this is already the case), but also and above all the security and cost of energy supplies.

The implementation of article 194 of the Treaty on the Functioning of the Union (TFU) introduced by the Lisbon Treaty provides a legal basis for this more comprehensive energy policy. The creation of a *"European Energy Community" on the pattern of the European Coal and Steel Community (ECSC) would constitute a symbolic initiative to match the scale of the challenge.* It could be established as an "enhanced cooperation", open to all Member States that wish to participate.

3. Providing effective content to an EU energy diplomacy

European political leaders must accept the objective of coordinating negotiations for energy supplies from outside the EU with major suppliers – notably Russia, which possesses 25% of the gas reserves in the world and supplies 25% of the natural gas and 20% of the oil consumed in the EU.

Given its eminently political character, the implementation of an energy diplomacy should be part of the strengthening of European diplomacy as a whole under the High Representative for the Common Foreign and Security Policy (CFSP). It should lead to strengthening ties and Europe's political, economic and even military presence in "diversification countries" (Turkey, Central Asia, North Africa).

B. A more realistic international strategy to combat climate change

Though European environmental policy has many components, some of which are longstanding and exemplary (protecting soil and biodiversity), nowadays it is strongly based on the EU's contribution to combating climate change. *The EU has sound political and industrial positions in this sector, constituting significant assets for the future.* It has already taken important measures in the framework of the Kyoto Protocol and the integrated "Energy-Climate" policy launched by the European Council in March 2007, which has since given rise to a legitimate debate:

- European climate change policy contributes to promoting an exemplary "European development model" on the international stage and strengthening the legitimacy of the EU in the eyes of its citizens;
- however, it can only be fully legitimate for economic players and effective in environmental terms if it is accompanied by an international strategy that seeks to engage EU partners and competitors – failing this, the competitiveness and employment capacity of European companies will be weakened, without any significant return in terms of climate improvement.

This debate reflects an important strategic challenge for the EU in the coming years, which could be taken up on the basis of an international strategy combining partnerships, cooperation agreements and even, as a last resort, coercive measures.

1. A climate policy that cannot remain isolated

The EU cannot curb global warming (or diminishing biodiversity) on its own; it must encourage its traditional partners (the United States) and its emerging partners (China, India) to step up their efforts, putting forward – if need be – its own exemplary role, without relying exclusively on this argument.

It is *all the more important to maintain this open or collective attitude in the short and medium term given that the EU's partners have, it appears, realised the need for better climate protection.* This realisation is particularly strong in the United States, but also in some emerging countries, including China, that up until now have not been bound by international obligations pursuant to the Kyoto Protocol but could agree to them in the future.

Establishing a concerted transatlantic approach to climate change is a priority for two reasons: first, because the United States produces a quarter of global CO_2 emissions; second, and most importantly, because transatlantic divergences on these subjects weigh heavily on the progress of international climate negotiations.

2. *A cooperative approach*

Although the contribution of the EU's emerging partners to environmental protection is lacking because of their stage of development or differing political choices, it may also be because they simply lack the means to do more. The EU is therefore duty-bound to cooperate better with them on the basis of its own resources, which are:

- industrial and technical, since, in the field of environmental economics, it has world-leading companies. The EU has considerable assets and experience in environmental protection that it can now make available to emerging countries in the context of its cooperative actions;
- political: the EU has a key role to play in demonstrating to its American and emerging partners the effectiveness of an emission quota trading system (European Trading System) and preparing for the post-Kyoto era (2012-2050).

3. *As a last resort, a more coercive approach*

If international post-Kyoto negotiations do not lead to the adoption of consensual measures validated by as many States as possible, could the EU envisage setting up Border Tax Adjustment (BTA) systems which would amount to a coercive means of making recalcitrant countries "partners" in global climate protection?

This would involve the EU imposing a tax on imported products that were not produced in conformity with environmental standards set by international agreements and, if the need arises, returning it for exported products that do conform.

This prospect gives rise to major objections, particularly from certain Member States that argue that any unilateral solution would expose the EU to harmful trade reprisals. It also raises certain technical issues.

The EU could study how to create such systems and attempt to establish clearly whether they are compatible with WTO regulations[2], particularly the principle of non-discrimination. In this respect, a recent WTO decision concerning tyre production in Brazil suggests that it is possible to assert environmental considerations in international trade disputes. This decision may open the way to BTA-type systems.

---

2 On this subject, see R. Ismer and K. Neuhoff (2004), "Border Tax Adjustments: A Feasible Way to Address Nonparticipation in Emission Trading", *Cambridge Working Papers in Economics*, No. 0409, and the conflicting position of the D4E – French Ministry for Ecology's Directorate of Economic Studies and environment evaluation – working paper by A. Berthier et C.Gros, Série Etudes 07-E0.

However, with this prospect in mind, it should be emphasised that invoking the "reciprocity principle" will not help the EU legitimise a BTA-type system when emerging countries are asymmetrically positioned with regard to the EU. This is, first, because the WTO charter allows for exemptions from this principle for developing countries (see above) and, second, because developing countries are not as yet subject to the same international obligations as developed countries that carry overwhelming responsibility for CO_2 emissions past and present (the notion of "environmental dumping" would seem particularly inappropriate in this respect).

C. A more consistent international normative strategy

Though the EU has sometimes been defined as a "normative power" – as opposed to a military power – it still needs a more coherent international strategy to promote the economic and social standards it develops on its own territory. Beyond the previously mentioned environmental standards and competition regulations, a more comprehensive approach to this subject would contribute to improved promotion of EU interests while creating the conditions for a more profitable and acceptable global competition.

The Mission is aware of the difficulties of such an approach, given the variety of "theatres of operation" concerned, as well as the need for discretion in implementing it.

1. A necessarily global normative approach

The need to respect regulations adopted by the EU – be they economic (*e.g.* intellectual property) or social (core labour standards) – is often brought up in international trade negotiations and often gives rise to calls to restrict (or impose conditions on) trade with various countries while, at the same time, arousing fairly widespread rejection within the EU. *In reality, it should be possible to achieve more significant results by not basing compliance with certain European standards solely on the Common Trade Policy*, which means taking the following additional steps:

- continued development of Internal Market rules (regulations, directives, technical standards) that third-country markets could be encouraged to follow because of the economic potential of the European market. The influence of European legal norms will be even stronger if the rules are both uniform and binding within the Single Market;

- increased European technical and financial cooperation with emerging countries to bring their economic, social and environmental norms up to standard;
- using the European trade policy to provide incentives by granting additional commercial advantages to countries that respect norms defined by the EU – on the General System of Preferences+ (GSP+) model – and, if need be, in a more coercive way;
- strengthening the EU's foreign, security and defence policy when exercising "hard power" would strongly influence our partners to take EU interests and norms into account.

2. An international strategy to suit each type of norm

On these foundations, a European normative strategy could be adapted to individual cases, depending on whether the EU is in a position of strength with regard to its partners and on the more or less asymmetric nature of its position compared to them:

- the EU has recently realised the extent to which its vast and prosperous internal market gives it a significant competitive edge in applying *industrial standards* throughout the world. In the automobile industry, for example, it has developed standards that have been adopted by most manufacturers in other countries, investing it with a leadership role that benefits its companies and workers. The EU must implement a strategy for all industrial sectors that have been standardised at the Community level and aim for more widespread international dissemination of those standards;
- with regard to *competition, investment and public procurement access rules* (described as "Singapore subjects" at the WTO and excluded from the Doha agenda), the EU must be more vigorously assertive with its partners in the bilateral negotiations it undertakes and demand more reciprocity from other OECD countries as well as emerging countries that are beginning to invest in European markets;
- as far as respecting *intellectual property* laws is concerned, the EU must also develop a strategy that incorporates better protection for European R&D breakthroughs (Community or even triadic patents), cooperation measures with third-countries and more robust sanctions against intellectual property violations and counterfeiting;
- the example of *financial and accounting standards* used internationally also reveals EU shortcomings. The adoption of accounting standards produced by the International Accounting Standard Board (IASB), for example, was not preceded by any political steps to ensure better European representation within this organisation and led to accounting

criteria that are sometimes destabilising for companies and that are now contributing to worsening the international financial crisis. Though the European Commission has started bilateral discussions about the financial standards applied by its main partners, these discussions would be more effective if a clear mandate was defined by the Council to which the Commission would have to answer on a regular basis in its negotiations;

• *"internationally recognised human and labour rights"*, as defined by the International Labour Organisation (ILO), should also be more actively promoted at the European level. The EU's 2005 recasting of the General System of Preferences (GSP) led to the creation of a GSP+ granting broader preferential access to European markets for countries that implement the main international agreements on human and labour rights[3]. In its current bilateral negotiations, the EU should consider going further, following the example of the United States at the conclusion of the North American Free Trade Agreement (NAFTA). A parallel agreement to NAFTA, called the "North American Agreement on Labour Cooperation" (NAALC), obliges its members to ensure that their labour legislation is enforced and, to this end, introduces a mutual monitoring and sanction system[4]. It is also important that the EU monitor the social responsibility of its companies and their code of conduct in emerging countries.

It goes without saying that the EU will not be able to obtain comparable results in all areas. The appeal of its Internal Market could help it make substantial progress with regard to industrial standards and the global challenge of climate change will favour a multilateral agreement, but social issues will doubtless fare differently since the application of core labour standards does not elicit overall consensus internationally.

D. An integrated European approach to developing countries and immigration

The EU is the developed economic zone with the most developing countries in its immediate neighbourhood; the relationships it builds with them will largely determine its economic and political future. Yet, unlike the United States and Mexico (with NAFTA) or Japan and the

3 In this context, the tariff preferences granted to Belarus were suspended in June 2007 because of violations of workers' rights condemned by the ILO.

4 A group of independent arbitrators, referred to once a complaint has been registered (30 complaints have been lodged so far), can impose a fine on a government when there has been "a persistent pattern of failure by the Party complained against to effectively enforce its occupational safety and health, child labour or minimum wage technical labour standards" with regard to its internal legislation.

countries of the Far East, *the EU is having difficulty putting into effect a comprehensive and effective strategy towards these countries*, apart from its enlargement policy, which now seems destined to concern only a limited number of countries.

The recently established European Neighbourhood Policy (ENP), along with the geographical processes launched here and there (*e.g.*, the Barcelona Process or the "joint Europe-Africa strategy") have not at this stage kept their promises. Beyond a particular policy, from now on the EU needs to take a new line with developing countries that is not centred on the aid it can give them but clearly accepts the need to establish a genuine strategic partnership with them. The EU needs developing countries just as these countries need the EU. This strategic partnership should be based on economic, migratory and financial agendas.

1. Economic agreements to formalise the strategic partnership between the EU and the developing world

Bilateral negotiations held by the EU with the ACP countries or Mercosur, and in the framework of the Neighbourhood Policy, should lead to trade-offs based on a strategic complementarity that is often talked about, but still needs to be given concrete shape:

- the EU has technical, industrial and financial resources that its southern Mediterranean partners need;
- as for the developing countries, they have raw materials (agricultural, mining and energy) and human resources required by Europe.

This *synergy should initially be formalised through trade agreements between the EU and the developing countries*, which mainly presupposes greater openness of European agricultural markets (already open to the Least Advanced Countries) and a reciprocal greater openness on the part of developing countries to EU industries and services.

A strategic partnership of this kind should also be based on technology transfers between the EU and developing countries, reinforced cooperation and training, stronger support for South-South economic integration (particularly help in setting up transport and energy networks) as well as concerted management of migratory flows.

2. A new European approach to migrants and "co-development"

Today, the EU seems to be conducting a restrictive policy towards immigration from outside the Community, even though the positions held by its Member States vary greatly in this respect, as do their respective needs. Demographic developments in the EU and its Member States should, however, lead them to adopt a much more open approach in the future. *For example, the Commission has recently estimated that European countries will need to attract 20 million qualified migrants over the next 20 years*. This migratory contribution is, in fact, essential for two reasons:

- first, to maintain the proportion of active workers within the total population in the context of European demographic aging (potential growth level, financing social protection regimes). In this respect, the commitment to a rise in employment rates made in Lisbon from 2000 will undoubtedly have run out of room for growth between now and 2010-2015, whereas the effects of a hypothetical European demographic recovery would only be felt 25 years later;
- second, to attract more qualified workers and "talent" from outside the Community, for whom global competition is already under way (particularly with North America); the result of that competition will partly determine the EU's dynamism and innovation capacity.

In this context, *the European immigration policy today seems less than effective for two reasons*:

- it is based on free movement within the EU and the Schengen area, but with separate management for access to European territory and regularisation methods for illegal workers;
- it is based, above all, on restricting immigration from outside the Community which has the effect of chasing highly qualified people towards other regions of the world (particularly North America) without preventing the less qualified from entering EU territory, often under poor conditions (illegal immigration, the unofficial economy).

In this context, the implementation of a European immigration policy should be based on the following principles:

- giving emphasis to the positive economic and social impact of migrations based, for example, on the lessons to be learned from the "Globalisation Migrations into the EU: main determinants and economic impact" report recently presented by the European Commission;
- *a clear policy line on the need to welcome more migrant workers from outside the Community, without necessarily resorting to the quota method* which is difficult for migrants to understand and automatically leads to illegal workers;
- *attracting migrants (particularly the more highly qualified) by offering more attractive conditions than those offered by other developed countries*. This should lead to granting some migrants (stu-

dents with master's degrees, seasonal and retired workers) free movement rights (return journeys) between their country of origin and the EU over a period of several years. As a matter of fact, the free movement of migrants between the EU and developing countries needs to be organised just as much as within the EU (the "blue card" project) where there is a risk of it remaining fairly limited (as is the case with European workers);

- *simplifying the formalities for applicants for EU migration*: establishing a single entry procedure for third-country citizens, as proposed by the European Commission; establishing joint consulates for EU countries in third countries; training and awareness-raising for the European staff in charge of the administrative processing of migrant requests, in Europe as in third countries;
- in parallel, at the national level: improving reception and integration policies since the benefits of immigration do not depend solely on migrants' entry qualifications but also on how successfully they are integrated. Effective integration policies should be implemented particularly in the field of education and professional training. This is the indispensable condition for improved acceptance of migratory flows from outside the Community into the EU.

The EU must also upgrade its development policy to a co-development policy, while making sure to:

- define with the countries concerned their own needs in terms of human resources (to avoid an immoderate "brain drain" effect). However, in seeking the right balance, the EU should not go so far as to deprive itself intentionally of qualified workers from developing countries, who would probably leave their countries anyway and settle in other developed countries if rejected by Europe;
- enlarge the scope of the "Erasmus Mundus" programme by extending it beyond 2008 and increasing its budget to three times its current level (only 300 million euros over 5 years), especially to attract more students from emerging countries to the EU;
- *facilitate funds transfers and "remittances" by immigrants to their countries of origin*, which greatly contribute to running local companies and economies, channelling funds more towards productive investments (tax incentives for productive local investments, etc.). For example, the EU could contribute financially and technically to making banking systems in countries of the South more secure so that immigrants make greater use of them for transfers rather than turn to private operators with very high fees;

- support migrants travelling between their countries and the EU by allowing them, for example, to create mixed jurisdiction companies (*e.g.* Euro-African) and by providing financial and technical support for their development projects (factory or school construction, etc.).

3. *A more Europeanised ODA*

The EU and its Member States are presently the world's leading donors of Official Development Aid (ODA) in terms of volume, with sums set at approximately 60 billion and 10 billion euros, respectively, in 2006 (*i.e.*, nearly three-quarters of the sums of money committed by OECD countries). But their efforts would be more effective if:

- *a greater share of ODA were committed in the framework of the EU*, to avoid the duplications and redundancies that beneficiary countries suffer from; this would involve increasing the current amounts jointly committed from 25% (including the European Development Fund) to at least 35% (joint level of humanitarian aid);
- *ODA committed by Member States were better coordinated*; strengthening geographical synergy between national aid strategies by relying on an EU "code of good practice"; joint project implementation, with much more systematic recourse to joint financing ("basket funds") and the designation of a leading country for each project;
- *there were continued improvement in European ODA management methods*; implementing "country" and "regional" strategies to make aid for beneficiary countries easier to foresee; resorting to financial aid rather than loans (the counter-example being China) with a "direct aid" component in national budgets brought up to the same level as the "project aid" component, in exchange for commitments to better management from beneficiary countries; increased aid for development projects undertaken by migrants; and lastly, an increase in the decentralisation of aid.

* *
*

The "Union for the Mediterranean" project, endorsed by the European Council of March 2008, can illustrate the new priority the EU means to grant to the region and the need for an integrated policy approach to these countries, backing up the initiatives begun within the framework of the Barcelona process. It aims to concentrate on implementing concrete sectoral projects (water, energy, environment, security, etc.) based on well-identified mechanisms, with strong private-sector involvement and giving tangible content to the strategic partnership to be built between the EU and its southern neighbours.

E. A new EC regulation to monitor certain sensitive investments

The geopolitical dimension that globalisation has taken on at the turn of the 21st century precludes Europe from disconnecting economic from security issues, as it has hitherto done. Foreign policy and common security must include an economic component and, likewise, the European strategy for globalisation must take into account the geopolitical dimension.

This is already the case for energy, the main conduit of geopolitics in the economic field. The measures presented by the Commission in September 2007 within the third "energy liberalisation package" allowed for a reciprocity clause (known as the "Gazprom clause") that aims to protect European companies from potential hostile takeover bids by integrated foreign energy groups, *i.e.*, groups that have not separated their production assets from their transmission assets. Strictly in the name of security and independence, this concern should be extended to any undesirable takeover of European strategic assets by players from outside the Community, as well as to some sensitive technology transfers.

The free movement of capital within the EU – the linchpin of the Single Market – has long made controlling foreign investments a taboo subject in Europe. In 1993, the Maastricht Treaty increased this freedom by stipulating that it should also be fully recognised for investments from third countries (article 56 of the EC treaty), which had not been provided for by the Treaty of Rome. Since then, ECJ case law has been constantly limiting Member States' leeway in defining regimes that are in derogation of the free movement of capital.

The spectacular rise in power of a new generation of Sovereign Wealth Funds (SWFs) from the major emerging countries with considerable exchange reserves – and the significant acquisition by these funds of holdings in the flagships of American finance, weakened by the subprime crisis – have recently drawn the attention of economic and political leaders to the need of monitoring the activity of such funds and other government-controlled entities at the international and European levels.

1. An inadequate response

So far, reflections on SWFs – as much at a multilateral level (IMF, OECD) as in a European context – have mainly focused on improving transparency and the governance of SWFs, given the financial volumes they control, in a context of international financial turbulence. This essential issue, taken up by the European Commission in its communication of 27 February 2008, should result in the development of codes of conduct and other concerted self-regulation instruments. This is a welcome move, but does not exhaust the subject, particularly in its geopolitical dimension.

The drive to set up a more restrictive monitoring system of potential "strategic" takeovers conflicts with the indisputably positive contribution of SWFs in the context of a global liquidity crisis and the need for the European economy to continue attracting foreign investment, as well as the opposition of more liberal Member States to any form of capital movement control. Also, as we have seen, this position has Community law in its favour.

At the same time, *SWFs help sharpen the divide in the global economy between a West that is converted to free market and an emerging world where the economy is still largely state-owned.* In the first place, the influence of the State in emerging economies creates competition distortions which, as we have seen, challenge the Common Trade Policy and the Competition Policy. But it can also present a geopolitical risk in terms of the takeover of strategic Western industries, companies or technologies. Faced with this prospect, the EU, unlike the United States, is at present powerless.

The Commission's communication concerning SWFs certainly touches on this preoccupation – shared in varying degrees by most Member States – but merely refers to the very limited exceptions to the principle of free circulation of capital authorised by Community law. In effect, the EC treaty (article 57, para. 2) allows Member States to adopt measures that amount to taking "steps backwards" as far as the liberalisation of capital movement from or to third countries is concerned. But this adoption is subject to the unanimity rule. Article 64 of the Lisbon Treaty on the Functioning of the European Union (TFEU) takes up this measure, holding that the Council "may unanimously, and after consulting the European Parliament, adopt measures which constitute a step backwards in EU law as regards the liberalisation of the movement of capital to or from third countries"[5].

---

[5] Article 64

[2] Whilst endeavouring to achieve the objective of free movement of capital between Member States and third countries to the greatest extent possible and without prejudice to the other Chapters of the Treaties, the European Parliament and the Council, acting in accordance with the ordinary legislative procedure, shall adopt measures on the movement of capital to or from third countries involving direct

Article 58 of the EC Treaty also validates certain restrictions for tax, prudential, public policy or public safety reasons. The Court of Justice of the European Communities specifies the range of these derogations, which it interprets restrictively. It recognises their legitimacy when they are correctly motivated and when they are public, proportional, necessary and open to appeal (Distrigaz ruling). Thus, in 2006, the Commission authorised France's "golden share" in Gaz de France. Lastly, the Treaty provides that the Council may, ruling with a qualified majority, take temporary safeguard measures in exceptional circumstances for reasons of economic (article 59) or political (article 60) public policy.

2. *The spread of national control measures*

This liberal attitude of the Community authorities encourages de facto adoption of national restrictive measures, often targeting investments from other Member States, and the Commission has had no hesitation in contesting their compatibility with Community law. This, for example, is the case with the French decree of 30 December 2005 which regulates foreign investments in certain sectors that are deemed strategic and the scope of which is doubtless insufficient in the new configuration of the world economy.

Germany is presently debating a bill to introduce a declaration regime for all investments from outside the Community that undermine "public policy and security" (as defined by Community law). In this respect, the preamble of the bill mentions making energy supplies secure, the security of means of telecommunication, electricity supply and certain so-called "strategic" public services. An optional system to notify the German authorities will be introduced whenever a foreign investor's share in the capital of the target German company exceeds 25% (a position also supported by Austria). Investors who, following checks, prove to have more than 25% of capital from outside the Community will be considered to be investors from outside the Community, notwithstanding their location within the EU.

In the absence of Community control, the probable spread of such national measures – that are more or less contrary to current Community law and more or less effective – will contribute to the fragmentation of the Single Market, the weakening of Community law and the disunity

investment – including investment in real estate – establishment, the provision of financial services or the admission of securities to capital markets.

[3] Notwithstanding paragraph 2, only the Council, acting in accordance with a special legislative procedure, may unanimously, and after consulting the European Parliament, adopt measures which constitute a step backwards in EU law as regards the liberalisation of the movement of capital to or from third countries.

(*i.e.*, lack of authority) of Europe over a major subject of preoccupation, whereas:

- SWFs manage considerable financial resources (an estimated 2.5 trillion dollars in 2007, 12 trillion dollars in 2015), enabling them to take over the biggest European and American companies on the market;
- unlike older sovereign funds, such as the Norwegian fund or the funds of certain Persian Gulf States, those recently set up by the major emerging powers such as China (200 billion euros) or Russia (100 billion euros) are capable of participating in the geopolitical strategies already openly implemented by these states;
- the EU is the only economic power in the world that does not have a monitoring instrument for foreign takeovers in strategic sectors.

The Committee on Foreign Investment in the United States (CFIUS), an inter-agency structure created in 1975, and the 1988 Exon-Florio legislation give the US government significant latitude to monitor foreign investment projects. As a last resort, this measure relies on the US President's evaluation of the risk to "national security". Prohibitions are rare, but the threat of a presidential veto makes it possible to impose substantial changes on takeover plans (Alcatel-Lucent) and occasionally discourage some of them from taking place (CNOOC/Unocal, Dubai ports).

The United States recently strengthened this legislative framework with a law passed on 26 July 2007. The main innovations concern:

- the explicit extension of national security considerations to transactions concerning critical infrastructures or technologies;
- increased monitoring of transactions involving entities controlled by a foreign state;
- the possibility for the government to re-examine a previously authorised transaction if the investor has violated the agreement entered into with the government; and
- reinforcing the administration's obligation to inform the Congress.

What is more, Washington has just bilaterally negotiated additional precautions concerning the nature of SWF investments with Abu Dhabi and Singapore.

In this new context, the limited approach to SWFs opted for at this stage by the European Commission does not seem up to the stakes. If the EU wishes to be a global player, it must, like all its partners and competitors, adopt a position from which it may prohibit, or subject to conditions, unsolicited takeover plans by non-Community players for assets that are deemed strategic to European security interests, all the more so if they are foreign states with which the EU may find itself in diplomatic conflict.

3. The need for a Community regulation

Accordingly, the Mission recommends introducing a specific Community regulation to address security concerns exclusively, following the example of the American Exon-Florio legislation, in lieu of similar national measures.

The legal basis for this new instrument would be the combination of articles 57 § 2 and 308 of the EC Treaty (the "flexibility clause"), adopted by the Lisbon Treaty. However, the scope of article 57 § 2 is too limited to the extent that it refers to the notion of capital movements constituting "direct investments". It would therefore be advisable to resort to article 308 of the EC Treaty as well in order for this Community instrument also to encompass capital movements that do not constitute direct investments. The flexibility clause is frequently cited in addition to other measures in the Treaty. Adopting such an act would require Council unanimity.

A detailed elaboration of such a measure goes beyond the scope of this report, but it should observe the following principles:

- it should only be directed at transactions that call into question security or other national or European strategic interests, excluding considerations of an economic, industrial or social nature, particularly those relating to employment and relocation (to which, if need be, other measures could apply). As is the case in American legislation, it is preferable not to predetermine sectors likely to be concerned, even if this means providing an indicative list in the form of guidelines;
- it should be applied to all acquisitions of holdings by investors controlled from outside the Community (including companies located in the EU), particularly (but not exclusively) foreign states. Here too it would be inadvisable in principle to fix a capital holding threshold;
- an investigation procedure should be triggered upon the optional notification of the investor or any Member State concerned and should be administered by a specific Community service using a procedure totally independent for merger control procedures, as is the case in the United States. This service should probably be located within the Commission because of the cross-sectoral nature of the policies concerned, but it should act in liaison with the High

Representative for the CFSP and the Member State(s) directly concerned by the transaction;

- the most difficult political question to resolve concerns the authority invested with the power to authorise – with or without conditions – or prohibit an investment targeted by this measure. This authority could be the President of the Commission or the President of the European Council. In the rare hypothetical situation of an authorisation decision (whether conditional or not) giving rise to opposition from a Member State directly affected, a tightly framed right of veto in favor of such Member State would, as a last resort, probably be preferable to the present legal void.

The Mission is aware of the difficulty of obtaining the agreement of all 27 Member States to such a measure in the current state of development of the concepts of "European interests" and, even more, "European security". More generally speaking, such a measure requires a degree of political unity and "self-awareness" that the EU has probably not yet attained.

What remains true is that the world around us will not stand by and wait, and Europe must possess the same legal weapons as the other major economic powers. In December 2003, the EU began defining a Security Strategy, the economic dimension of which has yet to be developed. It is therefore high time to start debating this subject.

CHAPTER IV

EuroWorld 2015: Conditions For Success

The post-2010 European strategy for globalisation will not succeed unless a number of political, doctrinal, institutional and financial conditions and evolutions are brought together. This chapter attempts to state what they are. As far as the institutional and financial components are concerned, our reasoning so far is based on treaties (including the Lisbon Treaty) and budgetary ceilings remaining constant between now and 2015. This realistic choice does not exclude the need to see further, particularly in legal and institutional terms, before this deadline.

I. A New Political Consensus For Stronger EU Leadership

The success of the strategic vision recommended by this report is based, in the first place, on political will, *i.e.*, a consensus among the 27 Member States regarding the new objectives of the European project. Such a consensus requires, in turn:

- a collective awareness of the issues, challenges and opportunities touched on in the first part of this report;
- the willingness to face these collectively, *i.e.*, the shared conviction that the EU is the appropriate and indispensable framework from which to prosper and exert influence in a world of continental scale nations;
- the courage to draw the necessary consequences thereof in terms of the institutional and financial means to put in place, particularly the launching of new common policies and, more generally, the revival of an integration process that has been dormant since the early 1990s.

To build political consensus on Europe's role and action in the global economy, we can start with what has already been achieved: the "Declaration on Globalisation" issued by the European Council in December 2007 closing the Portuguese presidency, and the convergence of a reputedly "protectionist" France and a reputedly "liberal" United Kingdom on the "Global Europe" theme, *i.e.*, a Europe heading for globalisation. Though the French and British positions may diverge concerning the instruments required for a European strategy for globalisation, it is important to deepen the convergence on the objective, based on the following considerations:

- the Lisbon strategy invites European states to adapt to globalisation on the basis of largely national structural reforms, the implementation of which takes into account the specific features of each country. A more comprehensive European strategy for globalisation should encourage a change of scale: if we now also wish to contribute to shaping globalisation, each Member State – whether "large" or "small" – is powerless to do so in isolation and the consequences of this paradigm shift should be drawn by expanding common policies and decision-making processes;
- *in particular, the EU should wake up fully to the fact that it is largely dependent on the world outside its borders*: it was strongly dependent on the external world during the Cold War in politico-military terms, seemed less dependent during the 1990s, but, in reality, remains dependent both economically and socially, because its development relies on vital contributions from the rest of the world (energy resources, immigration, exports and growth, reducing global warming);
- given their structurally open nature, small EU countries are often more keenly aware of this dependence than the largest ones, but historically they have counted on national strategies. The large countries, on the contrary, are more pervasively aware of the international role they can play and their assets in this respect; they often have the economic, diplomatic and military resources that the EU needs to wield greater influence internationally: it remains for them to work more collectively in the future to pool the assets of European countries to greater advantage, by reaching a greater awareness of their reduced individual influence in a multipolar world;
- *conversely, the EU now has the ability to exert much greater influence on the outside world, provided it has a real will to equip itself with the tools needed to realise its ambitions*. It should not live in constant fear of reprisals from its partners and must deal with them on equal terms while striving to promote its own model;
- lastly, the transatlantic dialogue should have pride of place in a European strategy for globalisation: over and above its ability to provide impetus for some Member States, close collaboration with the United States is a major precondition for the success of many components of such a strategy. Conversely, non-participation on the part of the United States would limit the scope of certain actions (climate negotiations) or enable third countries to take advantage of transatlantic discord (trade negotiations).

II. Doctrinal Modernisation

The "Copernican revolution" at work in the external reorientation of the European project also requires a few doctrinal adjustments.

A. Shifting from a logic of exemplarity to a logic of interests

Until the late 1980s, European unification pushed forward without any genuine strategic awareness because of its mainly inward-looking preoccupations on the one hand and American military protection on the other. The illusions of the post-Cold War decade confirmed the EU's sense of its position as a "soft power" or non-strategic and exemplary "civil power".

Since then, the return of geopolitics inaugurated by the attacks of September 11, 2001 and their multiple consequences, whether direct or indirect, has led Europe to develop its own embryonic strategic thinking, embodied in the publication of a "European Security Strategy" in December 2003.

So far, this noteworthy progress towards an EU strategic identity has only concerned the traditional dimensions of security, since the economic dimension was only tackled with regard to the integration of major emerging powers into the multilateral system. The EU must now incorporate the economic dimension into its security strategy, starting by defining common economic interests with an inventory of its insufficiently exploited assets and its insufficiently mastered handicaps. It should acknowledge the end of the "Atlantic era", marked by Euro-American dominance on the international stage.

This approach should lead Europe to complement its exemplary "soft power", capable of fashioning the world in its own image, with a more traditional and realistic attitude to power, at least in economic matters.

B. Revising the original pragmatism

For such a change in logic gradually to permeate attitudes and draw the EU's Member States together, it should be built on a case-by-case basis, "through concrete achievements which first create a *de facto* solidarity" in order to avoid yet another episode of the old debate between "Europe as a space" and "Europe as a power". For example, it is because each Member State will realise that it is not (or no longer) a question of defending an illusory "national energy independence", but of reducing the risks of the European energy dependence, that progress can be made in European energy diplomacy.

We also need to avoid restarting the great debate that traditionally pits partisans of unconditional openness of economic borders – accompanied by a drive to obtain the same treatment from emerging and developing countries – against proponents of an openness that is more directly subject to a notion of reciprocity. Here, too, this opposition could be put into perspective in view of the operational limits of the reciprocity principle and the observation that all European countries are externally dependent in economic terms, in addition to the realisation by supporters of unconditional free trade that governments and power strategies have made a comeback within the world's new growth poles.

As in days of old, there is no way Europe can progress along the external economic strategy path if it does not put ideological divisions behind it and search pragmatically for common interests that are sufficiently strong to prevail over divergent national interests.

C. Relaxing the unity and uniformity dogma

Implementing a European strategy for globalisation also requires *a clearer admission by the EU that it is now more politically, economically and socially heterogeneous than it was in the past* (in terms of domestic needs, collective preferences and, hence, national interests). Not only does this reality make decision-making more difficult, but it also hampers the very definition of the common interests that are capable of prevailing over divergent national interests. It makes it essential for the 27 – which, despite everything, need to act and unite to exert influence in the global economy – to favour paths of action that are appropriate in this new context:

a) Accepting differentiation for greater effectiveness

The adoption of *overall European objectives – stated by country or by country category* in accordance with their availability and capacities – is already practised for CO_2 emission reduction or for military initiatives within the framework of the European Security and Defence Policy (ESDP). We need to generalize this practice whenever necessary to implement Lisbon Plus (*e.g.* for 3% R&D, to be implemented clearly by country) to strengthen the degree of ownership and effectiveness of this strategy.

b) Favouring flexible, open cooperation

The implementation of European policies within a single Community framework applicable to all must remain the priority objective. But this unity and uniformity requirement, even though inspired by good European intentions, should no longer put obstacles in the way of limited initiatives by EU subgroups.

For many years, the plans envisaged in this direction have proved too rigid, whether they concerned a "hard core" or single vanguard pushing the path to integration or the "enhanced cooperations" that, up to now, have remained a dead letter. For want of an agreement by all 27 Member States in a given field, more flexible interest groups should henceforth be envisaged, on condition that they remain open and that their initiatives be fully compatible within the EU's existing framework.

The development of common policies and actions could therefore take the form:

- preferably, of common external policies (*e.g.* climate diplomacy);
- failing that, initiatives open to volunteer states bringing together a limited number of countries (*e.g.* the euro or the European Energy Community) in the framework of the new measures provided for by the Lisbon Treaty; or
- plurilateral cooperation outside the Community framework (*e.g.* Eureka for R&D).

III. Strong Institutions For Greater Coherence and Effectiveness

"Nothing is possible without men, nothing is lasting without institutions": Jean Monnet's words remind us that the success of a European strategy for globalisation must be based on the establishment of appropriate political and administrative structures.

Like the Lisbon strategy in the course of the 2000 decade, the implementation of the internal and external dimensions of the *EuroWorld 2015 Strategy* will face the challenges of effectiveness and coherence. In effect, both dimensions require a *cross-sectoral approach* interconnecting many fields governed by different logics and institutions. The national implementation of the Lisbon strategy has already experienced the difficulties of a cross-sectoral approach combining, for example, economics, higher education and research. The problem will be even greater when it becomes necessary to link the internal and external dimensions of a broader strategy.

When the Lisbon Treaty comes into effect, it will bring a number of useful innovations in this respect. However, these innovations constitute a necessary but insufficient condition for the success of this strategy, which requires more coherent political governance at Community and national levels and more Europeanised administrations.

We shall limit ourselves here to the external component and its linkage to the internal component of the *EuroWorld 2015 Strategy* as the institutional aspects of the latter have already been tackled under the heading of Lisbon Plus governance.

A. Making the most of the Lisbon Treaty's contributions (see Annex 6)

As far as the external dimension is concerned, *the Lisbon Treaty introduces a number of institutional innovations that are capable of serving the implementation of a strategy for globalisation*: the institution of a stable presidency of the European Council; the break-up of the old pillar-structure by allowing the High Representative of the EU for Foreign Affairs and Security Policy also to wear the hat of Commission Vice-President; clarifying the allocations of competences between the EU and its Member States and progress in Community jurisdiction in a number of relevant fields; the institution of a common "external action" service; the recognition of the EU's legal personality, etc. Taken together, these innovations should make it easier for Europe to assert itself on the international stage and link internal and external agendas.

But the new treaty is also likely to aggravate present difficulties. Without precisely defining their roles and interaction, the treaty brings into coexistence the new President of the Council, the President of the Commission, the High Representative/Vice-President of the Commission, the revolving presidency of the EU Council and the trio of presidencies. Obviously this congestion at the top risks jeopardising the coherence, effectiveness and legibility of the EU's internal and external action. It will be necessary to reduce these risks by transforming potential competition into complementary functions.

The task of the President of the European Council is thus to enhance the activity of the EU's supreme political organ while, at the same time, ensuring its external representation. The President must be a personality with strong internal legitimacy who also has genuine international stature. The High Representative will be the "Union Minister for Foreign Affairs", head of the common European External Action Service (EEAS) and the link between intergovernmental and Community dimensions (particularly in economic matters) for foreign and security policy. The President of the Commission, being in charge of the collegial operation of this key institution, needs to ensure the coherence of the internal and external components of the European strategy for globalisation. He must therefore work harmoniously in tandem with the President of the European Council.

B. The Commission: an irreplaceable centre of coherence

If a European strategy for globalisation is to succeed, the Commission must be maintained at the heart of the system since it is the vector of Community policies, the internal and external components of which must remain deeply interconnected. To play its role in full, however, the Commission must increase its efforts to synthesise the different policies concerned, since its present organisation in "silos" remains imperfect. An internal reorganisation of the Commission to fit the EuroWorld 2015 strategy is in order.

1. Increasing the coherence of common external policies

The creation of the High Representative post will increase the coherence of European foreign and security policy; but it is not his task to coordinate all the EU's external economic and social policies on his own.

To achieve this, a group of European commissioners in charge of external policies and in a position to forge a common, cross-sectoral vision should meet at least on a quarterly basis, under the aegis of the President of the Commission and in the presence of the High Representative for Foreign Affairs and Security Policy. This group should bring together commissioners for economic and monetary affairs, trade, development, enlargement, energy, the environment, the Internal Market, competition and migrations (a post yet to be created).

2. Preserving the group of "Lisbon Commissioners"

The group of "Lisbon Commissioners" instituted in 2005 should be called upon to continue working on everything that comes under Lisbon Plus. If need be, they could be open to press coverage to promote the ownership and better understanding of their progress and limits at national and Community levels.

C. A stronger intergovernmental dynamic

The issues and trade-offs involved in the *EuroWorld 2015 Strategy* are both political and cross-sectoral; they can only be effectively apprehended at the highest intergovernmental level.

1. A more hands-on European council

The European Council should devote more than one annual meeting (the spring meeting) to European and international economic and social affairs; it ought to meet formally every quarter and, on each occasion, address these matters. The appointment of a stable European Council President will help ensure better structuring and monitoring of this work. This mobilisation of the European Council is vital to establishing overall coherence since neither the General Affairs and External Relations Council (GAERC) nor the High Representative have sufficient legitimacy to carry out the required economic and social trade-offs.

2. *An operational college of "national Lisbon coordinators"* (see Chapter II of Part III)

D. An administrative mix

Lastly, the success of the EuroWorld 2015 Strategy involves developing more "mixed" administrative structures, adapted to the twofold Community and national character of the strategy.

1. *The common European External Action Service (EEAS): a promising start*

Beyond the removal of the pillar-structure adopted at Maastricht, setting up a common European External Action Service confirms that a European strategy for globalisation must, of necessity, combine Community and national action tools, which can only be well-coordinated if the services that manage them are on good working terms. Given the cumbersome administrative processes, the only way to promote such coordination is to bring national and European civil servants together within a single structure.

If the 27 are capable of reaching agreement on the creation of a common service in one of the most politically sensitive realms, foreign and security policy, they must be able to do the same for all the external components of a European strategy for globalisation (energy, climate change, migrations, etc.). In these areas, joint administrative structures should be established comprising Commission and Member State representatives who would be in a position to forge a common vision and work together to implement European policies, in liaison with their respective national governments.

2. *Increased contacts between national and Community administrations*

Besides the joint administrative structures created in Europe (in Brussels or elsewhere), contact between European and national administrations should be developed, not only on an individual basis (sending experts on temporary assignments) but with regular meetings, for example in the form of regular missions for Community administrations in national capitals.

This close coordination between national and Community administrations would seem particularly important externally, notably in third countries where national diplomatic services and Commission delegations will have to work out a common approach to issues and projects (such as development aid).

3. *Community regulatory bodies for pan-European flows*

It is very difficult to regulate the free movement of products, capital and workers within Europe on the basis of bilateral cooperation because too many such initiatives would need to be set up in an EU of 27 and they would struggle to take into account pan-European phenomena (*e.g.* the destabilisation of financial and labour markets).

Transnational flows of this kind require Europeanised control systems, *e.g.* for financial services and worker secondments. Since this Europeanisation cannot be based effectively on identifying a leading national controller, a European regulatory body needs to be created, dedicated to European movements of goods, capital and workers. This Europeanisation could be achieved by assigning national and Community civil servants to common regulatory structures.

IV. An Appropriate Mobilisation of National and Community Budgets

The review of the EU financial framework planned for 2008-2009 by the December 2005 European Council provides a good opportunity to start adapting the financing to be devoted to its strategy for globalisation, at national and Community levels.

This exercise should be undertaken in the framework of an aggregate approach and lead to increasing certain national expenditures, including joint expenditures, and concentrating the Community budget on expenditures with strong European added value.

A. The need for an aggregate financial approach

When it comes to financing, European public policies are most often studied through Community financing alone. This leads to errors in analysis. In effect, *the approach needs to be extended to all European financing – Community and national* – to be much more consistent with:

- the open method of coordination applied to the implementation of the Lisbon strategy which, in reality, relies much more on national than on Community financing;
- the current assessment of European external expenditures, the great majority of which also fall outside the Community budget;
- and, more generally, the reality of European public financing: the Community budget (approximately 1% of EU GDP) represents only 2.5% of total European public expenditures. Most of the financial resources required to implement a European strategy for globalisation, therefore, are to be found at the level of national ex-

penditures which, in total, account for nearly 44% of the EU GDP (with considerable variations from one Member State to another).

This aggregate vision of European public financing is, in part, already effective for R&D (since the objective of 3% of GDP, including 1% from public sources, cannot by its very nature concern the Community budget alone). But it has yet to spread to all EU budget categories to provide a coherent assessment of current European public financing and make a useful contribution to the debate on how that financing is to be adapted to the objectives of the strategy outlined in the preceding chapters.

B. The necessary increase in certain national expenditures (including joint expenditures)

1. *A strategy for globalisation based on new expenditures at the national level*

a) Increased expenditures for Lisbon Plus:

- on R&D: implementation of the 1% of GDP objective for public expenditures;
- on education, particularly higher education: increased national expenditures up to 3% of GDP;
- increased financing for innovation (a rise in the order of 0.3 or 0.4 points of GDP);
- establishing "flexicurity" (a rise of up to 2 points of GDP, depending on the country);
- increased expenditures on transport and energy infrastructures.

b) Increased expenditures linked to common external policies:

- increased development aid expenditures: the EU has become the biggest financial backer (55% of Official development assistance worldwide). At the European Council of Barcelona, to help achieve the "Millennium Objectives" the EU made a collective commitment at an average level of ODA of 0.33% to 0.39% of GNI between 2002 and 2006 and up to 0.7% by 2015;
- increased expenditures linked to external policy and defence, in accordance with the objectives defined by the Helsinki European Council[1];

[1] The "overall objective" set by the European Council at its meeting in Helsinki in December 1999 provides that Member States must be able to deploy within 60 days

- if required, increased national agricultural expenditures in the event of a drop in Community support for agriculture.

2. *The importance of "enhanced financial cooperation"*

Furthermore, spending by Member States could be undertaken in more of a joint framework, to enhance the cost-effectiveness ratio of projects supported by these States. These joint expenditures are already significant and would be subject to systematic assessment, which should also be part of European financial discussions.

Examples of common European (but non-Community) expenditures (Member States' contributions in 2005 in millions of euros)

	common expenditures		total	as a % of national expenditures	amount of Community expenditures
	compulsory	optional			
Technological Research & Development			*3302*	*4.81%*	*4613*
Eureka	270		270	0.39%	
CERN	636.3		636,3	0.93%	
ESA	694	1702	2396	3.49%	
Freedom, security and justice			*65.8*	*0.03%*	
EUROPOL	65.8		65.8		
Official development assistance			*2544*	*5.81%*	*6894*
EDF	2544		2544		
Defence			*1529.91*	*0.88%*	*68*
EDA	19.91		19.91	0.01%	
Athena	60		60	0.03%	
OCCAR	1450		1450	0.84%	
			7441.6448	*0.15%*	

Source: Centre d'analyse stratégique – (Amélie Barbier-Gauchard, Yves Bertoncini).
Data: Eureka, CERN, ESA, Europel, FED, EDA, Athena, OCC.

It is even more important to identify present and potential joint spending given that the development of Community expenditures would appear more difficult in a fairly heterogeneous EU, whereas common expenditures are necessary for the success of the internal and external components of a European strategy for globalisation.

---

and sustain for at least one year military forces of up to 50,000-60,000 persons capable of the full range of so-called "Petersberg" crisis management missions.

3. The possibility of increased recourse to private financing mechanisms

Taking into account increased social and health spending linked to aging European populations, Member States should broaden the room for manoeuvre by resorting to private financing mechanisms:

- increased EIB intervention to support innovative projects, guarantee student loans, build transport and energy infrastructures and finance external aid projects (particularly within the framework of the Union for the Mediterranean);
- more systematic introduction of public/private partnerships to finance transport and energy infrastructures, major European projects or training and research institutions;
- contributions to financing higher education (corporate endowments);
- increased household contributions to the financing of higher education, for which it would be legitimate for direct beneficiaries to participate to a greater extent.

C. A Community budget serving a European strategy for globalisation

The EU financial framework for the 2014-2019 period should also be adapted to the internal and external objectives of a European strategy for globalisation. For all parts of the strategy, this adaptation would seek to concentrate Community spending in areas with high European added value.

This budgetary redeployment raises the issue of the overall volume of the Community budget: are expenditures for the new innovation economy to be paid out of current spending or new financing? In the present European context, it is not realistic to aspire to a massive increase in the European budget. The trend is in fact towards a significant decrease, from 1.17% of European GDP to less than 1%, whereas the revival of the Lisbon strategy and enlargement towards the east would normally require an increase in financial investment.

Conversely, it is unreasonable to consider enhancing European policies without accepting the budgetary expression of that development.

For this reason, the Mission suggests *working on the basis of the planned financial ceiling for Community expenditures, i.e., 1.24% of European GNI, but using all available and presently unused margins.* Such an increase in Community spending would be a useful symbolic indication of the joint involvement of Community and national authorities in furthering a European strategy for globalisation.

This adaptation of the Community budget could be agreed upon at the planned 2008-2009 review and would mainly concern *the next financial framework, the duration of which should be harmonised with that of the Community legislature (i.e., 2014-2019)*. It could be based on the following indicative reference points, in accordance with the choices developed throughout this report:

1. Increasing investment in the knowledge economy and infrastructures

First of all, the presence of strong economies of scale justifies greater additional intervention by the EU compared to Member States' intervention in many areas, based on the following choices:

a) Increased expenditures on education, R&D and innovation
   - increased financing of common projects (Research and Development Framework Programmes (RDFPs), joint technological initiatives), provision of network facilities, exchange programmes (Erasmus and its variants) and linguistic programmes;
   - no financing planned for a series of leading European R&D organisations or for higher education, since it appears to be difficult to reach Community consensus on this subject.

b) Increased spending on transport and energy infrastructures
   - a massive increase in expenditures, underestimated by the Lisbon strategy (which focused greatly on ICTs), and now even more essential in the EU-27;
   - political consensus already reached concerning about thirty major Trans-European Networks (TENs) the introduction of which should be accelerated to give physical reality to the European Internal Market.

2. Increased adjustment and convergence expenditures

The EU is directly behind liberalisation processes, both internal (Internal Market and enlargement) and external (trade policy). Overall, liberalisation has had a very positive impact in terms of growth, competitiveness and employment. The EU is duty-bound, however, to take greater responsibility for their effects, which are sometimes non-egalitarian and negative, from both a social and territorial point of view:

a) An increase in social adjustment expenditures, in the context of European support for "flexicurity", on two fronts

- an increase in planned European Globalisation Adjustment Fund (EGAF) expenditures, which should not only be devoted to globalisation but (as is already partly the case) to all restructurings and relocations linked to European liberalisations (internal and external):
- the activation of expenditures from the European Social Fund (ESF) – one of the structural funds – which should be used like the EGAF mechanisms (direct investment in groups of workers).

b) An increase in regional and territorial development expenditures

- an increase in the level of structural funds to take into account not only the heterogeneousness of the EU-27 but also the limited absorption capacities of beneficiary territories, and the partial redeployment of these funds towards the most disadvantaged territories and countries; maintaining and respecting the allocation objectives of approximately two thirds of structural funds to "Lisbon projects" (education, R&D, etc.);
- an increase in Cohesion Fund (CF) expenditures which have the advantage of benefiting infrastructure and environmental projects, in line with the EuroWorld 2015 Strategy priorities.

3. Ambivalent growth of expenditures related to managing natural resources

The agricultural and environmental policies both rank among the main European policies and are intended to develop in accordance with the EU's political priorities:

a) A relative decrease in the overall level of agricultural and rural development expenditures

- a decrease in "first pillar" expenditures linked to the structural increase in world prices (making it possible to reduce support expenditures) and the requirements of WTO negotiations, the scale of the decrease depending on the new European political consensus on agriculture and food;
- the allocation of part of the social adjustment spending to farmers exposed to external liberalisation or reduced "first pillar" financing; an increase in national public financing in addition to Community social adjustment, rural development and structural expenditure;
- an increase in rural development expenditure and the allocation of a greater share of structural funds to rural areas.

b) An increase in environmental expenditures
in the framework of the Energy-Climate policy
   - increased spending on the "Environment" expenditure category;
   - an increase in RDFP subsidies and European external aid allocated to environmental projects;
   - for the record: an increase in Cohesion Fund expenditures, partly allocated to environmental projects.

4. *An increase in external expenditures*

The EU's external expenditures should increase because of the overall higher cost-effectiveness ratio for joint spending and to support the EU's new external policies.

a) An increase in Community development aid expenditures:
   - the proportion of joint development aid expenditures compared to total European expenditures could be increased to the current level of joint humanitarian aid expenditures (*i.e.*, approximately 33% of the total);
   - within official development assistance (ODA) expenditures, a priority increase in aid to emerging countries to upgrade their social and environmental standards (in the framework of a cooperative approach).

b) An increase in Common Foreign and Security Policy (CFSP) expenditures:
   - a larger share of common expenditures allocated to crisis management could be included in the Community budget;
   - at the same time, most CFSP expenditures seem to be destined to increase at the national level or in an intergovernmental framework (thus outside the Community budget).

5. *Figure-based expenditure growth assumptions, for the 2014-2019 period*

It may be useful to clarify prospective thinking about the Community budget by providing indicative figure-based content which, at this stage, serves purely as a rough guide but more concretely than the previously outlined strategic directions.

These figure-based assumptions show that significant increases in Community expenditures are possible in many areas and that they would modify the structure of the Community budget to a fairly large extent. The increases may sometimes be particularly substantial (multiplied by 4 or by 10) because the current level of Community expenditures is very low.

Of course, the assumptions should take into account European political realities and technical feasibility requirements (in particular, the capacity to manage and absorb Community funds). They may be modulated depending on the consensus reached for each of these areas and in relation to the overall level of the Community budget (which will increase in comparison with its present level, while respecting the limit set by Community law).

The expenditure growth perspectives expressed in figures and presented in the table below are based on the following calculation hypotheses:

a) Expenditures linked to the knowledge-based economy and infrastructures
   - multiplication by 2 for Community R&D expenditures and by 4 for Community education and training expenditures;
   - multiplication by 4 of Community expenditures to support innovation;
   - multiplication by 4 of Community expenditures dedicated to transport and energy infrastructures.

b) Adjustment and convergence expenditures
   - multiplication by 10 of planned EGAP funds;
   - a 10% increase in structural funds;
   - a one-third increase in Cohesion Fund expenditures.

c) Expenditures linked to "managing natural resources"
   - a one-third decrease in "first pillar" agricultural expenditures;
   - multiplication by 10 for rural development expenditures;
   - multiplication by 10 of expenses that come under the "Environment" heading.

d) External expenditures
   - an increase of approximately 50% in Community ODA expenditures;
   - multiplication by 10 for Community expenditures linked to the CFSP.

e) Other expenditures (*e.g.* Citizenship, Freedom, Security, Justice or Administration): maintained at current level

Community expenditures and the European strategy for globalisation: assumptions for the 2014-2019 period

Commitment appropriations (ceilings)	*2007-2013*			*2014-2019*		
	billions of euros per year* (average)	% of GNI	% of budget	billions of euros per year* (average)	% of GNI	% of budget
1.a. Competitiveness for growth and employment	*10.585*	*0.09*	*8.57*	*26.98*	*0.229*	*19.41*
Technological research and development	6.869	0.058	5.56	13.67	0.116	9.83
Transport, energy and communication	1.404	0.012	1.14	5.66	0.048	4.07
Education and training	0.965	0.008	0.78	3.77	0.032	2.71
Competitiveness and innovation	0.469	0.004	0.38	1.89	0.016	1.36
Social policy agenda	0.094	0.001	0.08	1.18	0.01	0.85
Other	0.785	0.007	0.64	0.82	0.007	0.59
1.b. Cohesion for growth and employment	*44.006*	*0.374*	*35.64*	*50.66*	*0.43*	*36.44*
Structural funds (ESF included)	35.218	0.299	28.52	*38.88*	0.33	27.97
Cohesion fund	8.788	0.075	7.12	*11.78*	0.1	8.47
2. Conservation and management of natural resources	*53.049*	*0.45*	*42.96*	*40.65*	*0.345*	*29.24*
Agriculture	41.872	0.355	33.91	*27.92*	0.237	20.08
Rural development	0.996	0.008	0.81	*9.43*	0.08	6.78
Fisheries	0.878	0.007	0.71	*0.82*	0.007	0.59
Environment	0.266	0.002	0.22	*2.36*	0.02	1.69
Other	0.068	0.001	0.06	0.12	0.001	0.08
3. Citizenship, freedom, security and justice	*1.539*	*0.013*	*1.25*	*1.53*	*0.013*	*1.1*
4. External relations	*7.066*	*0.06*	*5.72*	*12.02*	*0.102*	*8.64*
CFSP	0.249	0.002	0.2	*2.36*	0.02	1.69
ODA	5.668	0.048	4.59	*8.48*	0.072	6.10
Other	1.149	0.01	0.93	*1.18*	0.01	0.85
5. Administration	*7.114*	*0.06*	*5.76*	*7.07*	*0.06*	*5.08*
6. Compensations	*0.114*	*0.001*	*0.09*	*0.12*	*0.001*	*0.16*
Total	*123.474*	*1.048*	100	*139.03*	*1.18%*	100

Sources: European Commission, OJEU, Centre d'analyse stratégique calculations (figures rounded off).

* In billions of euros at 2004 prices (Source: European Commission, JOUE).

D. In parallel, reforming the Community budget financing system

The overall increase in the level of Community expenditures presented above will be undertaken if a sufficiently strong political consensus emerges around the need to implement a European strategy for globalisation, based on a coherent set of internal and external policies. However, it could be hampered for reasons connected to the Community budget's financing method, which should be assessed and modified accordingly.

a) A generally satisfactory resource structure

In this respect, *it does not appear that the present structure of Community resources should be challenged*: it is marked by the predominance of the GNI resource, which makes it possible automatically to cover any increase in the Community budget using a contribution method considered equitable by the Member States (being indexed to their relative levels of wealth).

The possible introduction of new Community resources, therefore, would serve mainly to meet objectives other than those of effectiveness and equity. Thus, an environmental-type taxation, applied to all internal CO_2 emissions or just those produced outside Europe, could serve the objectives of combating global warming while putting money into the Community budget (since all or part of the revenue from this tax would be allocated to it).

b) A more equitable financing

In reality, the main obstacle to an increase in the Community budget lies in the fact that it would lead to a rise in national contributions owed by certain Member States (*e.g.* France, whose net contribution has recently increased). These Member States could therefore consider this rise excessive compared to the anticipated benefits and the burden on their national budgets, both as an absolute value and compared to the benefits to and burdens on other states.

It must be recalled that the benefits gained from the Community budget should be assessed, first and foremost, at the EU level, which could serve to implement a strategy for globalisation on the basis of a suitable budget more effectively. They may also be assessed according to the benefits gained by each Member State, based on the following considerations:

– these benefits would be more fairly distributed if the Community expenditure structure corresponded better to spending deemed "in the common interest" (as is the case in the proposal above) and allocated in a more balanced fashion among Member States (which is also the case for the expenditures that are likely to increase). For example, a drop in the level of so-called "first pillar" agricultural expenditures would automatically reduce the net contribution level of countries like the United Kingdom or Germany, thus the compensation claims they make;

– any claim for compensation or financial correction should be based on the principle that the respective levels of contribution for the most prosperous Member States must correspond to their wealth-per-capita hierarchy. This means, for example, that countries like the United Kingdom and Ireland will see the current level of their Community budget contributions increase and, in the case of the former, the amount of its famous "check" will be reduced;

– since the "net contribution" to the Community budget of some Member States makes up for the economic and social benefits they gain from participating in European and global markets, it should not be reduced as a matter of principle except under a strictly budgetary reading of European financial negotiations. This observation holds true for all EU countries, including France.

Conclusion

Since the end of the Cold War, the European Union has been in search of a new impetus, or even a new *raison d'être*. The French and Dutch rejections of the Constitutional treaty in spring 2005, the Irish No to the Lisbon Treaty three years later, are only symptoms of a profound and already old crisis caused by the transition from the EU-12 to the EU-27, against the background of a transformed international system and accelerated globalisation.

The central question now faced by Europe – both as a political project and as a continental organisation – is that of its ability to avoid marginalisation from the competition between the United States and the new Asian powers that will mark the 21st century. This requires that the EU preserves its existence and specificity as a political enterprise and equips itself with the diplomatic, military and intellectual means to become a global player. To stay in the race, it must also address the economic and social challenges of growth that is too weak, insufficient innovation, a fledgling energy policy, deficient education and research, and demographic decline. None of this can be accomplished without a radical burst of ambition, accompanied by adequate means.

However, this set of challenges provides European leaders with the new mobilising project they have been looking for since the Single Market and the euro to replace peace and prosperity as the finalities of European unification. For Europe, it is quite simply a question of continuing to exist and weigh – that is, to defend its interests and identity – in a globalised world.

This call to action is patently of vital necessity and sufficiently general in character to mobilise all energies in all fields. It is perfectly in line with the Founding Fathers' project since – beyond the historic reconciliation of France and Germany – Europe has always been about pooling the resources of its nations to once again wield influence on the international stage. Today, globalisation, the emergence of new powers outside the Atlantic area, the return of power strategies and the turbulence of the international financial system only accentuate this necessity.

Europe is now moving forward under pressure from its external environment. It is high time for it to change scale and for a new generation of leaders to find the vision required to breathe new life into it. Contrary to the common view, there is no shortage of *raisons d'être*, objectives and challenges, from competitiveness to foreign policy and defence, from energy to immigration, from higher education to research and social cohesion. Public opinion expects more out of Europe, not less. All that is still lacking is collective ambition and means.

The EuroWorld 2015 Strategy outlined in this book endeavours to lay the foundations of a coherent response to all these challenges. It can help revive the European project on economic and social grounds, as was the case in 1957 and 1986. And, as in the past, in the coming months and years France has the opportunity to leave its mark by working together with Community institutions and its European partners.

Beyond Lisbon: A European Strategy For Globalisation

Executive Summary

1. The Lisbon strategy enjoys a broad consensus within the European Union because of the relevance of its long-term objectives. However, its results have been mixed, with wide variations from Member State to Member State. The non-binding method selected for its implementation – the "open method of coordination" – has had the virtue of introducing European coordination into largely national areas of competence, but is nevertheless at the origin of many deficiencies and has aroused criticism.

2. France is out of step compared to many other EU countries with its negative perception of the Lisbon strategy. The hitherto average or mediocre French performance in relation to Lisbon objectives and the low level of national ownership of the European agenda doubtless contribute to maintaining this negative perception.

3. The 2008-2010 cycle of the Lisbon strategy, which has just been decided on by the European Council of March 2008, is characterised by continuity with the previous cycle. This choice reflects the European consensus in favour of the status quo and a focus on implementation, in addition to the forthcoming end of the current Community legislature. As recommended in the Mission's Interim Report, the European Council has nevertheless invited the Commission, the Council and the national Lisbon coordinators to reflect on a post-2010 strategy without delay.

4. In France, much remains to be done to improve national performance and, by the same token, enhance credibility with regard to the Lisbon agenda. This is particularly true for employment market reform (flexicurity), knowledge-based policies, environmental and energy policy and the national ownership of the European strategy. Reforms introduced since the spring of 2007 should be pursued and expanded.

5. At the European level, the consensual nature of the Lisbon strategy should not blind us to the inadequacies of the process launched in 2000 in the face of new internal and external challenges and opportunities that confront the European Union in the medium and long term. These challenges and related opportunities are mainly the product of intensifying globalisation, the return of power-based strategies in the

economic realm (resulting from the rise of the major emerging countries), the issues of energy and the environment, and the impact of increasing heterogeneity and aging within the Union.

6. With its forthcoming EU presidency, France will have the opportunity to promote certain priority objectives such as stimulating the "knowledge triangle" (higher education, research and innovation) and strengthening the European financial market and the EU social agenda. It will also have the opportunity to influence the redefinition of Europe's post-2010 strategy for globalisation.

7. Indeed, the Lisbon strategy appears inadequate on two counts as the "European response to globalisation": on the one hand, it only deals with the internal dimension of such a response, and even in this respect its performance is not up to the mark; on the other, the critical external dimension of any strategy for globalisation falls, of necessity, within the province of common policies and not simply Lisbon-like intergovernmental coordination.

8. The EuroWorld 2015 Strategy outlined in this report includes as its first pillar an internal component, named "Lisbon Plus", which seeks to adapt the EU Member States to globalisation. Lisbon Plus is intended to continue the direction taken during the current decade in a more focused way, by relying on economic, social and environmental policies centred on promoting innovation. These policies should aim at strengthening the knowledge-based economy, enhancing the value of Europe's human capital and promoting a new "green economy".

9. Lisbon Plus must also be implemented on the basis of an improved governance based on better-targeted, better-differentiated and better-evaluated objectives, a timetable synchronised with that of the next European legislature (2009-2014), clearer mobilisation of EC legal and financial tools, more vigorous incentives for Member States to act and greater involvement of national political leaders.

10. As for its second, external pillar, the EuroWorld 2015 Strategy relies on common external policies designed to enable the European Union to help shape globalisation. It should lead to a greater or lesser updating of existing common policies – the Common Trade Policy, the Internal Market and Economic and Monetary Union (in their external dimension) and the Common Agricultural Policy. It should also rest on new external policies in respect of energy, climate change, international standards, development and migration issues and the monitoring of investments from outside the Community in sensitive sectors.

11. For the EuroWorld 2015 Strategy to succeed, a number of conditions must be met: a new European political consensus to enable Europe to exercise leadership at the international level; doctrinal renewal to shift

from a mere logic of exemplary conduct to one of interest, and to move forward with concrete projects that, if need be, initially bring together a limited number of Member States; the introduction of more coherent and effective institutions based on advances brought about by the Lisbon treaty; and last, the appropriate mobilisation of EC and national budgets thanks to a revised financial framework for the Union.

ATTACHMENTS

Mission Letter

Composition of the Mission Team

Composition of the Mission's Steering Committee

CDSEI Member Organisations

Consultations

Mission Letter

Translation from the French

Liberté • Égalité • Fraternité
RÉPUBLIQUE FRANÇAISE

Paris, 8 November 2007

Minister for the Economy, Finance and Employment

Minister for Labour, Social Relations, and Solidarity

Dear Sir,

At the instigation of the President of the Republic, France has undertaken a program of very wide-ranging structural reforms. Our ambition is to remove the obstacles that currently hinder growth and to better leverage our assets in order for our performance to catch up with that of the most dynamic countries. These reforms, some of which have already been launched, concern as much employment and the labour market as supporting innovation, research and professional training. They meet the EU's recommendations and converge with actions undertaken by our partners. France intends, therefore, to carry them through to a successful conclusion by setting them in the context of the development of European policies to which France intends to contribute fully by formulating concrete proposals.

In the coming months, the EU will be faced with important choices. The mid-term revision of financial perspectives will lead to a review of Europe's actions and commitments. Proposals for the second cycle of the Lisbon Strategy (2008-2011) must be formulated following the European Commission's strategic report scheduled for 11 December.

We believe it is essential for each of these occasions to be an opportunity to convey our vision of a Europe that is capable of combining economic growth, innovation and a high level of social protection and employment. The French presidency of the EU in the second half of 2008 will, therefore, constitute an important opportunity to promote this vision of Europe's role, but also to renew our thinking with regard to our policies and principles of action.

Accordingly, we wish to entrust you with the mission of reflecting on these major issues. We believe it is particularly important for you to draw on an assessment of the Lisbon strategy's implementation to formulate proposals concerning what the EU's strategy should be for the new cycle of this strategy (2008-2011), as well as concerning the post-Lisbon agenda. This will involve defining the guidelines to select to ensure that Europe strengthens its competitiveness, *i.e.* its ability to improve the living standards of its inhabitants on a long-term basis and provide them with a high level of employment and social cohesion. You should pay particular attention to the question of modernising industrial policy, enhancing Europe's appeal to attract innovation, research and production centres, and defining strategic sectors or functions and the protection they should possibly receive. Lastly, the question of implementing this new strategy should be studied thoroughly in the light of past experience to define methods of concerted action that are appropriate for this strategy's objectives. This reflection on governance could inspire the process of preparing the next national reform programme (2008-2011) that the government will submit to its European partners in October 2008.

We would like your approach to be as open and innovative as possible and conducted in close collaboration with our European partners and with Community institutions. It should also benefit from the many debates that take place at the European level. The directions followed by, and best practices of, our major partners should also shed light on your work.

In particularly, you should rely on the Social Dialogue Committee on European and international matters, and on qualified personalities who can contribute to your thinking. The main government services concerned will also provide you with support. The setting up of a steering committee will make it possible to ensure a strong involvement of all of these actors.

We would like you to submit an initial report on these major challenges by 15 January 2008. It should, in particular, include your proposals on the directions to take with respect to strategic sectors. A second report on possible methods of concerted action – especially with a view to preparing the next programme of national reform – should be presented by 15 March 2008. These reports will give rise to a debate in the Social Dialogue Committee on European and international matters.

Yours faithfully,

Christine LAGARDE
Xavier BERTRAND

Laurent COHEN-TANUGI
Attorney

Composition of the Mission Team

General Rapporteurs

Yves BERTONCINI
(Adviser on Europe and the Lisbon Strategy at the Centre d'analyse stratégique)

Olivier FERRAND
(Adviser to the Treasury and Economic Policy General Directorate of the Minister of the Economy, Industry and Employment)

Contributors

Virginie PARIZOT
(Consultant on European law at the Directorate for Legal Affairs, Ministry for the Economy, Industry and Employment)

Fausto ROTELLI
(Adviser for European and International Affairs to Luc Chatel, Secretary of State for Industry and Consumer Affairs, and to Anne-Marie Idrac, Secretary of State for External Trade)

Marie-Christine MOISON
(Mission Assistant, Executive Secretary at the Ministry for the Economy, Industry and Employment)

Composition of the Mission's Steering Committee

Anne-Laure de COINCY
(Deputy General Secretary – General Secretariat for European Affairs)

Bruno COQUET
(Head of Policy Assessment and Innovation Department – Representative to the Employment Committee – General Delegation for Employment and Vocational Training)

Sylvie GOULARD
(President of Mouvement Européen France)

Anton HEMERIJCK
(WRR – Scientific Council for Government Policy)

Agnès LECLERC
(Delegate for European and International Affairs – Ministry of Health – Ministry of Labour)

Christian MASSET
(Director of Economic and Financial Affairs at the Ministry of Foreign Affairs)

Philippe MILLS
(Chief Executive of Agence France Trésor at the Treasury and Economic Policy General Directorate)

Jean PISANI-FERRY
(Director – Bruegel)

Odile RENAUD-BASSO
(Secretary to the European Commission's Economic and Financial Committee)

Hélène REY
(Professor – London Business School)

Luc ROUSSEAU
(Director-General of the Enterprises DG at the Ministry for the Economy, Industry and Employment)

André SAPIR
(Professor – Free University of Brussels)

René SEVE
(Director-General of the Centre d'analyse stratégique)

Pierre TAMBOURIN
(Director-General of Genopole at Evry)

Jean-François TROGRLIC
(Director of the ILO Office, Paris)

Dominique VERNAY
(Technical Director of Thales Group)

Roger de WECK
(Editorial writer and President of the Graduate Institute of International Studies, Geneva)

Philip WHYTE
(Senior Research Fellow – Centre for European Reform)

Committee for Social Dialogue on European and International Matters (Comité du dialogue social pour les questions européennes et internationales, CDSEI)

Employee trade unions

- *Confédération française démocratique du travail, CFDT* (French Democratic Confederation of Labour)
- *Confédération française de l'encadrement – Confédération générale des cadres, CFE-CGC* (French Confederation of Management – General Confederation of Executives)
- *Confédération française des travailleurs chrétiens, CFTC* (French Confederation of Christian Workers)
- *Confédération générale du travail, CGT* (General Confederation of Labour)
- *Force ouvrière, FO* (Workers' Force)

Employer organisations

- *European Centre of Enterprises with Public Participation, CEEP*
- *Confédération générale des PME, CGPME* (General Confederation of Small and Medium-Sized Enterprises)
- *Confédération nationale de la mutualité, de la coopération et du crédit agricole, CNMCCA* (National Confederation of Mutual Societies, Co-operatives and Agricultural Credit)
- *Fédération nationale des syndicats d'exploitations agricoles, FNSEA* (National Federation of Farmers' Trade Unions)
- *Mouvement des entreprises de France, MEDEF* (Movement of French Enterprises)
- *Union nationale des professions libérales, UNAPL* (National Union of Liberal Professions)
- *Union professionnelle artisanale, UPA* (Trades Employers' Association)

Consultations

FRANCE

Government members

Christine LAGARDE
(Minister for the Economy, Industry and Employment)

Xavier BERTRAND
(Minister for Labour, Labour Relations, the Family and Solidarity)

Valérie PECRESSE
(Minister for Higher Education and Research)

Michel BARNIER
(Minister for Agriculture and Fisheries)

Bernard KOUCHNER
(Minister for Foreign and European Affairs)

Jean-Pierre JOUYET
(Secretary of State for European Affairs)

Eric BESSON
(Secretary of State for Forward Planning, Public Policies Evaluation and Development of the Digital Economy)

Martin HIRSCH
(High Commissioner for Active Solidarity againt Poverty)

Hervé NOVELLI
(Secretary of State for Small and and Medium-Sized Enterprises, Tourism and Services)

Political and administrative personalities

Georges BERTHOIN
(Former director of Jean Monnet's Office)

Sophie BOISSARD
(Deputy Director of the Office of the Minister for the Economy, Industry and Employment)

Gilles BRIATTA
(European Adviser to the Office of the Prime Minister and Head of the Secretariat-General for European Affairs)

Jean-François COPÉ
(Former minister – President of the UMP group)

Emmanuelle CORTOT
(Adviser on European Affairs to the Office of the Minister of Labour, Labour Relations, the Family and Solidarity)

Jacques DELORS
(Former President of the European Commission)

Antoine GOSSET-GRAINVILLE
(Deputy Director of the Prime Minister's Office)

Jean-Paul EMORINE
(President of the Senate Commission on Economic and Social Affairs)

Gérard ERRERA
(Former French Ambassador to the United Kingdom, Secretary General of the Quai d'Orsay)

Jean-Louis FALCONI
(Adviser on European Affairs to the Office of the Ministry of Foreign and European Affairs)

Valery GISCARD D'ESTAING
(Former President of the Republic, President of the Institute for Democracy in Europe)

Elisabeth GUIGOU
(Deputy for Seine-Saint-Denis, former Minister Delegate for European Affairs and Minister for Employment and Social Solidarity)

Raphaël HADAS-LEBEL
(Member of the Conseil d'Etat) (President of the Pensions Steering Council)

Pierre LEQUILLER
(President of the Delegation for the European Union at the French National Assembly)

Claude MARTIN
(Former French Ambassador to the FRG)

Pierre MOSCOVICI
(Deputy for Doubs, former Minister for European Affairs)

Xavier MUSCA
(Head of the Treasury and Economic Policy General Directorate, Ministry for the Economy, Industry and Employment)

Christian NOYER
(Governor of the Banque de France)

Patrick OLLIER
(President of the Commission of Economic and Social Affairs at the French National Assembly)

Admiral Alain OUDOT DE DAINVILLE
(Chief of Staff, French Navy)

François PEROL
(Deputy Secretary General to the French Presidency)

Pierre SELLAL
(Ambassador – Permanent Representative of France to the European Union)

René SEVE
(Director General of the Centre d'analyse stratégique)

Claire WAYSAND
(Head of Macro-Economic Policy and European Affairs at the Treasury and Economic Policy General Directorate – Ministry for the Economy, Industry and Employment)

Economic actors/Social partners

Jean-Paul BAILLY
(President and Director General of La Poste)

Henri de CASTRIES
(President of the AXA Board of Directors)

Bertrand COLLOMB
(Honorary Chairman of LAFARGE)

Maurice LEVY
(President of the Publicis Group SA Board of Directors)

Gérard MESTRALLET
(President and Director General of SUEZ)

Michel PEBEREAU
(President of BNP Paribas)

Denis RANQUE
(President and Director General of THALES)

Jérôme BEDIER
(President of the MEDEF Europe Commission and President of the Federation of Trade and Distribution Enterprises)

André-Luc MOLINIER
(Deputy Director for relations with government at MEDEF)

Marcel GRIGNARD
(National Secretary of CFDT)

Laurence LAIGO
(National Secretary of CFDT)

Mariano FANDOS
(Confederal Secretary of CFDT)

Patrick CORREA
(Europe/International Head of the Metallurgy Federation of CFTC)

Jean-François GENESTE
(CFTC Head of industrial policy questions at the European Metallurgy Federation)

Patrick PICANDET
(Adviser to the Europe/International Mission of the CFTC's Fédération Bâtiment-Mat-TP)

Anthony RATIER
(CFTC Technical Adviser – European Social Dialogue/CES)

Jean-Christophe le DUIGOU
(Secretary of CGT)
Denis MEYNENT
(Confederal Adviser – CGT Espace Europe International)
Maria NOWAK
(President of Association pour le Droit à l'Initiative Economique, ADIE)
Alain GRISET
(President of the Permanent Assembly of Chambers of Tradesmen and Crafts)
François MOUTOT
(Director General of the Permanent Assembly of Chambers of Tradesmen and Crafts)
Pierre SIMON
(President of the Paris Chamber of Commerce and Industry)
Jean-Louis SCARINGELLA
(Deputy Director General for studies, forward-planning and innovation, Paris Chamber of Commerce and Industry)
Jean-Claude KARPELES
(Adviser on European issues to the Paris Chamber of Commerce and Industry)
Pascal MORAND
(Director General of ESCP EAP – European School of Management)
Patrick FERRERE
(Director General of FNSEA)
Catherine LION
(Deputy Director General, Director of Economy and International Department, FNSEA)
Gaëtan BEZIER
(Social Affairs Department, FNSEA)

Hearings and written contributions

Philippe AGHION
(Professor at Harvard and member of the Conseil d'analyse économique)
Jean-Louis BEFFA
(President of Saint-Gobain)
Jacques BELTRAN
(Director of Public Affairs at Alstom)
Stéphane BOUJNAH
(Managing Director of Deutsche Bank)
Jean-Louis BOURLANGES
(European MP)
Bernard BRUNHES
(Vice President of BPI)
Didier CAHEN
(General Delegate – EUROFI) (written contribution)

Jean-Philippe COTIS
(Director General of INSEE – former Chief Economist and Head of the OECD Economics Department)

Josseline de CLAUSADE
(Member of Conseil d'Etat – General Rapporteur to the ATTALI Commission)

Jacques DELPLA
(Member of the Conseil d'analyse économique – Adviser, capital market, BNP Paribas)

Richard DESCOINGS
(Director of Sciences Po)

Francis DROUIN
(President Director General of OSEO)

Jacques DURON
(Adviser to the Economic and Social Council)

Philippe FAVRE
(President of the Invest in France Agency)

Evelyne GEBHARDT
(European MP – Rapporteur to the proposal for a directive on services in the Internal Market)

François GUINOT
(President of the National Academy of Technologies)

Philippe HERZOG
(President of Confrontations Europe)

Sylvain KAHN
(Associate Professor of History at Sciences Po)

Jean LAPEYRE
(Administrator to the General Secretariat of the European Economic and Social Committee)

Francis MER
(Former Minister – President of Safran)

M. Mario MONTI
(Former European Competition Commissioner and President of the Bocconi University in Milan)

Marie-José PALASZ
(Head of Mission to the General Economic and Financial Audit Department at the Ministry for the Economy, Industry and Employment, in charge of transposing the Services Directive)

Evelyne PICHENOT
(President of the Delegation for the European Union at the Economic and Social Committee)

Maria Joao RODRIGUES
(Special Adviser to the Portuguese Prime Minister)

Guillaume SAINTENY
(Director of Economic Studies and Environmental Impact Assessment, Ministry of Ecology and Sustainable Development)
Yves-Thibault de SILGUY
(Former European Commissioner, President of Vinci)
Mark SPELMAN
(Global Head of Strategy, Accenture)
Jérôme TUBIANA
(Director for Social Monitoring and Forward-Planning at Danone)
Pierre VELTZ
(Researcher)
Patrick VENTURINI
(Secretary General of the European Economic and Social Committee)
Patrick WEIL
(Research Director at the CNRS)

EUROPEAN UNION

European Commission

Joaquim ALMUNIA
(Commissioner for Economic and Monetary Affairs)
Jacques BARROT
(Commission Vice President and Transport Commissioner)
Danuta HUBNER
(Commissioner for Regional Policy)
Peter MANDELSON
(Trade Commissioner)
Hervé JOUANJEAN
(Deputy Secretary-General to the European Commission)
Petra ERLER
(Head of Cabinet of Commissioner Günter Verheugen, Vice President of the Commission and Commissioner for Enterprise and Industry)
Andris KESTERIS
(Head of Cabinet of Commissioner Andris Piebalgs, Commissioner for Energy)
Martin POWER
(Head of Cabinet of Commissioner Charlie McCreevy, Commissioner for Internal Market and Services)
Stephen QUEST
(Head of Cabinet of Commissioner Dalia Grybauskaite, Commissioner for Financial Programming and Budget)
Pierre SCHELLEKENS
(Deputy Head of Cabinet of Commissioner Stavros Dimas, Commissioner for the Environment)

Hervé DELPHIN
(Deputy Head of Cabinet of Commissioner Louis Michel, Commissioner for Development and Humanitarian Aid)

Antonio José CABRAL
(Adviser to the Cabinet of President José Manuel Barroso)

Jean-Claude THEBAULT
(Adviser to the Cabinet of President José Manuel Barroso)

Peter CARL
(Director General for Environment)

Jos DELBECKE
(Deputy Director General for Environment)

Philip LOWE
(Director General for Competition)

David O'SULLIVAN
(Director General for Trade)

Odile QUINTIN
(Director General for Education and Culture)

Gert-Jan KOOPMAN
(Director for Industrial Policy and Economic Reforms)

Xavier PRATS-MONNE
(Director for Employment Policy and Lisbon Strategy)

Jan H. SCHMIDT
(Director for structural reforms and economic assessment at the ECFIN DG)

Michel SERVOZ
(Director for Lisbon Strategy at the Secretariat-General)

Tonnie Erik de KOSTER
(Lisbon Strategy – Team Leader – Strategic Objective Prosperity – Secretariat-General)

Jérôme VIGNON
(Director of Social Protection and Integration)

Shane SUTHERLAND
(Adviser to the Cabinet of the Commissioner for the Internal Market and Services, Charlie McCreevy)

Rudiger BOOGERT
(Member of the Cabinet of Commissioner Neelie Kroes, Commissioner for Competition)

Jean-Philippe MONOD de FROIDEVILLE
(Member of the Cabinet of Commissioner Neelie Kroes, Commissioner for Competition)

Laurence GRAAF
(Adviser to the Cabinet of Commissioner Stavros Dimas, Commissioner for the Environment)

Nicolas THERY
(Principal Adviser to the Environment Directorate-General)

Julie RAYNAL
(Climate Strategy, International Negotiation and Monitoring of EU Action at the Environment Directorate-General)

Anna JAROSZ-FRIIS
(State Aid Strategic support and decision scrutiny at the Directorate-General for Competition)

Thomas DEISENHOFER
(Assistant to the Competition Directorate-General)

European Parliament

Pervenche BERES
(European MP – Chairwoman of the Commission on Economic and Monetary Affairs)

Robert GOEBBELS
(European MP – former minister)

Malcolm HARBOUR
(European MP)

Alain LAMASSOURE
(European MP – former minister)

Klaus-Heiner LEHNE
(European MP)

Jacques TOUBON
(European MP – former minister)

Ann van LANCKER
(European MP)

European Trade Union Confederation

John MONKS
(Secretary General)

Maria Helena ANDRÉ
(Deputy Secretary General)

Tom JENKINS
(Adviser)

Business Europe

Marc STOCKER
(Director of Economics Department)

Adrian van den HOVEN
(Director of International Relations Department)

Other Member States

GERMANY

Bernard de MONTFERRAND
(French Ambassador to Germany)

Chancellery

Mr. HERMES
(Head of Europapolitik bureau)

Federal Ministry of the Economy

Mr. BOTHE
(Head of Fundamental Issues bureau)

Mr. GERSTMANN
(Trade Policy Law bureau)

Mr. HESS
(Head of Lisbon Process bureau)

Mr. LEPERS
(Head of Fundamental Issues, Coordination bureau)

Mr. STOTZ
(Assistant Director responsible for European policy questions)

Mrs. WARNKEN
("Lisbon Process and European Parliament" bureau)

Federal Ministry of Finance

Mr. MERZ
(Head of European Economic and Financial Policy bureau)

Carsten PILLATH
(Head of the EU Policy Division)

Klaus BECK
(Europe Department, Confederation of German Trade Unions)

Jean-François BOITTIN
(Economic and trade counsellor to the French Embassy)

ITALY

Jean ROCHEREAU de la SABLIÈRE
(French Ambassador to Italy)

Ministry of Economy and Finance

Tommaso PADOA-SCHIOPPA
(Minister of Economy and Finance)

Lorenzo CODOGNO
(Head of 1st directorate, Economic and Financial Analysis, at the Department of the Treasury)

Maria Chiara RIONDINO
(Expert Committee, Department of the Treasury)

Ministry of European Affairs

Gianfranco DELL'ALBA
(Principal Private Secretary)

Massimo GAIANI
(Diplomatic adviser)

Ministry of Economic Development

Andrea BIANCHI
(Director of Competitiveness Department)

Ministry of Labour

Emilio GABALIO
(President of Labour Council)

Alfredo Durante MANGONI
(Diplomatic adviser)

CGIL

Marigia MAULUCCI
(Confederal Secretary)

Nicola NICOLOSI
Gianni VINAY
(Europe bureau)

CISL

Renzo BELLINI
Giacomina CASSINI
Luigi CAL
Claudio CAPPON
(Director General of RAI)

Matteo BUGAMELLI
Roberto TORRINI
(Economists)

Jean-Marie METZGER
(Minister Counsellor for Economic Affairs at the French Embassy)

Benjamin DELOZIER
(Economic Counsellor at the French Embassy)

CZECH REPUBLIC (MISSION AND TROIKA CONFERENCE)

Charles FRIES
(French Ambassador to the Czech Republic)

Vaclav BARTUSKA
(Roving Ambassador for energy security)
Marianne BARKAN-COWDY
(First Secretary at the French Embassy)
Bernard BOIDIN
(Economic and trade counsellor at the French embassy)
Lucie CHROUSTOVA
(Department of European and CIS countries – Ministry of Industry and Trade)
Petr DRULAK
(Director, Institute of International Relations)
Jiri HAVEL
(Professor at the Economic Institute of the Social Sciences Faculty)
Martin HOUSKA
(Deputy Director of the Dept. of Coordination with the EU, Ministry of Industry and Trade)
Karl Magnus JOHANSSON
(Södertörn University College – Sweden)
Martin KARLIK
(Section for the EU and International Relations, Ministry of Labour and Social Affairs)
Lucie LEKESOVA
(Department of EU Policies, Ministry of Foreign Affairs)
Miroslav MACHALEK
(Deputy Director of the Department of EU Policies, Ministry of Foreign Affairs)
Zdenek MALEK
(Vice President in charge of international relations for the CMKOS union)
Ivo MARCIN
(Deputy Director of the Conceptions and Analysis Department – Office of the Government)
Alena MARKOVA
(Department of Environmental Policy, Ministry of the Environment)
Zoran NERANDZI
(Director of the Department of Cohesion Policy, Ministry of Regional Development)
Michel PEROTTINO
(Secretary General of CEFRES)
Martin POTUCEK
(Director of the Centre for Social and Economic Strategies)
Jan PROCHAZKA
(Director of the Department of Coordination with the EU, Ministry of Industry and Trade)
Alexandra RUDYSAROVA
(Director of CzechInvest)

Thomas SEDLACEK
(Chief Economist at the CSOB bank)
Lukas SEDLACEK
(Representative of Mrs. M. MacDonagh-Pajerova, President of the "Yes for Europe" Association)
Miroslav SEVIK
(Director of the Liberal Institute)
Martin TLAPA
(Vice Minister of Industry in charge of European affairs)
Catherine von HEIDENSTAM
(Swedish Ambassador to Prague)

UNITED KINGDOM

Edward BANNERMAN
(Counsellor on European Affairs at the British Embasy in France)
Neil MCMILLAN
(Director, European & Global Issues Secretariat – European Secretariat – Cabinet Office)
Robert SPECTERMAN
(Head of Strategy, Growth & Innovation Branch European Economic Reform – HM Treasury)

SLOVENIA

Chantal de BOURMONT
(French Ambassador to Slovenia)
Ziga TURK
(Minister for Growth)
Gonzalo CAPRIROLO
(Chief Economist – Ministry of Finance)
Andrej CVELBAR
(Secretary – Ministry of Higher Education, Science and Technology)
Dimitri GRCAR
(Secretary – Ministry of the Economy)
Milan JAZBEC
(Assistant Professor – Minister Plenipotentiary – Ministry of Foreign Affairs)
Ales MIHELIC
(General Director – Ministry of Higher Education)
Dunja PERKO
(Senior Adviser at the Governmental Office for European Affairs)
Jana POLJAK
(Adviser – Government Office for Growth)
Vlasta TUREL
(Under-Secretary – Government Office for Growth)

Martin ZDOVC
(Financial System Directorate – Ministry of Finance)
Magda ZUPANCIC
(Directorate for Labour Market at the Ministry of Labour, Family and Social Affairs)
Jadran LENARCIC
(Director of the Jozef Stefan Institute)
Janez SUSTERSIS
(Associate Professor – University of Primorska – Faculty of Management Koper)
Dominique LAPIERRE
(Economic and Trade Counsellor at the French Embassy)
Pierre LEGUELTEC
(First Counsellor at the French Embassy)

SWEDEN

Joël de ZORZI
(French Ambassador to Sweden)
Per HOLMSTROM
(Plenipotentiary Minister at the Swedish Embassy in France)
Daniel WOLVEN
(First Secretary at the Swedish Embassy in France)

Prime Minister's Office

Hakan JONSSON
(Minister of State for European Affairs)
Anna ODHNER
(Assistant Director and person in charge of coordinating the Lisbon Strategy)
Katarina ARESKOUG
(Assistant Director and person in charge of European questions)

Ministry of Foreign Affairs

Olof EHRENKRONA
(Ambassador and Counsellor on globalisation to the Swedish Minister of Foreign Affairs)
Daniel BLOCKERT
(Assistant Director in charge of WTO negotiations)

Ministry of Finance

Jens GRANLUND
(Assistant Director in charge of questions related to the Lisbon Strategy)
Lennart LINDSTROM
(Counsellor in charge of coordinating International Affairs)

Ministry of Industry

Olof SANDBERG
(Counsellor in charge of questions related to innovation and sustainable development policy)

Parliament

Margareta CEDERFELT
(Deputy and member of the Committee on European Affairs)

Carl B. HAMILTON
(Deputy and member of the Committee on European Affairs)

Bengt-Anders JOHANSSON
(Deputy and member of the Committee on European Affairs)

Anna KINBERG-BATRA
(Deputy and President of the Committee on European Affairs)

Marie KORNIAS-WEIBULL
(Deputy and member of the Committee on Industrial Affairs)

Centre for Business and Policy Studies

Stefan LUNDGREN
(Director General)

Arvid WALLGREN
(Director of Studies)

Globalisation Council

Pontus BRAUNERHJELM
(General Rapporteur)

Liberal Think Tank TIMBRO

Johnny MUNKHAMMAR
(Counsellor)

Confederation of Swedish Enterprise

Anita LUNDIUS
(Assistant Director General)

Thérèse KRAUS
(Director of Coordination and International Affairs)

The Swedish Trade Union Confederation

Dan ANDERSSON
(Senior Economist)

Monika ARVIDSSON
(Economist and General Rapporteur to the President of the Union Confederation, Mrs. Lundby-Wedin)

Olivier ROUSSEAU
(Economic Counsellor to the French Embassy in Sweden)

Out of European Union

ISRAEL

Jean-Michel CASA
(French Ambassador to Israel)
Alexis DUTERTRE
(First Economic Advisor, French Embassy in Israel)

Prime Minister's Office

Shmuel ABRAMZON
(Economist)
Yulia EITAN
(Economist)

Ministry of Finance

Ami LANDAU
(Senior Deputy Accountant General)
Oded BROOK
(Deputy General Manager - International Affairs)

Office of the Chief Scientist

Mina GOLDIAK
(Deputy Chief Scientist)

Delegation of the European Commission in Israel

Jonathan CLARIDGE
(Director of the political and trade section)

Weizmann Institute of Science

Professor Mudi SHEVES
(Vice President for Technology Transfer)

The Manufacturers' Association of Israel

Dan CATARIVAS
(Director-Division of Foreign Trade and International Relations)

Ministry of Industry, Trade and Labor

Gaby BAR
(Senior Regional Director of Foreign Trade Administration)

WORLD TRADE ORGANIZATION

Pascal LAMY
(Director General)

THINK TANKS

Centre for European Policy Studies

Daniel GROS
(Director of Research)

Notre Europe

Board of Directors

European Policy Centre

Stanley CROSSICK
(Director and Founding President)

Hans MARTENS
(Chief Executive)

Eurifri

Pierre DEFRAIGNE
(Director) (written contribution)

Fondation pour l'innovation politique

Scientific Council

Institut Montaigne

Claude BÉBÉAR
(President of AXA)

Philippe MANIÈRE
(Director General of the Institut Montaigne)

Lisbon Council

Paul HOFHEINZ
(President)

SELECTED BIBLIOGRAPHY

Europe in the global economy: the state of play

The Lisbon Strategy: A mixed balanced sheet

Works and articles

BARYSCH K., TILFORD S. and WHYTE P., *The Lisbon Scorecard VIII – Is Europe Ready for an Economic Storm?*, Centre for European Reform (CER), 2008.

BEGG I., *Lisbon II, Two Years On: an Assessment of the Partnership for Growth and Jobs*, Special CEPS Report, 2007.

BERTONCINI Y., WISNIA WEILL V., *La stratégie de Lisbonne : une voie européenne dans la mondialisation*, Fondation Schuman-Centre d'analyse stratégique, 2007.

DAVERI F., *Why is There a Productivity Problem in Europe?*, *CEPS Working Document*, No. 205, Centre for European Policy Studies (CEPS), Brussels, 2004.

DEFRAIGNE P., *What's Wrong with Lisbon? From Low to High Quality Growth*, Eur-IFRI, 2005.

Estrategia (Review), *The Lisbon Strategy: Reaching Beyond Europe*, Bizancio, No. 22-23, 2007.

FITOUSSI J.-P. and LE CACHEUX J., (eds.), *L'état de l'Union européenne*, OFCE, Paris, Fayard/Presses de Sciences Po, 2007.

GELAUFF G. and LEJOUR A., *The New Lisbon Strategy, an Estimation of the Impact of Reaching Five Lisbon Targets*, Industrial Policy and Economic Reforms Papers, No. 1, European Commission, 2006.

Lisbon Council, *European growth and jobs monitor – Indicators for success in the Knowledge Economy*, The Lisbon Council and Allianz, 2008.

PISANI-FERRY J. and SAPIR A., *Last Exit to Lisbon*, Bruegel, 2006.

RODRIGUES M.J., *European Policies: For a Knowledge Economy*, Edward Elgar Publishing, 2003.

RODRIGUES M.J., *The New Knowledge Economy in Europe, a Strategy for International Competitiveness and Social Cohesion*, Edward Elgar Publishing, 2002.

SAPIR A., *Current Issues in Evaluating Structural Reforms within the Lisbon Process, Comments and Recommendations about the Lisbon Methodology (LIME) Working Group*, Bruegel, 2007.

Official Reports and Communications

European Commission, *"A Year of Delivery"*, Annual Report on Growth and Employment, 2006.

European Commission, *Strategic report on the renewed Lisbon Strategy for growth and jobs: launching the new cycle (2008-2010) – Keeping up the pace of change*, 2007.

European Commission, *Statistical Annex to the European Commission's December 2007 Annual Report on growth and employment*, 2007.

Economic and Social Council, Processus de Lisbonne : contribution du Conseil économique et social à la préparation du sommet de printemps 2008, *Journaux officiels, 2007.*

DURON J., *Contribution du Conseil économique et social français au rapport de synthèse du Comité économique et social européen préparatoire au sommet de printemps 2008*, Journaux officiels 2007.

DUTHILLEUL A., *Suivi de la situation de la France au regard des indicateurs de Lisbonne*, Economic and Social Council, Journaux officiels, 2007.

KOK W., *Facing the Challenge – The Lisbon Strategy for Growth and Employment*, Report from the High Level Group, 2004.

2000-2008: New challenges, new opportunities

Works and articles

AHEARNE A., *European and Asian Perspectives on Global Imbalances*, Asia Europe Economic Forum, Bruegel, 2007.

AHEARNE A., PISANI FERRY J., SAPIR A., VERON N., *The EU and the Governance of Globalisation*, Bruegel, 2006.

BRIMMER E., *Seeing Blue: American Visions of the European Union*, Institute for Security Studies, 2007.

CHOPIN T., FOUCHER M. (eds.), *Schuman Report 2008 on the State of the Union*, Schuman Foundation, 2008.

COHEN-TANUGI L., *Guerre ou paix, Essai sur le monde de demain*, Grasset, 2007.

DELGADO J., *Europe's Arsenal to Fight Climate Change*, Bruegel, 2008.

DELGADO J., *Why Europe is not Carbon Competitive*, Bruegel, 2007.

DESSILLONS S., MAURISSE T., *Les nouveaux conquérants: qui a peur des entreprises des pays émergents ?*, Editions Mines Paris, Paristech, 2007.

Deutsche Bank Research, *Sovereign wealth funds*, 2007.

DULLIEN S. and FRITSCHE U., *Anhaltende Divergenz bei Inflations – und Lohnentwiclung in der Eurozone: Gefar für die Währungsunion?*, Vierteljahshefte zur Wirtschaftsforschung, 2007.

FABRY E., *Les Européens face à la mondialisation*, Kairos Future – Fondation pour l'innovation politique, 2007.

FOUCHER M., *L'Union européenne un demi-siècle plus tard : état des lieux et scénarios de relance*, Fondation Schuman, 2006.

GAYMARD H., *Un nouvel usage du monde : Propositions pour une France plus active dans les pays émergents*, Mille et une nuits, 2006.

GEISS R., *Après le Japon, la France... Faire du vieillissement un moteur de croissance*, Notes de l'Institut Montaigne, 2007.

GNESOTTO N. and GREVI G., *The New Global Puzzle: What World for the EU in 2025?*, Institute for Security Studies, 2006.

HEIKKILA T., BOUCHER S., *Raison et flexibilité : atteindre l'équilibre entre souveraineté et harmonisation dans la mise en place du système européen des échanges de quotas d'émissions (SEEQE)*, Notre Europe, 2006.

IFRI, 2007 Ramses Report, *L'Europe et le monde*, 2007.

LISBONNE-DE VERGERON K., *L'Europe vue de Chine, regards contemporains*, Notes de la Fondation Schuman, 2007.

LISBONNE-DE VERGERON K., *L'Europe vue d'Inde, regards contemporains*, Notes de la Fondation Schuman, 2006.

PELLION A., *Renouveler la production d'énergie en Europe : un défi environnemental, industriel et politique*, Notes de la Fondation Schuman, 2008.

PISANI FERRY J., *Rougher Times Ahead for the Euro Area*, Bruegel, 2008.

RIFKIN J., *Engager la troisième révolution industrielle*, Fondation pour l'innovation politique, 2008.

ZABOROWSKI M., *Facing China's Rise: Guidelines for an EU Strategy*, Institute for Security Studies, 2006.

Official Reports and Communications

International Energy Agency, *World Energy Outlook*, 2007.

European Central Bank, *Review of the International Role of the Euro*, 2007.

OECD, *Main Science and Technology Indicators*, 2007.

World Intellectual Property Organization (WIPO), *Patent report: statistics on worldwide patent activity*, 2007.

STERN S.N., *Review on the Economics of Climate Change*, Cambridge University Press, 2006.

The short term (2008-2010)

The 2008-2010 cycle of the Lisbon Strategy

Official Reports and Communications

European Commission, *Strategic report on the renewed Lisbon Strategy for growth and jobs: launching the new cycle (2008-2010) – Keeping up the pace of change*, 2007.

European Commission, *Communication from the Commission to the Spring European Council: Integrated Guidelines for Growth and Jobs (2008-2010)*, 2007.

European Commission, *Strategic Report on the Renewed Lisbon strategy for Growth and Jobs: Launching the New Cycle (2008-2010): Companion Document*, 2007.

European Commission, *Proposal for a Community Lisbon Programme, 2008-2010*, 2007.

European Commission, *Commmunication from D. Hübner and V. Spidla entitled Member States and Regions delivering the Lisbon strategy for growth and jobs through EU cohesion policy, 2007-2013*, 2007.

Recommendations for the French EU presidency

Works and articles

DAVIDENKOFF E., KAHN S., *Les universités sont-elles solubles dans la mondialisation ?*, Hachette, 2006.

DUTHEILLET DE LAMOTHE O., *Politique de l'emploi et dynamique des entreprises*, Liaisons, 2005.

WAHL P., *Avoir des leaders dans la compétition universitaire mondiale*, Institut Montaigne, 2006.

Official Reports and Communications

European Council, *Country-specific integrated recommendations, Report from Council to the European Council*, 2008.

AGHION P. *et al.*, *Mondialisation : les atouts de la France, Rapport du Conseil d'analyse économique*, 2007.

ARTUS P. and CETTE G., *Productivité et croissance, Rapport du Conseil d'analyse économique*, No. 48, La Documentation française, 2004.

ATTALI J., *Commission pour la libération de la croissance française, 300 décisions pour changer la France*, La Documentation Française, XO Editions, 2008.

LEVY M. and JOUYET J.-P., *L'économie de l'immatériel, Rapport au Ministre de l'Economie, des Finances et de l'Industrie*, 2006.

VEDRINE H., *La France et la mondialisation : Rapport au Président de la République*, La Documentation française, 2007.

EuroWorld 2015: a European strategy for globalisation (2010-2015)

"Lisbon Plus": adapting more effectively to globalisation

Works and articles

AGHION P., DEWATRIPONT M., HOXBY C., MAS-COLELL A., SAPIR A., *Why Reform Europe's Universities?*, Bruegel, 2007.

AGHION P., *A Primer on Innovation and Growth*, Bruegel, 2006.

ALÉCIAN Jean, *Après Erasmus, Amicus – Pour un service civique universel européen*, Institut Montaigne, 2007.

BARROT J., *L'Europe n'est pas ce que vous croyez*, Fondation Schuman, 2007.

BLANCHARD O. and GIAVAZZI F., 2003, *Macroeconomic Effects of Regulations and Deregulation in Goods and Labour Markets, Quarterly Journal of Economics*, 118, No. 3, 2003.

CONWAY P., ROSA D., NICOLETTI G. and STEINER, F., *Regulation, Competition and Productivity Convergence*, OECD Economics Dept, *Working Paper*, No. 509, September, 2006.

DELGADO J, *The Economics of the Services Directive*, Bruegel, 2008.

GIDDENS A., *Le nouveau modèle européen*, Hachette, 2007.

HERZOG P., *Un nouvel acte unique – Pour une mutation du modèle économique et social européen*, 2008.

JAMET J.-F., *Où va l'industrie européenne?*, Questions européennes, Fondation Schuman, 2007.

PHILIPPON T. and VÉRON N., *Europe's Saplings Need Financial Fertiliser*, Bruegel, 2008.

PISANI-FERRY J., *Financial Integration and European Priorities*, Bruegel, 2006.

SANTOS I., *Is structural spending on Solid Foundations?*, Bruegel, 2008.

SCHLENKER J.-M., *Innovation, enseignement supérieur et recherche publique: réussir est possible*, En temps réel, Les cahiers, 2008.

TABELLINI G. and WYPLOSZ C., *Réformes structurelles et coordination en Europe*, Rapport du Conseil d'analyse économique, No. 51, La Documentation française, 2004.

VON WEIZSÄCKER J., WASMER E., *A Better Globalisation Fund*, Bruegel, 2007.

Centro Europa Ricerche, *Which Way Forward After the Lisbon Strategy?*, 2008.

MEDEF, *Leadership Europe*, 2007.

European Trade Union Confederation, Syndex, Istas, Wuppertal Institute, SDA, *Climate Change and Employment. Impact on employment in the European Union-25 of climate change and CO_2 emission reduction measures by 2030*, 2007.

Official Reports and Communications

AGHION P., COHEN E., PISANI-FERRY J., *Politique économique et croissance en Europe*, Rapport du Conseil d'analyse économique, No. 59, La Documentation française, 2006.

BOISSARD S. *et al.*, *Quelle dimension sociale pour le projet politique européen ?*, Centre d'analyse stratégique, 2007.

European Commission, *Economic Reforms and Competitiveness*, Commission Staff Working Document, SEC(2006) 1467/2, 2006.

European Commission, *Interim Forecasts, October 2006 and February 2007*, 2007.

European Commission, Communication on "*A single market for 21st century Europe*", 2007.

European Commission, *European job mobility action plan 2007-2010*, 2007.

European Commission, *A lead market initiative for Europe*, 2007. European Innovation Progress Report, 2006.

European Commission, *European Innovation Progress Report*, 2007.

European Commission, *Global Europe – Competing in the world – A contribution to the EU's growth and jobs strategy*, 2006.

European Commission: *The European Interest: succeeding in the age of globalisation – Contribution of the Commission to the October Meeting of Heads of State and Government*, 2007.

European Policy Centre, *Challenge Europe – Dragons, elephants and tigers: adjusting to the new global reality*, 2006.

GRIFFITH R., HARRISON R. and SIMPSON, H., *The Link Between Product Market Reform, Innovation and EU Macroeconomic Performance*, European Commission, DG Economic and Financial Affairs, *Economic Papers*, No. 243, 2006.

STRAUSS-KAHN D., *Building a political Europe, 50 proposals for tomorrow's Europe*, Report submitted to Romano Prodi, 2004.

Common external policies to help shape globalisation

Works and articles

CHAMBON N. *et al.*, *Quel cadre pour l'agriculture après 2013 ? What Future Framework for Agriculture after 2013 ?*, Notre Europe, 2007.

COHEN-TANUGI L., *L'influence normative internationale de l'Union européenne : une ambition entravée*, note de l'IFRI, 2002.

DE VASCONCELOS A., *An Open Europe in a Multipolar World: Lessons from the Portuguese Experience*, Notre Europe, 2007.

M. KIMMITT R., *Sovereign Wealth Funds and the World Economy*, Foreign Affairs, Vol. 87, 2008.

MANDELSON P., *The European Union in the Global Age*, Policy Network, 2007.

MEUNIER S., *L'Union fait la force – L'Europe dans les négociations commerciales internationales*, Les Presses Sciences Po, 2006.

RUBIO E., *La question de l'impôt européen : bénéfices, aspects pratiques et possibilités pour doter l'UE d'une véritable ressource propre*, Notre Europe, 2008.

SAPIR A., *Globalisation and the Reform of European Social Models*, Bruegel, 2005.

SAPIR A. *et al.*, *Fragmented Power: Europe and the Global Economy*, Bruegel, 2007.

TRAN THIEN J.-P., *Quelle politique de l'énergie pour l'Union européenne ?*, Institut Montaigne, 2007.

Official Reports and Communications

European Commission, *Globalisation Migrations into the EU: Main Determinants and Economic Impact*, 2007.

Institute for Security Studies, *A secure Europe in a better world, European Security Strategy*, 2003.

MANDELSON P., *Global Europe, European Commission*, 2006.

EuroWorld 2015: conditions for success

Works and articles

AHEARNE A., PISANI FERRY J., SAPIR A., VERON N., *Global Governance: an Agenda for Europe*, Bruegel, 2006.

ALLEMAND F., WOHLGEMUTH M., BRANDI C., *Faire l'Union à 27 : tenter de nouvelles méthodes ?*, Fondation pour l'innovation politique, 2007.

BERTONCINI Y, *La révision du budget de l'Union européenne : pour une analyse politique globale*, Horizons stratégiques, 2007.

BERTONCINI Y., CHOPIN T., *Le Traité de Lisbonne : des réponses utiles, mais partielles, aux défis politiques lancés à l'Union européenne*, Questions européennes, Fondation Schuman, 2008.

DU GRANRUT C., FABRY E., ALLEMAND F., TRESALLET D., PINI S., *Ce que change le Traité de Lisbonne*, Fondation pour l'Innovation politique, 2008.

KURPAS S., CRUM B., DE SCHOUTHEETE P., KILLER J., DEHOUSSE F., ANDOURA S., MISSIROLI A., HAGEMANN S., BRIBOSIA H., *The Treaty of Lisbon: Implementing the Institutional Innovations*, European Policy Centre, Egmont, CEPS, 2007.

LE CACHEUX J., *European Budget: the poisonous budget rebate*, Notre Europe, 2005.

MULLER A., *Quels moyens pour l'Europe ? Débat sur le budget de l'Union européenne*, Fondation Schuman, 2005.

SAPIR A., *An Agenda for a Growing Europe*, Report to the President of the European Commission, 2004.

Official Reports and Communications

Foreign and Commonwealth Office, *Global Europe, Meeting the Economic and Security Challenges*, 2007.

De La Loyère G., *Quel budget de l'Union européenne au service de la croissance et de l'emploi ?*, Economic and Social Council, Journaux officiels, 2007.

Haenel H., Sénat, *Rapport d'information fait au nom de la délégation pour l'Union européenne sur le Traité de Lisbonne*, 2007.

TABLE OF ANNEXES

ANNEX 1

Assessement of the Lisbon Strategy by Figure-based Objectives and by Country

1. Growth and employment objectives that the EU has gotten closer to and that some of its Member States are achieving

Reviewing the implementation of the Lisbon strategy involves, in the first place, evaluating the performance of the EU and its Member States with regard to the final objectives set by the European Council, with the aim of producing "growth and jobs", according to the formula used by the European Commission since 2005. By the yardstick of these objectives, such an evaluation shows:

- relatively encouraging results, sometimes demonstrating clear progress compared to the year 2000, even though they do not necessarily guarantee that the objectives set for 2010 will be achieved;
- fairly mixed results from one European country to another, which were quite predictable given the very different starting-points of these countries and their economic and social heterogeneity and which also express unequal degrees of mobilisation.

Somewhat disappointing growth rates, despite a recent upturn

Though the objective of a 3% growth rate was not achieved by the EU for the 2002-2006 period, more than half the Member States have nevertheless attained higher results.

Growth rate of GDP in volume – in the EU (in %)

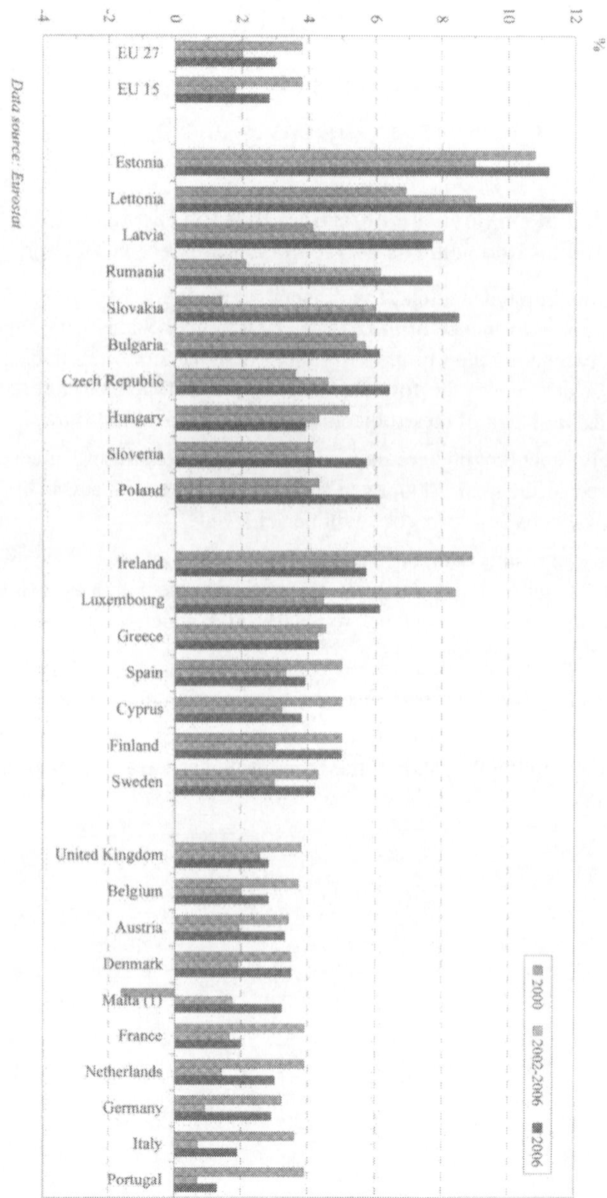

Closer analysis reveals that:

- 17 EU countries had a growth rate higher than 3% for the 2002-2006 period: these were the 10 central European countries that joined the EU in 2004 and 2007, and which were carried along by a catch-up dynamic, and 7 other countries with very different characteristics but all of which shared a certain economic vitality;
- France, Germany and Italy – the three biggest continental economies (representing nearly 50% of the EU's GDP between them) – were relatively mediocre in performance during the 2002-2006 period: this was an important factor behind the weakening of the EU-27's average growth rate (1.9% for the same period).

Furthermore, it is worth emphasising that:

- 2006 was a recovery year for the EU-27, with a growth rate estimated at 3%, *i.e.* the highest level since 2000;
- for the same year, 20 of the EU-27 countries had a growth rate higher than 3% and four others had growth rates higher than 2.5%;
- forecasts for 2007 seem to confirm this upturn (2.9% growth rate for EU-27) following the upswing in terms of employment, and this could herald more favourable results for the 2005-2010 period.

Noteworthy progress in employment rates for the EU and its Member States

Though it is as yet lower than the targets set by the European Council, the employment rate situation overall and for women and older workers has developed positively since the launch of the Lisbon strategy.

It can thus be observed that the overall employment rate has increased by 2.1 points in the EU-27 between 2000 and 2006 and that this increase reflects varied developments in several "groups of countries":

- 5 EU countries have already reached and exceeded the 70% employment rate objective (Denmark, Sweden, the Netherlands, the United Kingdom and Austria);
- 9 other countries exceeded 65% in 2006 and the next 6 crossed the 60% threshold, whereas the employment rate in 7 EU countries in 2006 was below 60%;
- furthermore, if one analyses developments in trend, one observes that 7 countries with low employment rates experienced an increase higher than 3.5 points between 2000 and 2006, and in some cases in excess of 5 points (Spain and Latvia); and that only 3 countries in the EU-27 – Poland, Portugal and Romania – suffered a drop in their overall employment rate for this period.

As the charts below indicate, a relatively positive assessment can also be made of employment rate developments for women and older workers:

- even though they remain for the time being below the objectives set for 2010, the employment rates for women and older workers have increased by 3.4 and 6.6 points respectively in the EU-27 between 2000 and 2006 (and 4.3 and 7.5 points in the EU-15);
- in 2006, 13 countries in the EU-27 had an employment rate for women higher than 60% and 3 others approached this threshold; however, the employment rate for women remained lower than 50% in 11 other EU countries, though with significant progress in most of them but a decrease in Poland and, above all, in Romania;
- in 2006, only 9 EU countries exceeded the objective of an employment rate for older workers higher than 50%, while 11 countries had a rate lower than 40%; however, all the EU-27 countries made clear progress between 2000 and 2006, apart from Romania (where this rate dropped), Poland and Portugal (where the rate was more or less maintained, but beyond 50% for the latter).

Total employment rate in the EU in %

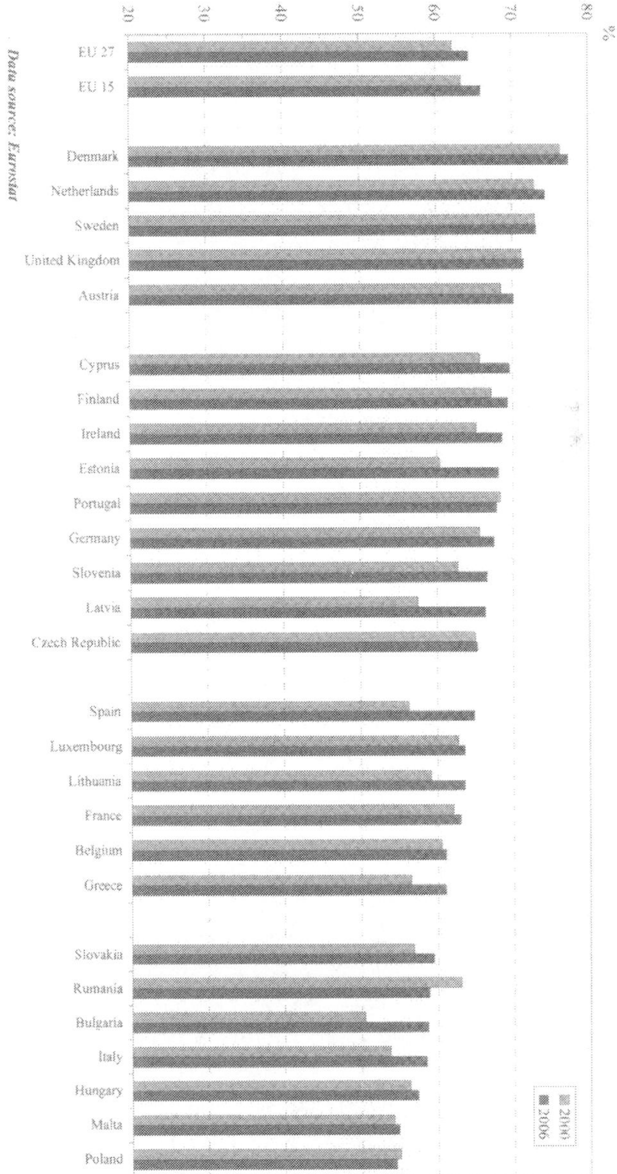

Employment rate of women in the EU in %

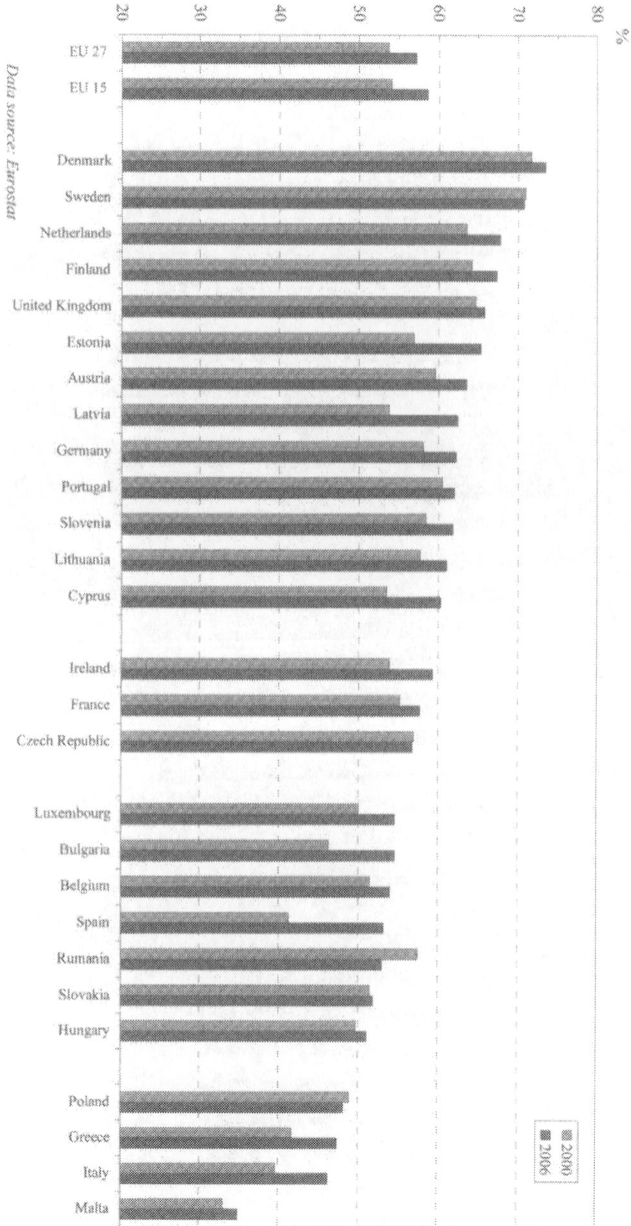

Employment rate of elderly workers in the EU in %

2. Very mixed European and national results, but fairly positive, with regard to the intermediate and related objectives of the Lisbon strategy

Evaluating the situation of the EU and its countries with regard to the figure-based "intermediate" objectives identified by the European Council is all the more necessary since the results recorded may, in part, foreshadow the EU's ability to achieve its "final" objectives in terms of "growth and jobs" by 2010. This evaluation confirms that the implementation of the Lisbon strategy has produced fairly encouraging results, though they vary according to the objectives and the countries concerned.

A relatively stable budgetary situation, but significant national evolutions

Since the compliance with the measures of the Stability and Growth Pact is an integral part of the Lisbon strategy, it is primarily in relation to its two main elements that the results need to be evaluated.

- Public debt generally stable and limited in the majority of EU countries

As far as the level of public debt is concerned, it can be observed that:

- the situation of the EU-27 has remained almost stable over the period, with public debt at an estimated level of 61.7% of GDP at the end of 2006, compared to 62.9% in 2000; however, it should be noted that, in its October 2007 forecasts, the European Commission indicated that the 60% of GDP threshold may be respected for the first time by the EU in 2007 (59.7%);
- 17 countries had a level of public debt that was lower than the 60% of GDP limit while 10 countries remained above this limit;
- 7 of these 10 countries experienced unfavourable developments in their public debt between 2000 and 2006 (Germany, France, Cyprus, Hungary, Malta, Greece and Portugal).

Government debt in the EU in % of GDP

- Budget deficits relatively under control

An analysis of the results recorded for the 2002-2006 period and at the very end of the period shows that:

- after first being weak, the EU-27 balance improved at the end of the period, reaching in 2006 a level that was certainly higher than that recorded in the early years of the 2000 decade (-1.6% compared to +0.6%) but lower than the 3% limit set by the Stability and Growth Pact (the EU balance for the 2002-2006 period reaching -2.5%);
- 16 of the EU-27 countries respected the 3% maximum deficit threshold for the 2002-2006 period and in 2006 (and half even showed a positive balance);
- among the 11 countries with a deficit higher than the 3% threshold for the 2000-2006 period, only 5 remained below this threshold in 2006, one having reduced its deficit compared to the previous year (Portugal) and the 4 others experiencing a deterioration in their situation (Hungary, Italy, Poland and Slovakia).

General government balances in the EU in % of GDP

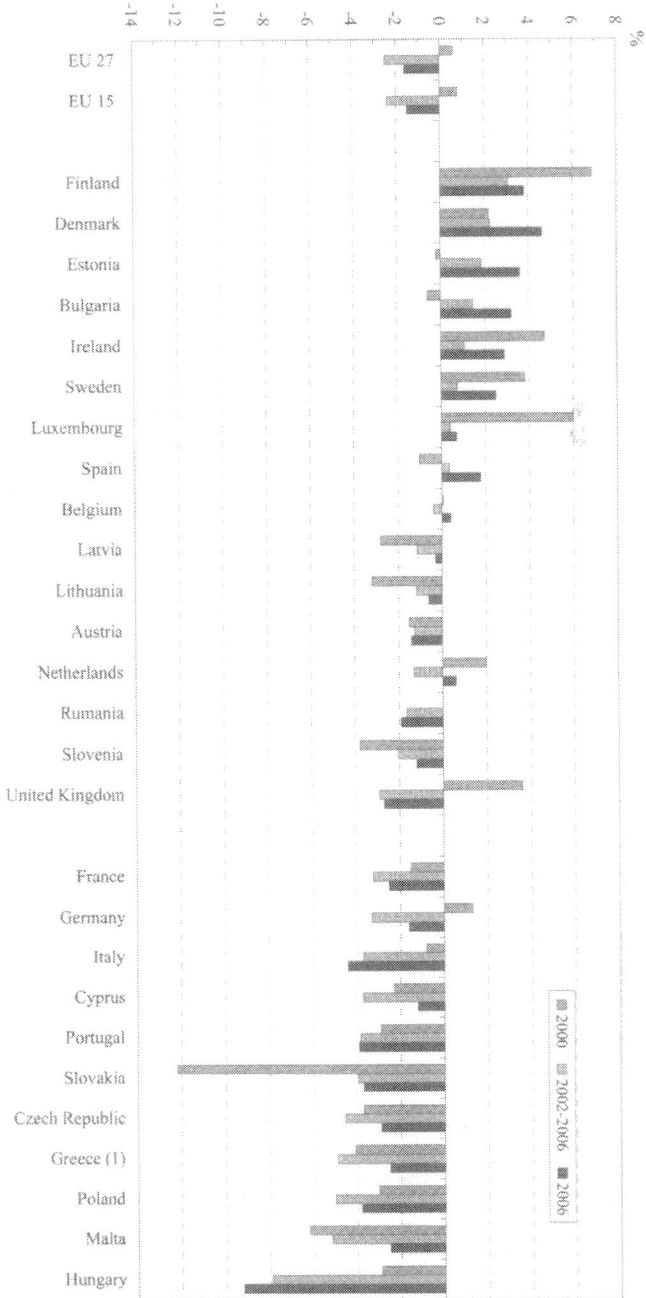

Data source: Eurostat

Very mixed developments with regard to the objectives relating to the knowledge-based economy

The promotion of a "knowledge-based economy", founded on education, training, research and development and innovation constitutes one of the linchpins of the Lisbon strategy, which should therefore also be evaluated by this yardstick, particularly on the basis of the three figure-based objectives set by the European Council.

- Limited progress in terms of overall R&D expenditure

The analysis of the development in national R&D expenditure shows that:

- in 2006, only Finland and Sweden exceeded the 3% of GDP objective, 4 countries (Denmark, Germany, Austria and France) were between 2 and 2.5%, whereas the expenditure of 11 other countries was lower than 1%;
- for the 2000-2006 period, 17 countries increased their internal R&D expenditure, whereas the level of expenditure in 10 other countries (including France and the UK) dropped or stagnated;
- given the absolute and relative importance of R&D expenditure in the two last-mentioned countries, this performance explains why the EU's overall average investment has remained generally stable between 2000 and 2006, which contravenes the commitments made in Lisbon and Barcelona.

R&D expenditure in % of GDP

Data source: Eurostat

- A fairly positive development in the level of education in EU countries between 2000 and 2006

Population of 20-24 years having reached at least higher secondary education (in %)

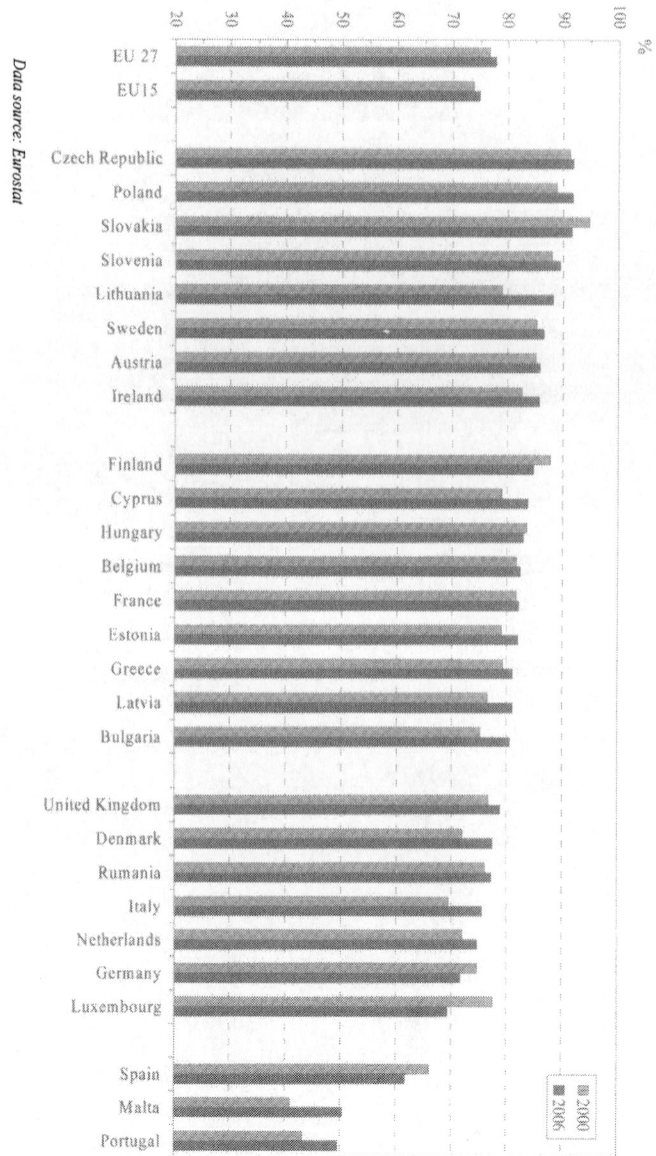

As far as the level of education in EU countries is concerned, we can observe that:

- 8 of the EU-27 countries have already reached or exceeded the 85% objective for an age group in higher secondary education, and 9 others exceeded the 80% limit;
- between 2000 and 2006, the level of education advanced in 21 EU-27 countries (including France), sometimes substantially (Lithuania, Malta, Greece, Portugal);
- however, 3 countries that have not reached the 85% objective recorded a significant decrease for the same period (Germany, Spain and Luxembourg), whereas Finland seems to have dropped below the 85% threshold;
- the relative size of the population of Germany and Spain in the EU explains the limited progress in the percentage of the population aged between 20 and 24 having reached at least a level of higher secondary education, though it nevertheless rose from 76.6% to 77.8% between 2000 and 2006.

- Varied development in the early dropout rate

As far as the premature school leaving rate is concerned, it can be observed that:

- in 2006, only 6 EU-27 countries had premature leaving rates that were already lower than the 10% objective set by the Lisbon strategy, while 11 others had a rate of below 14%;
- in 2006, 10 EU-27 countries had rates higher than the European average (15.3%) and sometimes exceeding 20% (Spain, Italy) or even 30% (Malta, Portugal), consequently modifying the average rate;
- over the 2000-2006 period, 21 of the 27 EU countries improved their results and the rate of premature school leaving for the EU-27 dropped from 17.6% to 15.3%: if this trend continues, it would enable the EU-27 to close in significantly on the 10% maximum objective set for 2010.

Dropout rate from school system of 18-24 year olds

Positive development with regard to the Internal Market objectives[1]

Consulting the "Internal Market Scoreboards" that are regularly drawn up by the European Commission shows that the situation of EU countries in relation to the objectives set by the Lisbon strategy is positive.

- The level of State aids has increased in conformity with the wishes of the European Council

Analysing the development in the level of State aids compared to GDP reveals that:

- 17 of the EU-25 countries reduced their level of State aid between 2001 and 2005;
- in 2005, only 6 of the 8 others had a level of State aids higher than the European average;
- in total, the level of State aid in the EU-25 dropped from an average of 0.64% to 0.59% of GDP between 2001 and 2005.

1 See the "Internal Market Scoreboard" at: http://ec.europa.eu/internal_market/score/index_en.htm.

State aids in the EU as a % of GDP (excl. railways)

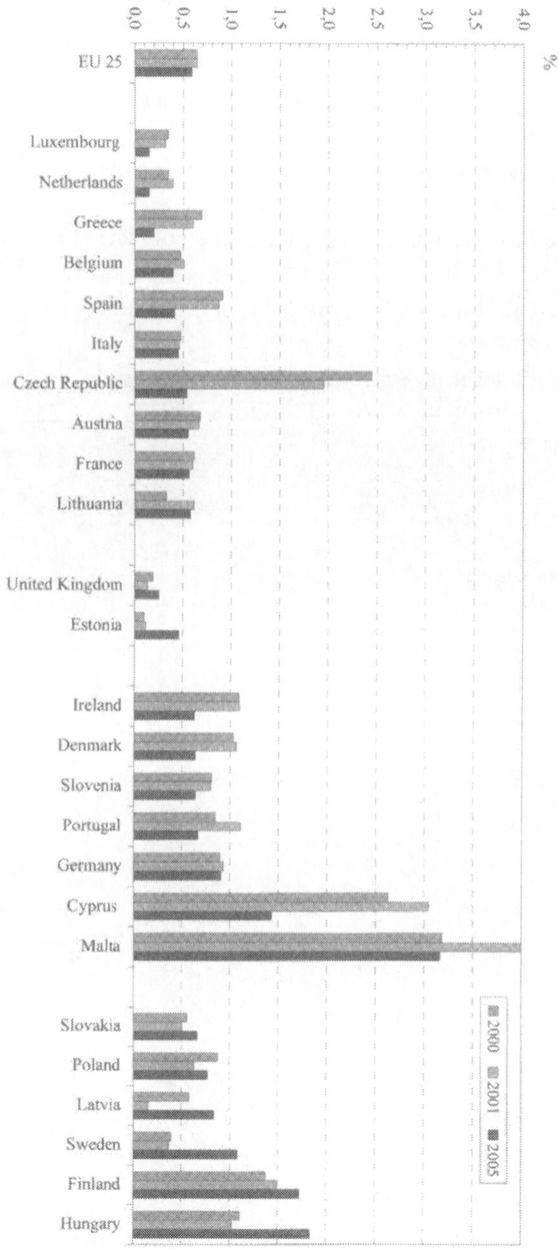

Source: Eurostat

- Improved integration into national law of directives relating to the Internal Market

Furthermore, the EU-27 Member States have become more effective in transposing directives relating to the Internal Market to national law, despite a slight end-of-period falling off:

- in 2007, 16 Member States respected the 1.5% objective for the maximum number of directives transposed beyond the deadline set by the European Council;
- among the EU-15 countries (for which a 2000-2007 comparison is possible), 10 made progress over the period, and that progress was sometimes substantial (*e.g.* France);
- in total, the rate of EU-15 directives transposed on schedule rose from 97% to 98.2% between 2000 and 2007, the latter rate being also that of the EU-27.

This generally favourable development led the March 2007 European Council meeting to invite Member States to attain a new objective of a 1% maximum between now and 2009 at the latest.

Implementation deficit of EU directives (as a %)

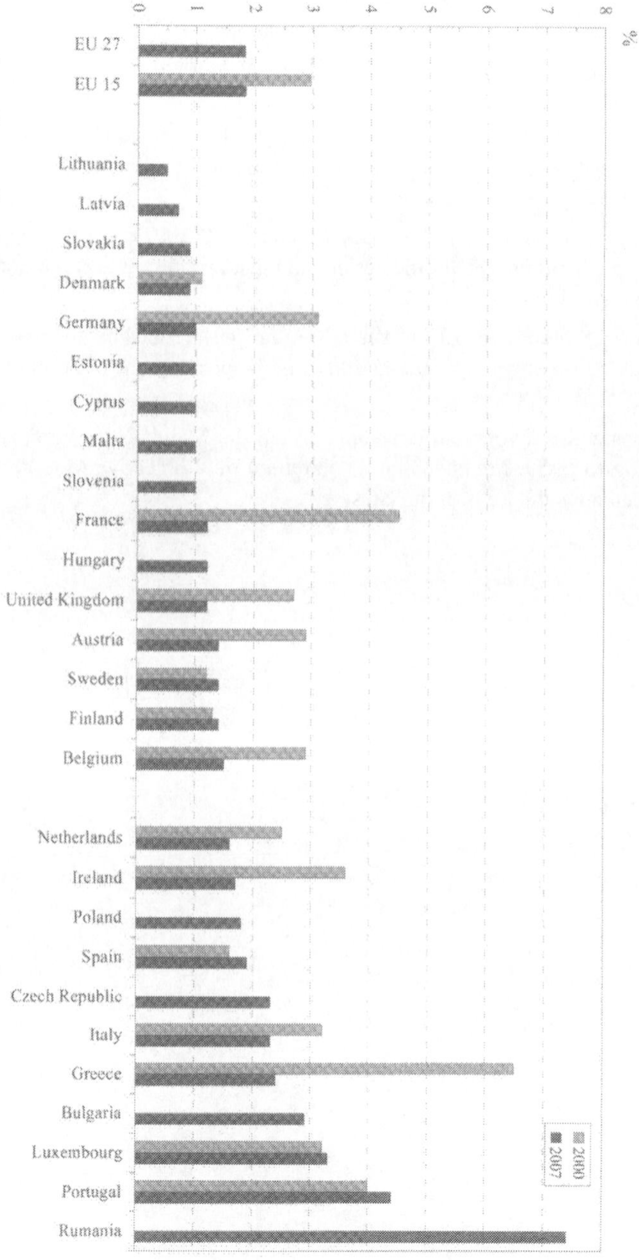

Source: European Commission

Often limited progress with regard to the Lisbon strategy's other economic and social objectives

- A slight increase in the effective age for retiring from the labour market

Average exit age from the labour market in the EU

Source: Eurostat

As the table above shows, the perspective of an approximately 5-year increase in the effective retirement age gave rise to a few noteworthy developments in EU countries:

- 24 EU-27 countries registered a rise in their average retirement age and 6 of them had a rise of 2 points or more (Belgium, Spain, Luxembourg, Hungary, Poland and Romania), *i.e.* a pace that is more or less in line with the objective set for 2010;
- 3 countries (Denmark, Italy, Latvia) experienced a drop in the average retirement age, which was more noteworthy in the case of the second of these countries since this average age is below 60 years;
- in total, the average retirement age increased by 1 point in the EU-27 between 2000 and 2006 (from 59.9 to 60.9), which would not seem to presage the effective achievement of the 2010 objective set by the Barcelona European Council meeting.

However, it should be emphasised that these intermediate results do not take into account the predictable effects of the "pension reforms" that have recently been put into effect in several EU countries, including Germany, France and Italy: since these reforms have sometimes led to an increase in the age at which one can retire on full pension, they may contribute to raising the average retirement age by 2010.

- A slight drop in the youth unemployment rate

As far as the youth unemployment rate is concerned, the situation changed little between 2000 and 2006 in the EU-27; even though this rate rose to 19.2% in 2004, in total a slight drop was registered for the period.

Unemployment rate of young people (18-24 years) in %

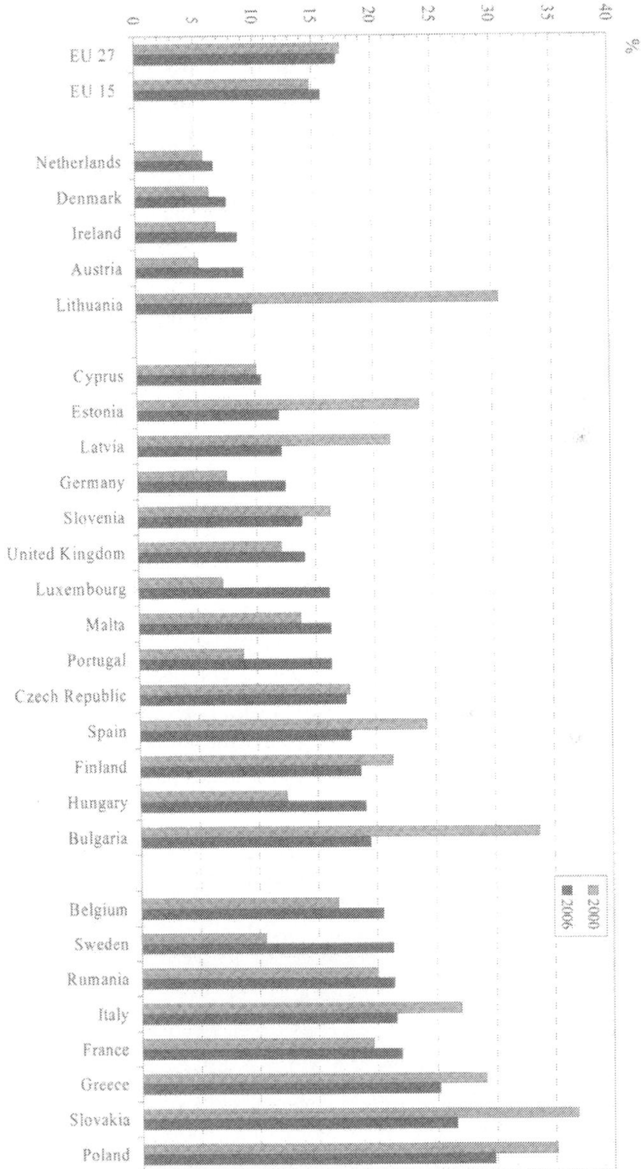

Source: Eurostat

Once again, very mixed situations and developments lie concealed behind this situation:

- in 2006, 5 EU-27 countries (Denmark, Ireland, the Netherlands, Lithuania and Austria) had a youth unemployment rate that was lower than 10%;
- among the 22 other countries, 11 registered a drop in their youth unemployment rate between 2000 and 2006, while 11 experienced a rise (including France);
- in 2006, 8 EU-27 countries (including France) had a youth unemployment rate that was higher than 20%.

- The improvement in childcare facilities

As far as childcare facilities for young children in the EU are concerned, and despite the partial nature of the available data, it is possible to note that the EU countries are in a relatively satisfactory situation with regard to one of the two objectives set by the European Council, which 15 of those countries have already achieved.

Drawing on a recent study that also analysed care facilities for children aged 0 to 3 years[2], the OECD confirms that the situation of European countries is relatively good compared to non-European OECD countries:

- on the one hand, because subsidised childcare facilities for children aged 3 and over are a statutory right in nearly all EU European countries within the OECD (except the Netherlands and Ireland), whereas this statutory right is set at the age of 4 or 5 in most other OECD countries;
- on the other, because, according to the OECD, 4 EU countries have already achieved the two objectives set by the EU for childcare facilities: these are Belgium (Flanders), Denmark, France and Sweden, to which one should add Finland, a country in which the level of facilities increases substantially if one excludes from the calculation children taken care of by their parents, the vast majority of whom benefit from specific leaves;
- lastly, because – once again, according to the OECD – many EU countries have made headway towards these two objectives in the course of the last few years.

[2] See *Starting Strong II* (2006), OECD.

Pre-school children in subsidised daycare in 2004 (in %)

Also, modest progress with regard to the objective of reducing greenhouse gas emission rates

In order to take into account the 2005 refocusing on the objectives of growth and jobs, it is advisable to consider the reduction in greenhouse gas emission rates not as one of the final objectives of the Lisbon strategy but as a "related objective" the achievement of which is, moreover, often referred to in the spring European Council meetings.

From this viewpoint, analysing the increase in the rate of greenhouse gas emissions and the efforts undertaken by the EU to apply the Kyoto protocol leads to the following observations:

- in 2005, 13 of the EU-27 countries (and 4 of the EU-15) produced results in line with the maximum emission objective set for them by the EU;
- 11 EU-27 countries registered a reduction in their level of greenhouse gas emissions between 2000 and 2005, 4 of which (Belgium, Denmark, Germany and the Netherlands) thereby came close to their objective;
- however, all in all, over the 2000-2005 period there was a total rise in emissions of 1.4 points for the EU-27 and the EU-15, *i.e.* a trend that was hardly in line with respecting the objective of an overall reduction by 2010.

Index of total greenhouse gas emissions in the EU in CO_2 equivalents (base year = 1990)

Source : European Environment Agency - Eurostat

ANNEX 2

The European Gap in terms of Wealth, Productivity and Innovation

The Economic Foundations of the Lisbon Strategy[1]

The observation made at the time of the launch of the Lisbon strategy is a reminder that, in addition to fierce intra-European competition, the EU countries' main competitors are countries that have reached a comparable stage of economic development, primarily the United States and Japan. This observation is greatly coloured by the economic context at the turn of the millennium, characterised by the advent of a "new economy" based on knowledge and information and communication technologies, but also by relatively strong growth in Europe (around 3%). It nonetheless determined the orientations adopted at Lisbon, and is still relevant in an era when the economic progress of emerging countries is increasingly becoming an issue.

Europe's gap in terms of wealth and productivity

The Lisbon strategy is above all based on empirical results and data, all of which underline the EU's "deficit" compared with its main competitors and, in particular, the United States[2].

In terms of wealth, it was thus observed that Europe experienced a period from the post-war to the mid-1970s during which it caught up with the United States:

- European GDP per capita was around 40% that of the United States at the end of the war;
- it then stabilised at a little over 70% of that of the United States.

Since the 1990s (see the table below), this growth momentum has however been losing steam:

---

1 This annex is, to a great extent, inspired by the work of Y. Bertoncini and V. Wisnia Weill, *La stratégie de Lisbonne, une voie européenne dans la mondialisation* (*The Lisbon Strategy, a European Route to Globalisation*), Centre d'analyse stratégique, Robert Schuman Foundation, October 2007.

2 For a more in-depth analysis of this deficit, see the work by Aghion P., Cohen E. and Pisani-Ferry J., (2006), *Politique économique et croissance en Europe* (*Economic policy and growth in Europe*), Report No. 59, Conseil d'analyse économique, La Documentation française.

- the GDP per capita in France, which represented 82% of the reference level set by the United States (75% for the EU-15) in 1990, dropped to 76% in 2004 (71% for the EU-15);
- the average annual rate of growth of GDP per capita was 0.4 points less in the European Union (EU-15) compared with that of the United States[3].

GDP /capita[4] (in purchasing power parity)

United States = 100	1991	1995	2000	2004
France	82	79	77	76
EU-15	75	73	72	71

Source: OECD.

The differential in wealth (GDP/capita) between the United States and Europe is manifest, resulting from both a difference in level and a difference in variation. These differences are the result of several factors that implicate the components of the GDP/capita[5]: ratio of employment, average length of employment, percentage of the population of working age and hourly labour productivity.

Breakdown of GDP/capita in 2005

	GDP/capita as a percentage of the level in the United States	Hourly productivity as a percentage of the level in the United States*	Number of hours worked per capita
France	72%	101%	617
EU-19**	67%	79%	726
United States	100%	100%	865

Sources: OECD (Labour productivity report 2006) and European Commission (Competitiveness Report 2006) **GDP per hour worked; **Members of the European Union belonging to the OECD.*

The difference in level of GDP is first and foremost due to a "quantitative" differential that results both from the lower number of hours worked on average by Europeans and by the lower rate of employment.

---

3 See Aghion P., Cohen E. and Pisani-Ferry J., (2006), *op. cit.*

4 For a full presentation of the evolution of the level of GDP/capita in the 27 EU countries, consult Eurostat: http://epp.eurostat.ec.europa.eu/portal/page?_pageid=1996,39140985&_dad=portal&_schema=PORTAL&screen=detailref&language=fr&product=EU_strind&root=EU_strind/strind/ecobac/eb011.

5 GDP/capita = productivity per hour worked x hours worked per capita = productivity per hour worked x average duration of work x rate of employment x percentage of the population of working age out of the total population.

Employment / Population,
people aged between 15 and 64 in percentages

	1994	*2001*	*2002*	*2003*	*2004*	*2005*
France	5.4	6.0	6.2	6.5	62.4	62.3
EU-15	5.9	6.1	6.3	6.4	64.9	65.4
United States	7.0	73.1	7.9	7.2	71.2	71.5

Source: OECD, *Employment Outlook*, 2006.

Compared with the United States, Europe suffers from a higher rate of unemployment, and is also lagging in terms of economic integration of the population of working age. The lower rates of employment and length of work (weekly and in lifetime) registered in Europe bear down upon the economic growth of EU countries.

This observation was highly influential in the call made in the Lisbon strategy to increase the rate of employment in Europe, on the assumption that Europeans want to maintain, and even increase, their relative level of wealth, and that this will require them to play a greater role in the labour market.

The difference in the level of GDP is also due to other more "qualitative" factors, in particular a difference in hourly productivity. While some European countries, France in particular, have an hourly productivity level that is seemingly comparable with that of the United States, the structure effects of the economically active population must however be taken into consideration. It is therefore possible to consider that such noteworthy productivity levels are in part attributable to the exclusion of a percentage of less productive elements from the labour market: according to some experts[6], it is possible to calculate a *de facto* structural productivity that highlights even more clearly the difference in levels between the United States, France and Europe.

Observed and structural hourly productivity
as a percentage of the level of the United States in 2002

	"Observed" hourly productivity as a percentage of the US level			Effect as a percentage of the gap compared with the United States		**"Structural" hourly productivity** as a percentage of the US level		
	OECD (a)	Eurostat (b)	VA-MG* (c)	of the length of work (d)	of the rate of employment (e)	(f) (a)-(d)-(e)	(g) (b)-(d)-(e)	(h) (c)-(d)-(e)
United States	100	100.0	100.0	0.0	0.0	100.0	100.0	100.0

6 See Artus P. and Cette G., (2004), *Productivité et croissance*, *op. cit.*

EU	91	88.2	91.6	4.4	5.3	81.3	78.5	81.9
France	103	106.6	107.8	5.2	7.5	90.3	93.9	95.1
Japan	72	67.5	73.1	0.1	2.6	69.3	64.8	70.4
OECD	81	0.0	78.1		4.7	76.3		73.4

* Van Ark and Mc Guckin; Source: Artus P. and Cette G., (2004), *Productivité et Croissance* (*Productivity and growth*) Report No. 48, Conseil d'analyse économique, La Documentation française.

While the difference in levels of productivity can, on one hand, be thus qualified, on the other hand, a marked deficit in terms of variations of productivity nonetheless subsists. Since the mid-1990s and for the first time in several decades, the growth of European productivity has begun to notably lag behind (see the table below).

Hourly labour productivity in the United States and Europe, 1950-2003

	Average annual growth rate of productivity		European Union as a percentage of the United States	
	United States	EU-15		
1950-1973	2.77	4.77	1973	79
1973-1995	1.48	2.25	1995	94
1995-2003	2.33	1.15	2003	85

Source: Conseil d'analyse économique / Gordon, 2004.

After a catching up phase between 1979 and 1995, during which European productivity grew at a faster rate than that of the United States, the phenomenon has been reversed. The convergence of levels of productivity has given way to a divergence that is against Europe[7]:

- productivity grew by 2.2% per year in Europe compared to 1.4% per year in the United States between 1979 and 1990;
- the differential was even more markedly in favour of Europe from 1990 to 1995 at 2.3% in Europe compared with 1.1% in the United States;
- this phenomenon then suffered a reversal from 1995 to 2001: American productivity then began to grow by 2.3% per year and only by 1.7% in Europe; while this differential with the United States may have seemed of a short-term nature for a time, most economists are now in agreement as to its structural character.

7 See Gordon R., (2004), "Why Was Europe Left at the Station when America's Productivity Locomotive Departed?", Discussion Paper, No. 4416, Centre for Economic Policy Research.

This shortfall in hourly productivity in Europe is due in part to differences in performance in the field of innovation.

European' deficit innovation

While the disappointing performance of Europe in terms of productivity can be explained by several factors (volume of labour, etc.), economic literature grants innovation a central position, because of its decisive role in the global productivity of production factors. This pre-eminence is also at the heart of the strategy adopted in Lisbon in March 2000, in a context coloured by the strong development of information and communication technologies.

Europe's lack of momentum in terms of innovation is both a symptom and a cause of the EU's economic performance differentials and concerns two main fields:

- resource differentials: R&D, higher education, ICT investments;
- "results" or intermediate indicator differentials: scientific publications and awards, patents, growth of certain innovative industrial sectors, lesser product innovation, reorganisation or reallocation of production activities[8].

In terms of resources, the discrepancy between the EU and the United States can be measured in relation to the proportion of domestic spending on R&D: in 2001, this accounted for 1.94% of the GDP of the EU-15 compared with 2.76% for the United States. This public and private spending differential in favour of R&D largely underpins the European objective of obtaining public and private funding for R&D equal to 3% of the GDP. A significant percentage of this differential is due to the poor level of R&D investment on the part of European businesses.

The low levels of European investment in the production and use of information and communication technologies (ICT) in comparison with the United States is one of these reasons[9]. It alone cannot however explain the productivity differential observed on either side of the Atlantic, particularly at the beginning of the 2000s, *i.e.* the period following the ICT investment boom in the United States[10].

---

8 It should be stressed that these intermediate indicators are sometimes also used to measure the effectiveness of investments in favour of research and innovation.

9 See Gomez-Salvador R., Musso A., Stocker M. and Turunen J., (2006), "Labour Productivity Developments in the Euro Area", European Central Bank, Occasional Paper Series, No. 53.

10 Investments made in the ICT field are converted into productivity gains on condition that the companies involved in such a process carry out significant changes to their organisation in parallel (Askenazy and Gianella, 2000, for the United States; Janod and Saint-Martin, 2003, for France). The same reservations apply to all physical investments: the need to renew the stock of fixed capital is higher in Europe than in the United States, but this element alone is not sufficient to explain Europe's deficit: Europe must also prove capable of deriving advantages from newly acquired equipment (Aghion, 2006).

In the opinion of many observers, it would seem, more globally, that Europe suffers from a shortage of companies active in "innovative" sectors and from the paucity of the average sums invested by such companies.

Among the other indicators[11] of the European deficit, one can also point to the number of patents and the percentage of high added-value companies in the economy, which would seem to confirm Europe's shortcomings in the field of innovation compared with the United States:

- EU countries possessed 23% of international patents in 2000, a slight decline, compared with 38% for the United States;
- 56% of the world's top ICT firms are based in the United States compared with 13% in Europe; the discrepancy between Europe and the United States is even greater in the case of so-called "new technological paradigm" (ICT, biotech, etc.) industries.

The innovative performance of a country or a continent depends de facto on a series of interrelated factors: public and private investment in research and the quality of this investment, links between research and business, corporate environment, sector-based positioning of an economy, etc. It depends, to an even greater extent, on the "performance" of educational and research systems: in this context, the European Commission confirmed Europe's structural deficit compared with the United States in the domain of high calibre research[12], and the systemic approach to innovation would seem to highlight the differences in the field of higher education, which are a decisive element in the economic discrepancy between the EU and the United States.

Breakdown of the population and rates of employment according to the level of education in Europe and the United States in 2005[13]

	Breakdown of 15-64 year olds in percentage			Rate of employment in percentage		
Level of education	France	EU-15	United States	France	EU-15	United States
Less than the second cycle of secondary education	37.6	35.6	21.3	47.8	49.2	43.0
Second cycle of secondary education	40.2	43.8	52.3	69.9	70.1	71.1
Higher education	22.2	20.6	26.5	73.6	82.5	82.9

Source: Center for European Policy Studies.

11 In this field, numerous methodological limits are apparent and indicative of the need to develop a suitable European measurement system of R&D effectiveness.

12 See for example, European Commission, (2007), European Innovation Progress Report 2006.

13 NB: the current table integrates the population aged between 15 and 64, unlike the table on page 76 that considers the population aged between 25 and 64.

An initial static approach thus reveals that with similar qualifications, Europeans and Americans benefit from comparable rates of employment and that higher education graduates enjoy the highest rates of employment. It also demonstrates that the number of American higher education graduates is 6 points higher than that in Europe. The population structure effects in terms of educational level therefore act mechanically on employment rates, and thus on the growth of the European Union. This empirical data explains why the Lisbon strategy grants such importance to education and training.

ANNEX 3

Lisbon: A Strategy in Progress

Since 2000, the method of implementation of the Lisbon strategy has been constantly adjusted, including a significant step in 2005 that involved a refocus on growth and employment and a clearer breakdown of responsibilities. Between 2000 and 2007, changes have occurred in the six areas covered in the table below.

Scope of the Lisbon strategy	**Extraordinary meeting of the European Council in Lisbon in March 2000: three main areas of focus are selected for the Lisbon strategy**: (i) investment in scientific research and technological development, education and vocational training; (ii) completion of the implementation of the large community-wide single market by the suppression of obstacles still subsisting in numerous sectors; (iii) a more active employment policy, targeted in particular at elderly workers and women.
	European Council of Gothenburg in June 2001: specifies the environmental dimension of the Lisbon strategy by the adoption of a sustainable development strategy.
	European Council of Brussels in March 2005: In the wake of the *KOK report, a refocus on growth and employment* takes place. The European Council makes all forms of knowledge and innovation the driving forces of sustainable growth in Europe: launch of the 7th framework programme for research and development 2007-2013, creation of a European Research Council, the 2010 initiative that places the accent on research and innovation in the ICT field, and an action plan in favour of biotechnologies and bio-innovations in relation to energy.
	Informal European council of Hampton Court in October 2005: discussion of the "*European social model*" concept that underpins the Lisbon strategy.

Strategic guidelines of the Lisbon strategy	**Extraordinary meeting of the European Council in Lisbon in March 2000**: • The **Broad Economic Policy Guidelines** (BEPG) under article 99 of the EC treaty and in existence since 1997, make up the general framework that the guidelines of Member States must comply with in relation to employment and employment policies. In 2000, they become one of the guideline documents of the Lisbon strategy. • The **Employment guidelines** (EG) under article 128 of the EC treaty and in existence since 1998, become the second guideline document of the Lisbon strategy in 2000. From then on, the European employment strategy and the Lisbon strategy mutually fuel each other.
	European Council of Brussels in March 2005: A **new method of establishing Lisbon strategy guidelines** is developed. On the basis of a strategic report, or a "summary document" by the Commission, the Council must adopt a series of "*Integrated Guidelines*" made up of BEPGs, composed of macro- and micro-economic aspects, and Employment guidelines. Established for the 2005-2008 period, 24 guidelines were laid down.
Objectives and monitoring indicators	**European Council of Lisbon in 2000**: - 3% growth per year - Average employment rate of 70% - Women employment rate of 60% - 85% of an age category with baccalaureate level
	European Council of Stockholm in 2001: - Elderly workers employment rate of 50% - Public deficit lower than 3% of GDP - Public debt lower than 60% of GDP - 98.5% transposition of internal market directive in national law within the set deadlines, reduction of the global level of State aids in percentage of GDP by 2003.

	European Council of Barcelona in 2002: - 8% reduction in greenhouse gas emissions compared to 1990, - 3% of GDP allocated to R&D spending, 2/3 of which by private funding, - Raise the effective age of retirement by 5 years, Ensure that subsidised structures exist for 90% of children between 3 years and the compulsory schooling age, and for 33% of children under the age of 3.
	European Council of Brussels in 2006: - Educational dropout rate less than 10%, - Offer of employment, training, internships within a maximum of 4 months for 18-24 year olds.
	In addition to these quantitative objectives, "**structural indicators**" were adopted by the European Commission to compare nation- and community-wide performance, and to assess results. The number of these indicators has been cut from 42 in 2003 to **14 today** (some of the quantitative objectives are also structural indicators, such as R&D and GDP rates, for example).
Involvement of the European Union	Adopted in **July 2005** for three years, the **Lisbon Community Programme** bears witness to the involvement of the Community's institutions in the implementation of the Lisbon strategy.
	European Council of Brussels in June 2005: the Luxembourg process for employment, the **Cardiff process** for market reform and finally the **Cologne process** for macro-economic dialogue, community strategies related to the Lisbon strategy, were simplified. From then on, national documents related to the Lisbon strategy are presented in a **format that combines all three processes**.
Involvement of Member States	**Extraordinary meeting of the European Council in Lisbon in 2000**: the **open method of coordination**, created as part of the European employment strategy launched by the European Council of Luxembourg in December 1997, and based on the identification of common objectives, jointly defined measuring instruments and benchmarking, becomes an instrument of the Lisbon strategy.
	European Council of Brussels in March 2005: Member States are invited to present **national reform programmes** for the 2005-2008 period, focused on defined Integrated Guidelines for growth and employment for the same period.

	Since 2006, the Council has adopted **country-recommendations** based on an assessment of the implementation of the Lisbon strategy in each member country.
Involvement of political stakeholders	**Since 2000**, each **spring European Council** is devoted to **monitoring the Lisbon strategy**.
	In June 2002, a **Competitiveness Council** is created, resulting from the fusion of the "Internal market", "Industry" and "Research" Councils.
	European Council of Brussels in March 2005: each national administration *appoints a* **"Mr." or "Ms" Lisbon** entrusted with the task of ensuring the implementation of reforms agreed in the framework of the Lisbon strategy.
Financial framework of the Lisbon strategy	**European Council of Brussels in March 2005**: the functioning of the stability and growth pact (adopted in 1997) is eased, to better take into account investment spending (R&D, employment policy, for example) when the Commission examines if an excessive deficit exists in a Member State.
	European Council of Brussels in December 2005 adopts a 2007-2013 multi-annual financial framework, endeavouring to align it with the Lisbon strategy.

ANNEX 4

2000-2008: New Challenges and Opportunities For the European Union

A. New Global Challenges

1. Emerging countries

Increase in the relative weight of emerging countries in the worldwide economy

Average yearly rate of GDP growth between 1996 and 2005 (in %)

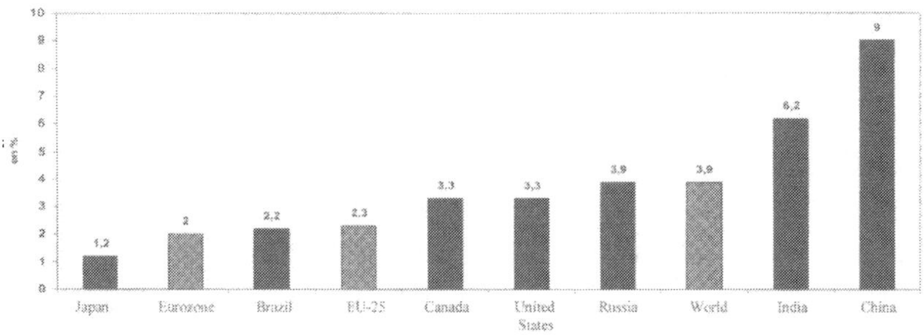

Source: IMF.

Over the last decade, the economies of the major emerging countries have continued to catch up while the EU-25 has shown a growth deficit compared with the United States.

Shares of worldwide GDP for the 2001-2030 period (in %)

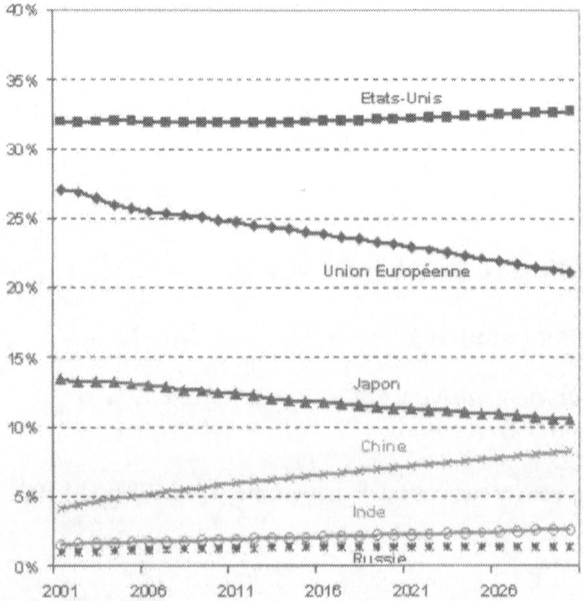

Source : Poncet(2006).

Key: United States, European Union, Japan, China, India, Russia.

This trend is confirmed when one looks at the share of the six geographical zones in worldwide GDP during the 2001-2030 period. The United States maintains its share, while that of the European Union drops significantly. China and India on the other hand are constantly progressing.

Even though the EU remains the world's number one exporter, ahead of the United States and China, etc.

Shares of the world export market for good and services in 2005 (in %)

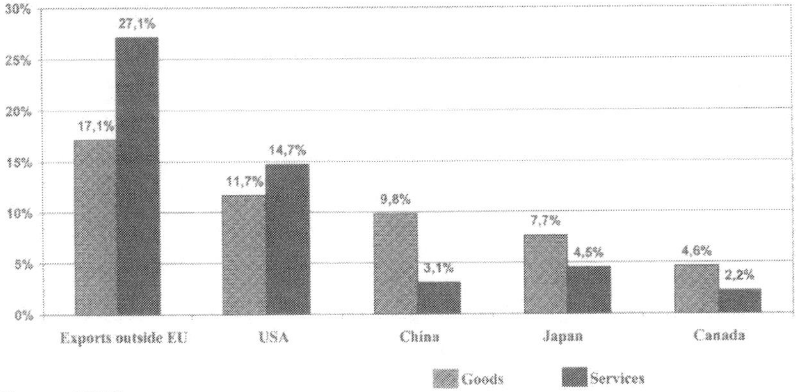

Source: WTO.

Shares of six geographical zones in world exports from 2001 to 2030 (in %)

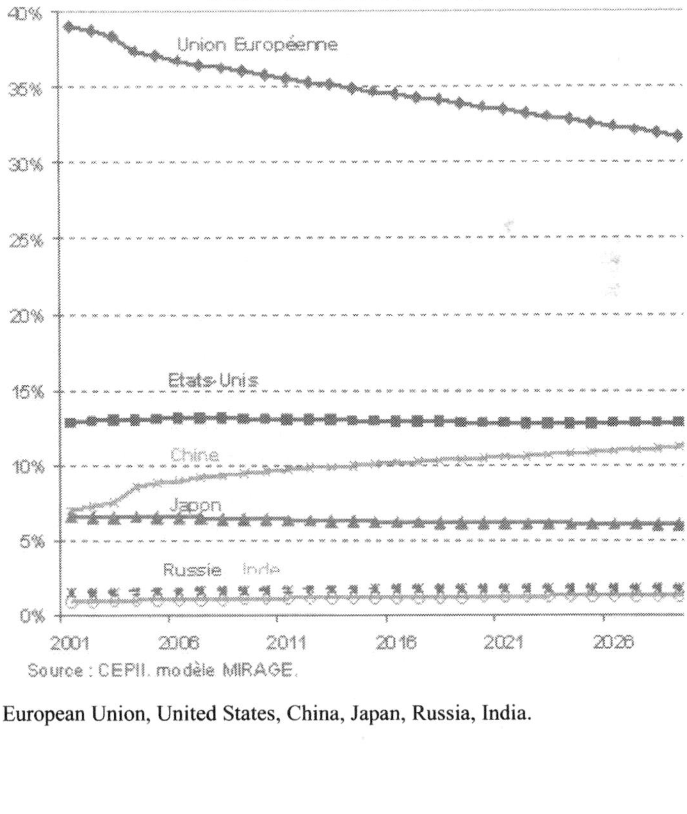

Source : CEPII. modèle MIRAGE.

Key: European Union, United States, China, Japan, Russia, India.

… the contribution of European Union countries to world trade has dropped recently and this trend is confirmed over the 2001-2030 period. The European Union's share of world exports is dropping faster than that of GDP.

Breakdown of foreign direct investments in the EU-15 in 2005

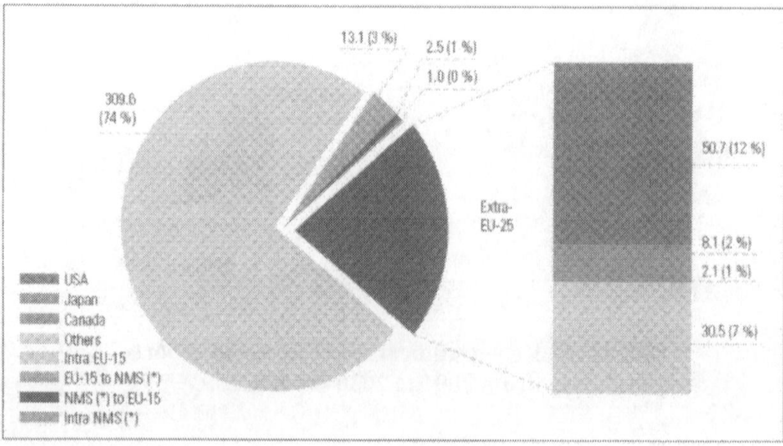

(*) NMS: New Member States
Source: European Commission (2005a).

Foreign direct investments by European countries are, to a very great extent, focused in EU countries (78%), while the USA is their first outside beneficiary (12%).

EU-25 outward FDI stocks in the BRIC countries at end-2005 (in million EUR)

	2001	2002	2003	2004	2005
Extra-EU	2 017 386	1 904 845	2 011 069	2 048 346	2 380 303
BRIC	187 475	145 965	184 795	208 301	252 085
Brazil	73 492	44 369	59 214	70 768	80 069
Russia	10 693	10 220	14 786	20 983	31 324
India	6 276	6 398	6 764	9 713	13 682
China	97 014	84 978	104 031	106 837	127 010
of which					
Hong Kong	77 705	65 009	85 326	85 559	95 740

Source: Eurostat.

In BRICs, direct investment on the part of the EU-25 is primarily aimed at Hong Kong and Brazil.

Between 2001 and 2005, direct investment by the EU-25 outside the EU increased by 17.9%. Investments in BRICs represented 9.3% of FDI outside the EU in 2001 and 10.6% in 2005.

The breakdown of FDI in BRICs evolved immensely from 2001 to 2005:

- Brazil, which represented 39.2% in 2001 of FDI by the EU in BRICs, only represented 31.7% in 2005;
- Russia, which only represented 5.7% of FDI in BRICs in 2001, represented 12.4% in 2005;
- India's share of FDI increased from 1.7% in 2001 to 5.4% in 2005;
- Finally, China's share has remained stable (from 51.7% in 2001 to 50.4% in 2005), although the concentration of FDI in Hong Kong has declined (from 41.4% in 2001 to 37.9% in 2005).

The European Union's investments in BRICs are more profitable than investments outside the EU globally. Revenue from China represented 50% of the 23 billion EUR income generated by the European Union FDI outflows.

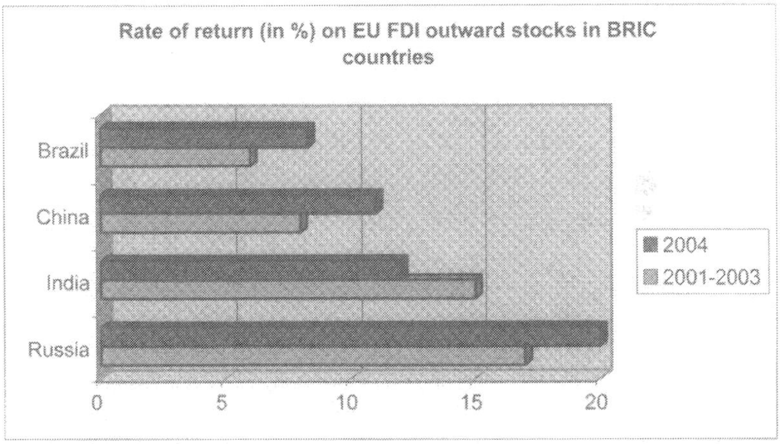

Source: Eurostat.

Moreover, the BRICs are investing more and more in Europe.

EU-25 FDI inflows from BRIC countries (in million EUR)

	2001	2002	2003	2004	2005
ExtraEU	145,867	126,567	123,541	53,072	94,149
BRIC	11,975	4,240	2,167	8,812	11,287
Brazil	1,023	599	- 878	4,014	5,488
Russia	752	342	704	196	4,107
India	108	133	615	1	220
China	10,092	3,166	1,726	4,601	1,472
Of which Hong Kong	9,545	2,925	1,436	4,748	1,071

Source: Eurostat.

Growth in research and development investments by emerging economies

Number of patents filed from 1883 (date of the signature of the Paris Convention on the protection of industrial property) to 2003

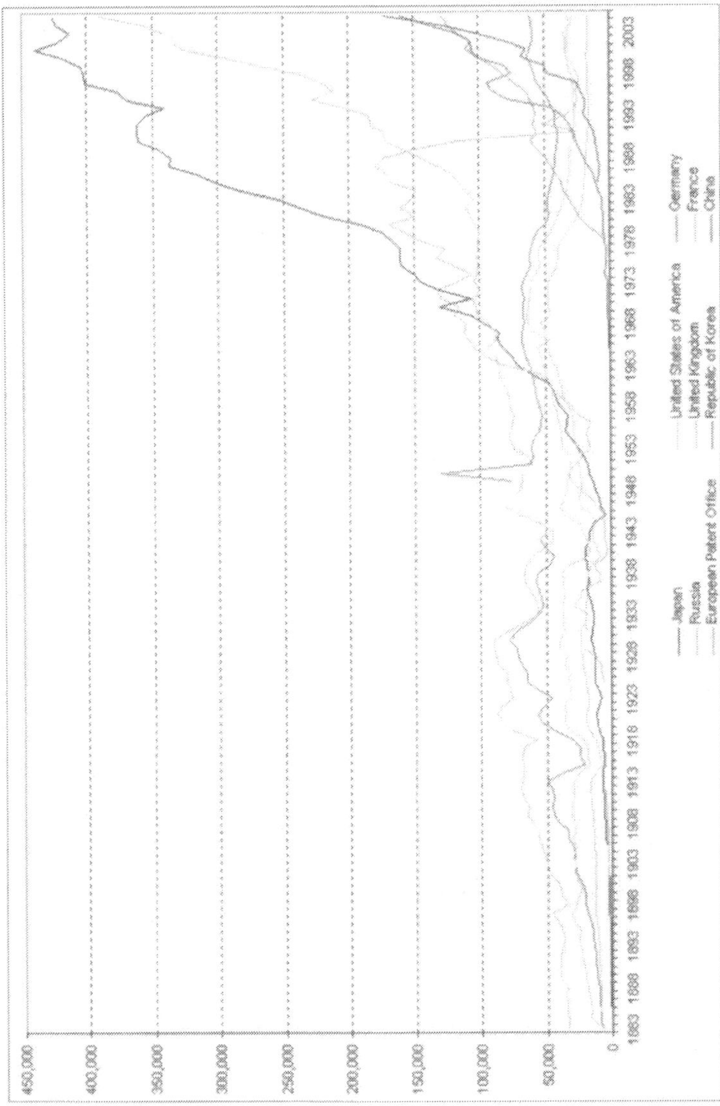

Source: World Intellectual Property Organization, Patent Report: Statistics on Worldwide Patent Activity (2007 Edition).

Number of engineering diplomas awarded by the United States, India and China in 2004

Degree Field	United States[1]	India[2]	China[3] *
Total Bachelors and Subbaccalaureate Engineering, Computer Science and Information Technology Degrees	**222,335**	**215,000**	**644,106**
Number of Bachelors Degrees	137,437	112,000	351,537
in Engineering (Excluding CS and Electrical)	52,520	17000	---
in CS, Electrical and IT	84,917	95,000	---
Number of Subbaccalaureate Degrees **	84,898	103,000	292,569
in Engineering	39,652	57000	---
in CS and IT	45,246	46,000	---

* This data provided by the Chinese Ministry of Education may include additional engineering and technology degrees outside traditional engineering fields, CS majors and IT specializations (example: auto mechanics)

** Subbaccalaureate degrees refer to Associates degrees in the United States, Short-Cycle degrees in China, and three-year diplomas in India

Note: The National Center for Education Statistics reports the total US engineering bachelors degrees granted in 2004 to be 63,558 This number differs from the American Society of Engineering Education's (ASEE) 2004 statistic of 72,893. This variation is due to the way each of these organizations classifies and categorizes engineering graduates.

Sources:
1 National Center for Educational Statistics (NCES). 2003-4 Table 249, 2003-4 Table 253. NCES. Obtained from NCES Annual Reports Program Director
2 National Association of Software and Service Companies (2005). 2005 Strategic Review: Chp 6: Sustaining the India Advantage. NASSCOM. Pg 158
3 Chinese Ministry of Education. Number of Students in Regular HEIs by Field of Study. Ministry of Education. http://www.moe.gov.cn/edoas/website18/info14477.htm

Source: Duke University, December 2005.

China and India are training increasing numbers of engineers and now have a manpower level that is close to that of the United States.

Total full-time researchers in the European Union, United States and China in 2006

EU-27	1 301 022
United States	1 394 682
China	1 223 756

Source: OECD, Main science and technology indicators, October 2007.

Moreover, the number of full-time researchers in China in 2006 was similar to that of the EU-27 and the United States.

New economies, new markets: the example of China

European Union exports to China have increased sharply since 1999. Emerging countries are also potential new markets and are in this sense a source of opportunity.

EU-27 exports to China for the top 5 products between 1999 and 2006

Sector	Exchange value 2006 (in billion EUR)	Rate of growth 1999-2006 (in %)
Vehicles, aircraft, ships	27,936	14.8%
Base metals and products for base materials	7,744	24.6%
Chemical industry products and related	4,385	17.7%
Medical, optical and musical instruments, watches	2,944	23.4%
TOTAL	63,707	18.3%

Source: Eurostat.

The financial power of emerging countries

Foreign currency reserves in the main emerging countries (2000 = 100)

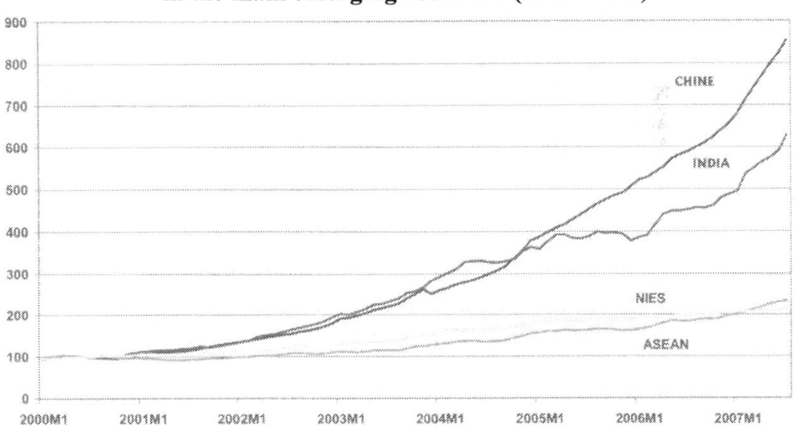

Source: IMF.

The foreign currency reserves of the main emerging countries have increased over the recent period and those of China and India have multiplied by respectively 8 and 6 since 2000.

Distribution of official monetary reserves in 1996 and 2006

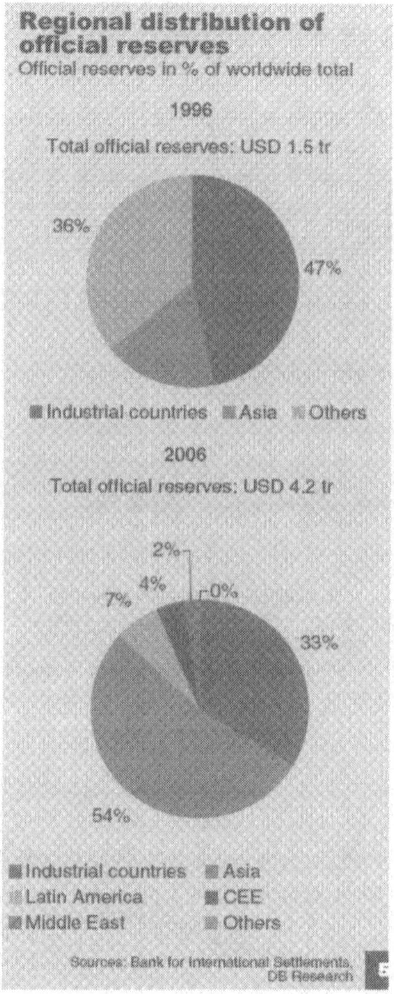

Source: Deutsche Bank Research, Sovereign wealth funds, 2007.

The distribution of official monetary reserves evolved hugely between 1996 and 2006. Two highly significant evolutions can be highlighted:

- Asia, that only owned 17% of the world's monetary reserves in 1996, owned 54% in 2006;
- Industrialised countries, that held 47%, almost half the world's reserves in 1996, only held 33% by 2006.

Sovereign wealth funds

Amounts held by the main sovereign wealth funds (in billion USD)

Abu Dhabi (Adia)	1300
Singapore (GIC)	330
Norway (GPF)	315
Saudi Arabia (various)	300
Kuwait (KIA)	250
China (CIC)	200
Russia (SFRF)	158
Singapore (Temasek)	115

Source: NATIXIS, November 2007.

At the end of November 2007, sovereign wealth funds possessed some 3,337 billion dollars…

SWF assets growth (2006-2016) (in %)

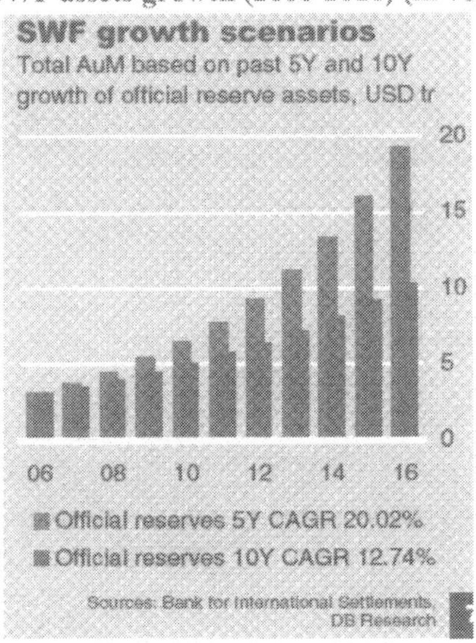

Source: Deutsche Bank Research, Sovereign wealth funds, 2007.

… and this figure is expected to increase over the next ten years.

2. The rise in commodity prices and the rise in value of the Euro compared with the dollar and the yen

Commodity price indices (January 2002 = 100)

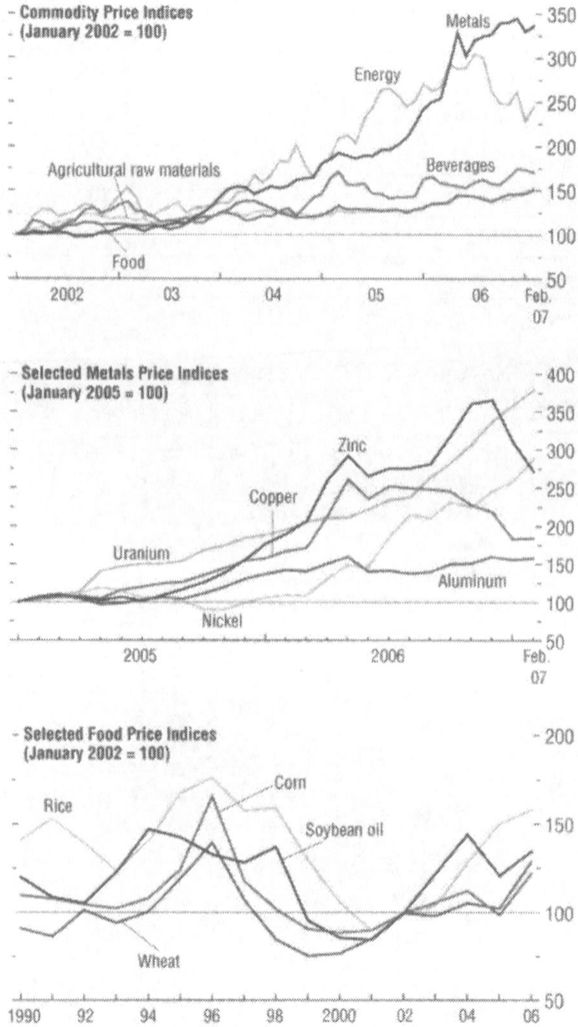

Source: IMF, *World Economic Outlook*, 2007.

Commodity prices rose between 2003 and 2007. The prices of metal and energy have increased the most dramatically, rising by 330% and 230% respectively since 2003.

Nominal exchange rate and real exchange rate of the Euro, Dollar and Yen from 2000 to 2007 (2000 = 100)

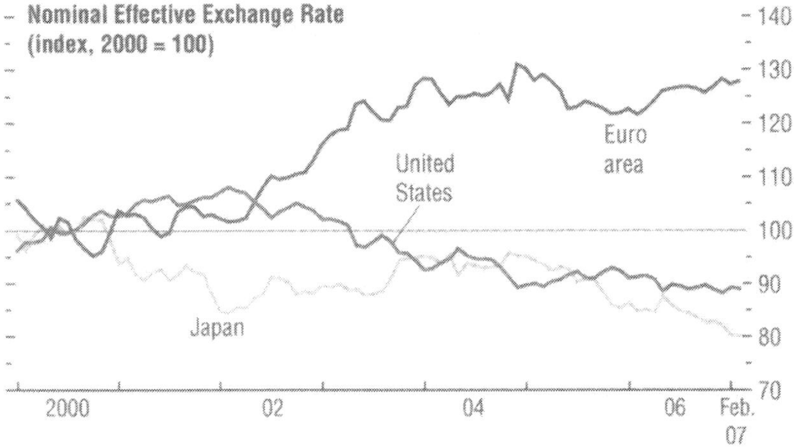

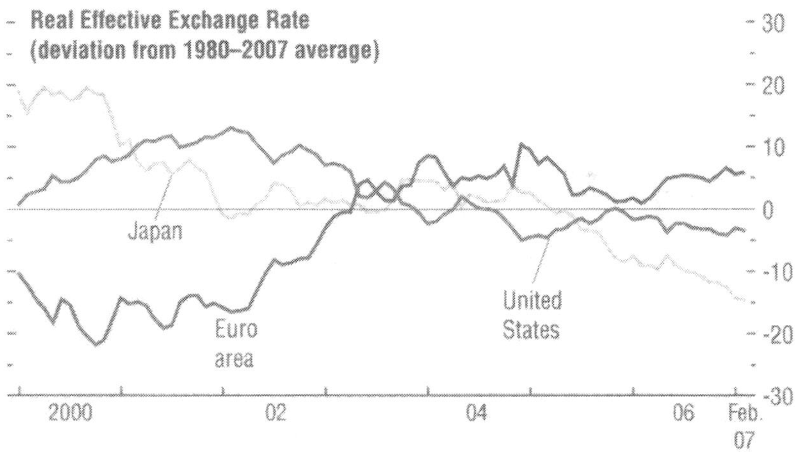

Source: IMF, *World Economic Outlook*, 2007.

Since 2000, the euro has noticeably increased in value compared with the dollar and the yen.

3. Energy and climate

Worldwide energy consumption, 1980-2030

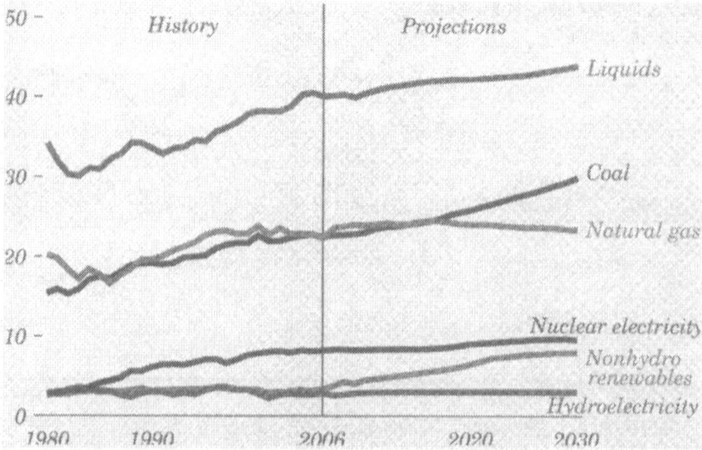

Source: Energy Information Administration, *Annual Energy Outlook*, 2007.

The demand for all energy sources will increase up until 2030.

The rates of energy dependence vary substantially from one state to another of the European Union from –36.8% in Denmark in 2006, for example, to 102.5% for Cyprus. The average European rate is 53.8%.

CO_2 emissions in 2003 and by 2030 (in millions of tons of CO_2)

	2003	2030	Increase in %
North Africa	295	604	+104%
Brazil	303	626	**+106%**
Sub-Saharan Africa	468	1031	+120%
Latin America	547	1153	+110%
Russia	1515	2003	+32%
Middle East	1102	2191	+99%
India	1050	2283	**+ 117%**
OECD Pacific	2025	2319	+14%
Asia	1291	3052	**+136%**
EU	3789	4219	**+11%**
China	3760	7173	**+90.7%**
OECD North America	6620	8387	**+26%**

Source: International Energy Agency, *World Energy Outlook*, 2005.

Up until 2030, CO_2 emissions will increase moderately in the European Union, the majority of OECD countries and Russia, but will increase dramatically elsewhere.

Energy consumption, net imports and dependence rate, 2006

	Gross inland energy consumption		Net imports		Energy dependence rate[4] (%)
	Mio. toe	% change 2006/2005	Mio. toe	% change 2006/2005	
EU27	**1 825.2**	**0.0**	**1 010.1**	**2.4**	**53.8**
Belgium	60.4	-1.2	53.5	-0.5	77.9
Bulgaria	20.5	2.8	9.5	0.3	46.2
Czech Republic	46.2	2.0	12.9	0.3	28.0
Denmark	20.9	6.1	-8.1	-22.5	-36.8
Germany	349.0	0.5	215.5	0.1	61.3
Estonia	5.4	-2.5	1.9	28.1	33.5
Ireland	15.5	2.6	14.2	4.1	90.9
Greece	31.5	0.5	24.9	6.0	71.9
Spain	143.9	-0.5	123.8	-0.1	81.4
France	273.1	-1.2	141.7	-1.8	51.4
Italy	186.1	-0.6	164.6	2.2	86.8
Cyprus	2.6	5.8	3.0	5.5	102.5
Latvia	4.6	3.0	3.2	5.8	65.7
Lithuania	8.4	-2.2	5.5	7.1	64.0
Luxembourg	4.7	0.0	4.7	0.9	98.9
Hungary	27.8	-0.8	17.3	-1.0	62.5
Malta	0.9	-6.4	0.9	-6.4	100.0
Netherlands	80.5	-2.3	37.2	-3.0	38.0
Austria	34.1	-0.1	24.9	0.8	72.9
Poland	98.3	4.7	19.6	16.2	19.9
Portugal	25.3	-6.3	21.6	-11.7	83.1
Romania	40.9	4.2	11.9	9.9	29.1
Slovenia	7.3	0.6	3.8	0.4	52.1
Slovakia	18.8	-1.2	12.0	-3.5	64.0
Finland	37.8	9.1	20.9	8.5	54.6
Sweden	50.8	-1.7	19.8	-1.9	37.4
United Kingdom	229.5	-1.6	49.3	52.7	21.3

Source: Eurostat.

B. New Internal Challenges Facing the European Union

1. Increased heterogeneity

Increased European Union heterogeneity in economic terms

GDP per capita in Purchasing power standards (EU-27 = 100)

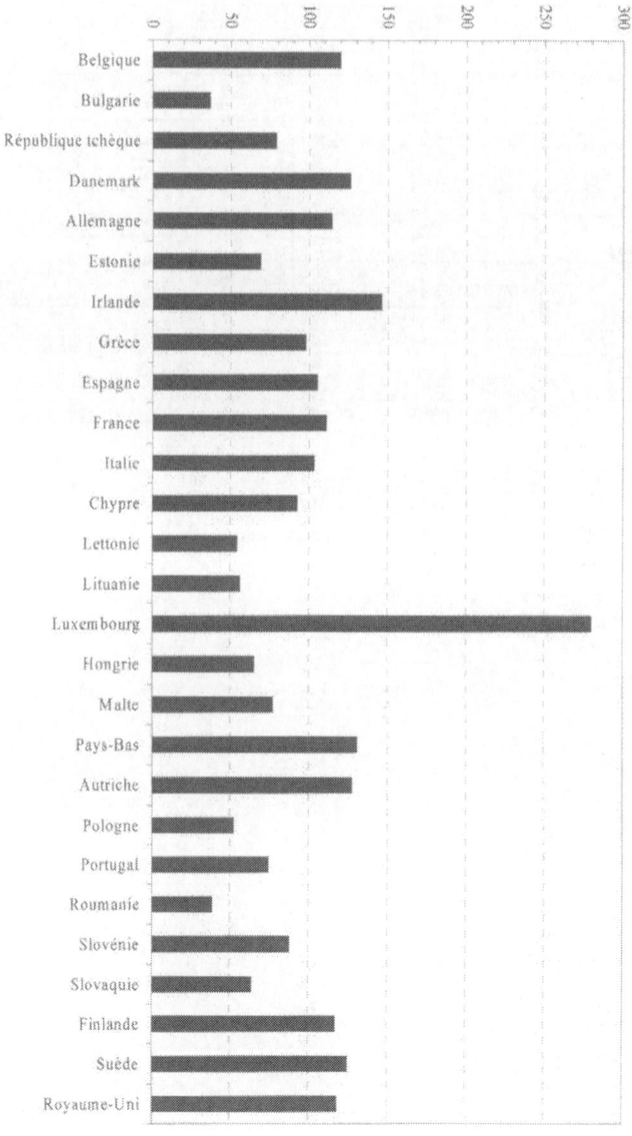

Source : Eurostat

GDP per capita in PPS in 2006 (EU-27 average = 100)

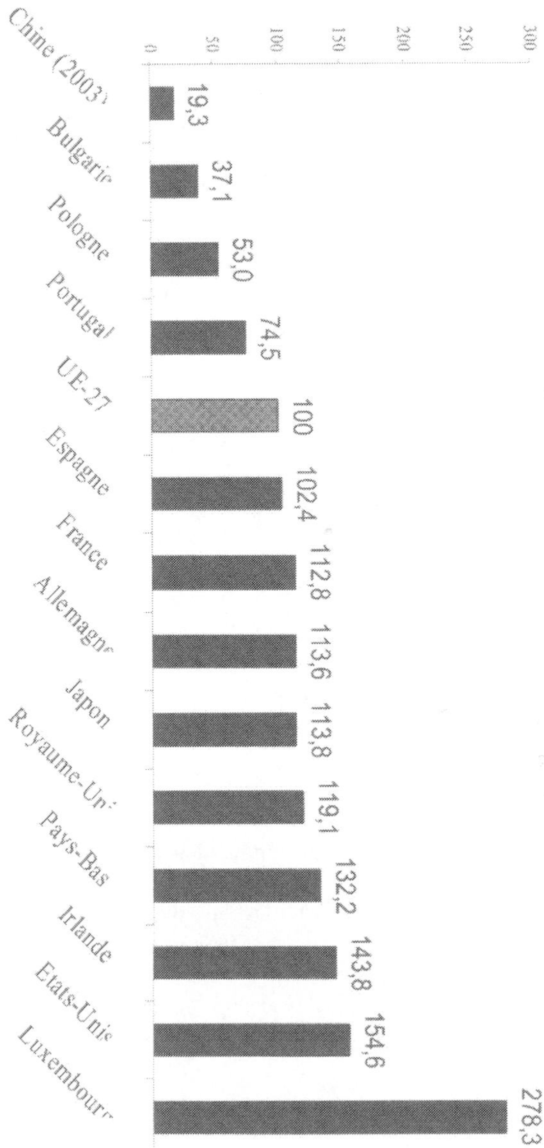

Source: Eurostat.

Economic differences within the European Union are notably illustrated by differences in GDP per capita that vary from around 1 to 7.
Substantial differences also exist between minimum wages in some European Union countries and the United States.

Minimum wages in some European Union countries and the United States in 2006 (in purchasing power standards)

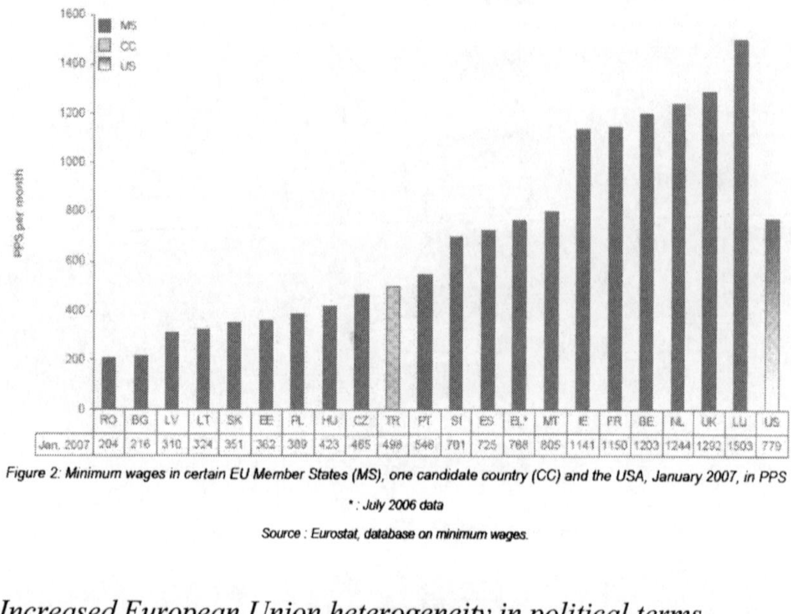

	RO	BG	LV	LT	SK	EE	PL	HU	CZ	TR	PT	SI	ES	EL*	MT	IE	FR	BE	NL	UK	LU	US
Jan. 2007	204	216	310	324	351	362	389	423	465	498	546	701	725	768	805	1141	1150	1203	1244	1292	1503	779

Figure 2: Minimum wages in certain EU Member States (MS), one candidate country (CC) and the USA, January 2007, in PPS

** : July 2006 data*

Source : Eurostat, database on minimum wages.

Increased European Union heterogeneity in political terms

Significant differences also emerge concerning their perception of globalisation, *i.e.* whether or not it represents an opportunity for them and/or a threat to employment in their country. The graph illustrates the differences in 9 states.

Significance of globalisation according to Europeans: opportunity or a threat to national employment? Question asked: what does globalisation mean to me

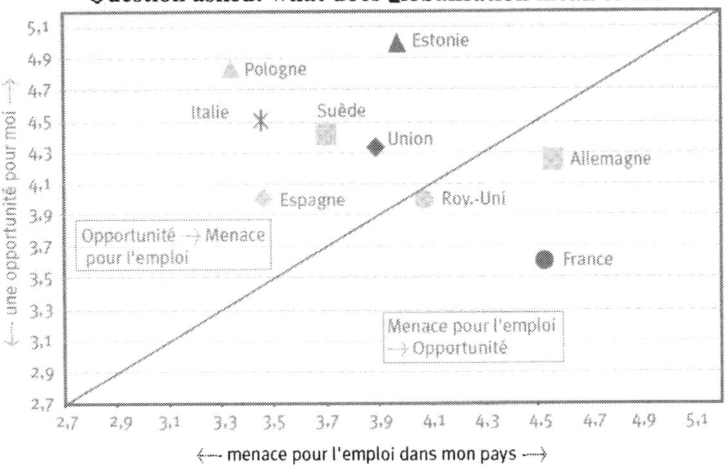

Source: European youth in a global context 2007, Kairos Future – Fondation pour l'innovation politique, 2007.
Key: Vertically "an opportunity for me", horizontally "a threat to employment in my country".
From top to bottom and left to right: Estonia, Poland, Italy, Sweden, EU, Germany, Spain, United Kingdom, France.

The results are on a scale of 1 to 7. Interpreting the graph:

- the higher a country is located, the more globalisation is perceived as an opportunity;
- the more a country is located to the right, the more globalisation is perceived as a threat to employment.

Europeans' perception of globalisation differs as the variations shown by this survey illustrate. Another survey indicates that the proportion of Europeans that associate globalisation with *relocation* varies from *11% to 57% depending on the state* and from *10% to 47%* concerning *opportunities in terms of new openings for businesses* (see table below).

The consequences of globalisation are multiple.
What does the word "globalisation" make you think of first of all?

	Relocation of some companies to countries where labour is cheaper	Opportunities for (NATIONALITY) companies in terms of new outlets	Increased competition for (NATIONALITY) companies	Foreign investments in (OUR COUNTRY)	Other (SPONT.)	DK
EU27	35%	22%	15%	14%	3%	11%
BE	44%	22%	14%	14%	2%	4%
BG	20%	17%	13%	21%	1%	28%
CZ	31%	21%	21%	19%	2%	6%
DK	28%	47%	14%	7%	2%	2%
DE	46%	30%	12%	7%	1%	4%
EE	13%	28%	22%	16%	2%	19%
EL	50%	15%	18%	17%	0%	0%
ES	28%	18%	14%	16%	6%	18%
FR	57%	16%	13%	7%	1%	6%
IE	33%	16%	13%	18%	2%	18%
IT	26%	24%	17%	18%	4%	11%
CY	19%	13%	25%	27%	5%	11%
LV	15%	19%	28%	18%	2%	18%
LT	11%	28%	16%	17%	3%	25%
LU	45%	17%	19%	9%	1%	9%
HU	29%	17%	16%	27%	1%	10%
MT	18%	22%	26%	18%	1%	15%
NL	31%	34%	14%	8%	6%	7%
AT	46%	15%	13%	19%	3%	4%
PL	20%	21%	19%	20%	2%	18%
PT	38%	10%	19%	16%	1%	16%
RO	11%	18%	16%	25%	3%	27%
SI	35%	22%	18%	16%	1%	8%
SK	31%	20%	16%	21%	1%	11%
FI	46%	21%	17%	6%	6%	4%
SE	34%	41%	12%	6%	3%	4%
UK	34%	22%	14%	13%	2%	15%
HR	28%	10%	22%	26%	2%	12%
TR	11%	15%	11%	23%	1%	39%
MK	17%	20%	12%	28%	1%	22%

Source: Eurobarometer 67 – Spring 2007.

Europeans do not have the same societal expectations (level of taxation, level of protectionism and liberalism). Such differences are illustrated by these graphs that demonstrate the differing aspirations between European Union populations.

Societal aspirations of Europeans according to age.
Question asked: What are the characteristics of your ideal society?

NB: – "J" indicates a result of the 30-50 year old panel and "A" a result of the 16-29 year old panel.
– The results are on a scale of 1 to 7.

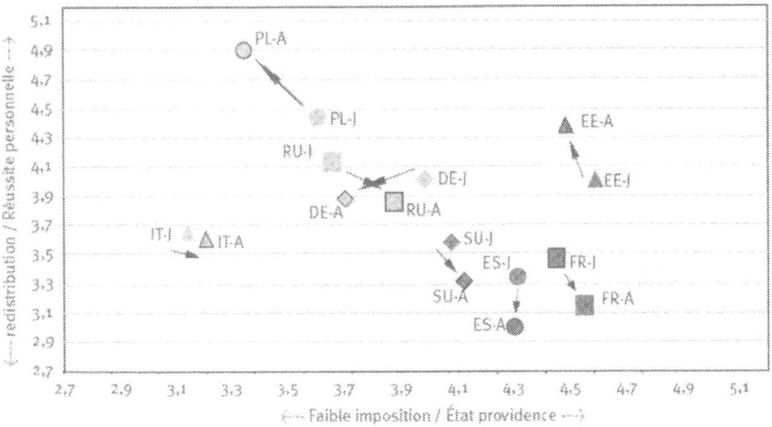

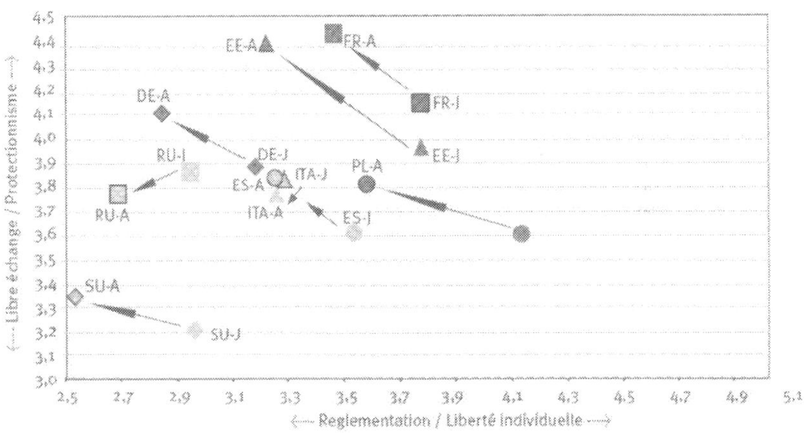

Source: European youth in a global context 2007, Kairos Future – Fondation pour l'innovation politique, 2007.
Key – Graph 1: Vertical scale – redistribution/individual success / Horizontal scale – low taxation/welfare state.
Key – Graph 2: Vertical scale – free trade/protectionism / Horizontal scale – regulation/ individual freedom.

2. Demography-migration

With 1.5 children per woman, the European Union has the lowest fertility rate in the world.

Synthetic fertility index, 2006

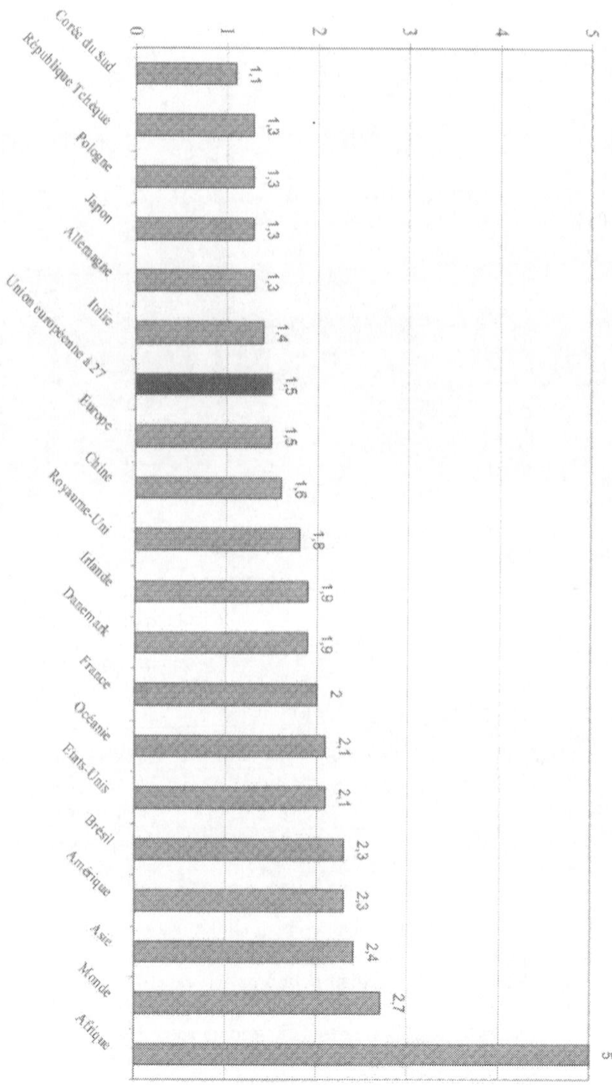

Source: INED and World Population Data Sheet 2007.

Europe is the only region in the world whose population will decrease as from 2025.

Population by world region in 2005, 2025 and 2050

		Population (in millions of inhabitants)	Change between 2005 and 2050
Sub-Saharan Africa	2005	770	+ 128.5%
	2025	1193	
	2050	1760	
Latin America and the Caribbean	2005	558	+ 37.8%
	2025	688	
	2050	769	
Middle East and North Africa	2005	416,8	+81.9%
	2025	588	
	2050	758,3	
Europe	2005	731	-9.2%
	2025	715	
	2050	664	
China	2005	1312	+7.3%
	2025	1445	
	2050	1408	
India	2005	1134	+46.2%
	2025	1447	
	2050	1658	
United States	2005	300	+34%
	2025	355	
	2050	402	
Russia	2005	144	-25%
	2025	128	
	2050	108	

Source: United Nations Department of Economic and Social Affairs, Populations Division. http://esa.un.org/unpp.

The breakdown of age brackets within the working-age population will change significantly from 2025, when 25-40 year olds will no longer be the most represented segment of working-age Europeans.

Proportion of the economically active population aged under 40 (2000-2025)

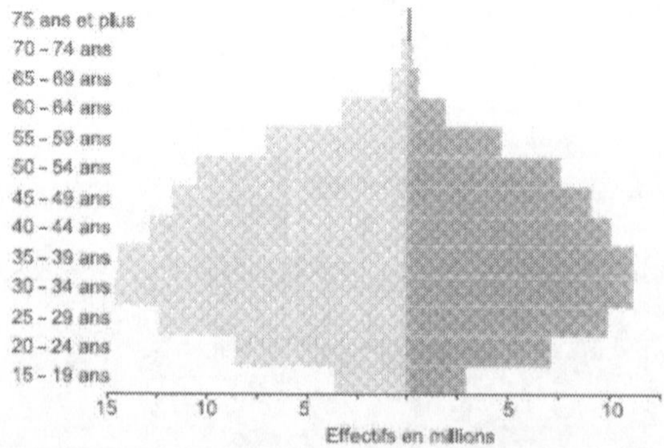

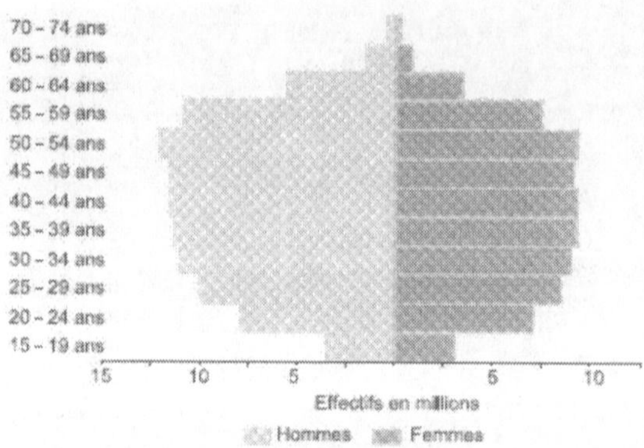

Source: Institut Montaigne, *Ageing and competitiveness*, 2003.

Key – Graph 1: Age pyramid for economically active Europeans (2000). In millions, Men/ Women.

Key – Graph 2: Age pyramid for economically active Europeans (2025). In millions, Men/ Women.

Change in the total amount of public spending related to the aging of the population in the European Union (27) from 2004 to 2050 (in % of GDP)

Table 1-1 Total age-related public spending: pension, health care, long-term care, education and unemployment transfers (% of GDP) – baseline scenario

	2004	2005	2010	2015	2020	2025	2030	2035	2040	2045	2050	Change 2004-
BE	25.4	25.3	25.1	25.5	26.6	28.2	29.9	31.1	31.6	31.8	31.7	6.3
DK	26.8	26.5	27.0	27.8	28.6	29.5	30.8	31.7	32.1	31.9	31.6	4.8
DE	23.7	23.4	22.5	22.2	22.9	23.8	24.7	25.4	25.7	26.1	26.4	2.7
GR *	8.9	8.9	8.7	8.7	8.7	8.9	9.1	9.4	9.7	9.9	10.2	1.2
ES	20.1	20.0	19.7	19.8	20.4	21.7	23.4	25.2	27.3	28.7	28.6	8.5
FR	26.7	26.8	26.7	26.9	27.6	28.1	28.6	29.4	29.6	29.7	29.6	2.9
IE	15.5	15.2	15.4	16.3	17.1	18.0	18.8	19.7	20.7	22.1	23.3	7.8
IT	26.2	26.2	25.7	25.6	25.9	26.4	27.3	28.1	28.7	28.6	28.0	1.7
LU	19.5	19.5	19.4	20.6	21.6	23.5	25.0	26.6	27.4	28.1	27.8	8.2
NL	20.9	20.5	20.6	21.5	22.4	23.4	24.7	25.7	26.2	26.1	25.8	5.0
AT	25.2	24.9	24.2	24.0	24.2	25.2	26.0	26.5	26.1	25.7	25.3	0.2
PT	23.6	24.2	24.2	24.9	26.3	27.1	28.0	29.5	31.1	32.8	33.6	9.7
FI	25.4	25.2	25.6	26.5	27.7	28.8	30.1	30.6	30.7	30.6	30.6	5.2
SE	29.6	29.2	28.2	28.3	28.6	29.5	30.9	31.7	31.9	31.7	31.8	2.2
UK	19.6	19.5	19.4	19.5	19.9	20.7	21.8	22.5	22.9	23.2	23.6	4.0
CY	16.4	16.4	16.5	16.7	17.6	18.8	20.6	21.9	23.4	26.0	28.2	11.8
CZ	19.3	19.3	18.8	18.6	19.2	20.0	21.0	22.4	24.1	25.6	26.4	7.2
EE	17.1	17.6	16.5	15.4	15.1	15.0	14.8	14.6	14.3	14.3	14.4	-2.7
HU	20.7	20.9	21.0	21.3	22.3	22.9	23.6	24.7	26.4	27.4	27.7	7.0
LT	16.0	16.0	15.3	14.8	15.1	15.7	16.3	16.6	16.8	17.0	17.4	1.4
LV	17.5	15.9	14.6	14.1	14.0	15.6	16.0	16.2	16.2	16.1	16.2	-1.3
MT	18.2	18.2	18.1	19.7	20.4	20.5	20.0	19.5	19.2	18.9	18.5	0.3
PL	23.7	23.4	20.2	18.1	17.9	17.7	17.6	17.5	17.3	17.1	17.0	-6.7
SK	16.2	16.5	15.4	14.9	15.3	15.9	16.6	17.1	17.7	18.3	19.1	2.9
SI	24.2	24.2	24.0	24.5	25.5	27.0	28.6	30.2	31.7	33.0	33.8	9.7
EU25	23.4	23.3	22.7	22.7	23.2	24.0	24.9	25.6	26.4	26.7	26.8	3.4
EU15	23.5	23.3	22.9	23.0	23.5	24.4	25.4	26.3	26.8	27.1	27.2	3.7
EU12	24.0	23.9	23.4	23.5	24.1	24.9	26.9	26.9	27.5	27.8	27.8	3.7
EU10	21.1	21.0	19.4	18.4	18.7	19.0	19.4	19.9	20.5	21.0	21.4	0.2
EU9 (EU10-PL)	19.3	19.3	18.8	18.7	19.3	20.0	20.8	21.8	23.0	23.9	24.7	5.4

1) Total expenditure for GR does not include pension expenditure. The Greek authorities have agreed to provide the pension projections in 2006. In the context of the most recent assessment of the sustainability of public finances based on the Greek stability programme, public spending on pensions was projected to increase by 10.3% of GDP between 2004 and 2050.
2) Total expenditure for: GR, FR, PT, CY, EE, HU does not include long-term care
3) The projection results for public spending on long-term care for Germany does not reflect current legislation where benefit levels are fixed. A scenario which comes closer to the current setting of legislation projects that public spending would remain constant as a share of GDP over the projection period.
Note: these figures refer to the baseline projections for social security spending on pensions, education and unemployment transfers. For health care and long-term care, the projections refer to "AWG reference scenarios"

Source: European Commission, Directorate-General for Economic and Financial Affairs.

The aging of the European population has already led to a substantial increase in social spending. Between 2000 and 2005, the amount spent on social welfare by the EU-25 rose by 22.8%. In the same period, pension spending increased by 18.5%.

This acceleration in social spending will be confirmed over the 2005-2050 period: the total amount of public spending relating to the ageing of the population will increase by 3.5% of GDP between 2005 and 2050.

In most European countries, immigrants represented a growing proportion of the working-age population over the 1992-2004 period.

Share of migrants in the working-age population in several European Union countries, the United States and New Zealand from 1992 to 2004 (in %)

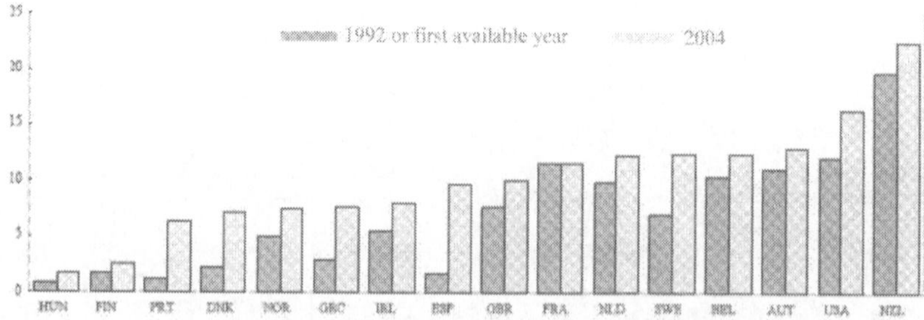

Migrants are making up an increasing share of the male working age population.
Source: OECD

The share of migrants in skilled occupation is increasing globally in EU countries and in particular in Portugal, Spain and Denmark.

Share of migrants in skilled occupation in several European Union countries, the United States and New ealand from 1992 to 2004 (in %)

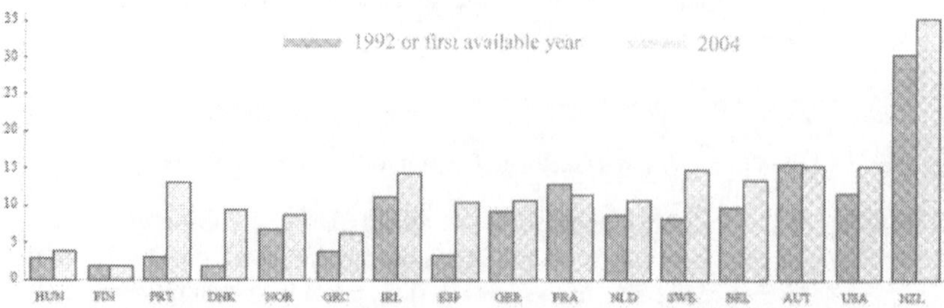

Note : The figures relate to men only for reasons of data availability. Workers are counted as migrants when they are foreign-born.
Working age population is defined as people aged 16-64. The first year is 1992 except for Australia 1995, Finland 1996, France 1993, Hungary 1997, Netherlands 1996, Norway 1996, Sweden 1995, New Zealand 1997, United States 1994.

The share of migrants is also rising among highly skilled male workers.
Source: OECD.

ANNEX 5

Perceptions of Globalisation and France's Relative Specificity

This graph examines whether European countries view globalisation as an opportunity for business by opening markets or as a threat to employment in their country.

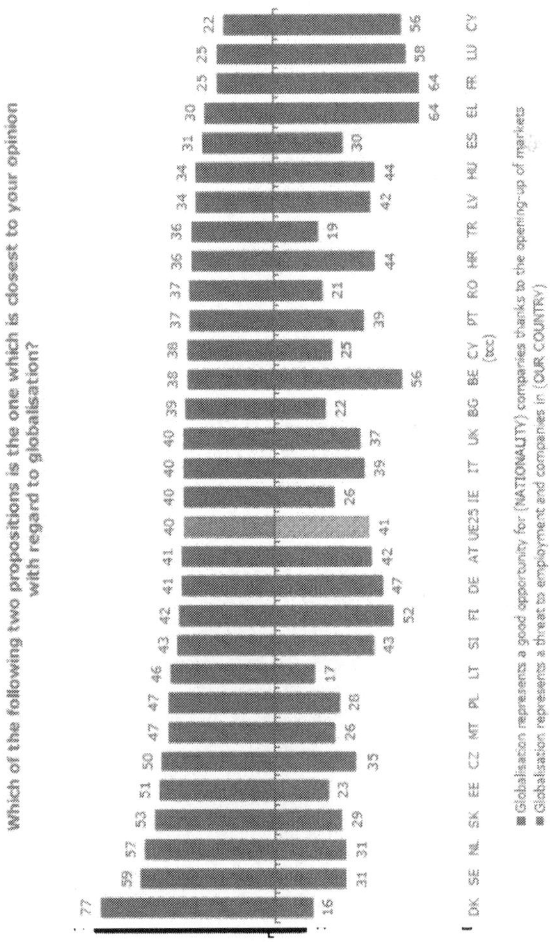

Source: European Commission, Eurobarometer 2006.

Significance of globalisation according to Europeans: individual opportunity and/or threat to national employment?

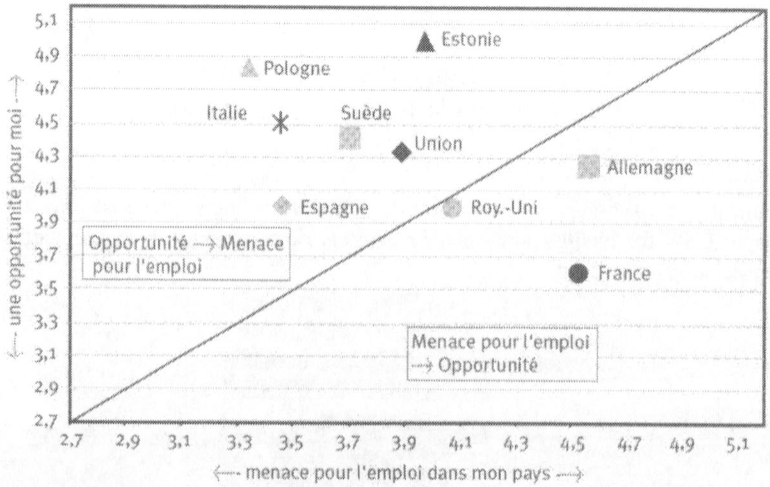

Source: European youth in a global context 2007, Kairos Future – Fondation pour l'innovation politique, 2007.
Key: Vertical scale "an opportunity for me", horizontal scale "a threat to employment in my country".
From top to bottom and left to right: Estonia, Poland, Italy, Sweden, EU, Germany, Spain, United Kingdom, France. The results are portrayed on a scale of 1 to 7.

While Europeans may have very contrasting perceptions of the impact of globalisation on businesses and employment, the French manifest the highest level of defiance. Many more French citizens consider that globalisation represents a threat to employment rather than an opportunity compared to their European neighbours.

The consequences of globalisation are multiple.
What does the word "globalisation" make you think of first of all?

	Relocation of some companies to countries where labour is cheaper	Opportunities for (NATIONALITY) companies in terms of new outlets	Increased competition for (NATIONALITY) companies	Foreign investments in (OUR COUNTRY)	Other (SPONT.)	DK
EU27	35%	22%	15%	14%	3%	11%
BE	44%	22%	14%	14%	2%	4%
BG	20%	17%	13%	21%	1%	28%
CZ	31%	21%	21%	19%	2%	6%
DK	28%	47%	14%	7%	2%	2%
DE	46%	30%	12%	7%	1%	4%
EE	13%	28%	22%	16%	2%	19%
EL	50%	15%	18%	17%	0%	0%
ES	28%	18%	14%	16%	6%	18%
FR	57%	16%	13%	7%	1%	6%
IE	33%	16%	13%	18%	2%	18%
IT	26%	24%	17%	18%	4%	11%
CY	19%	13%	25%	27%	5%	11%
LV	15%	19%	28%	18%	2%	18%
LT	11%	28%	16%	17%	3%	25%
LU	45%	17%	19%	9%	1%	9%
HU	29%	17%	16%	27%	1%	10%
MT	18%	22%	26%	18%	1%	15%
NL	31%	34%	14%	8%	6%	7%
AT	46%	15%	13%	19%	3%	4%
PL	20%	21%	19%	20%	2%	18%
PT	38%	10%	19%	16%	1%	16%
RO	11%	18%	16%	25%	3%	27%
SI	35%	22%	18%	16%	1%	8%
SK	31%	20%	16%	21%	1%	11%
FI	46%	21%	17%	6%	6%	4%
SE	34%	41%	12%	6%	3%	4%
UK	34%	22%	14%	13%	2%	15%
HR	28%	10%	22%	26%	2%	12%
TR	11%	15%	11%	23%	1%	39%
MK	17%	20%	12%	28%	1%	22%

Source: Eurobarometer 67 – Spring 2007.

More French citizens, compared to their European neighbours, associate negative effects with globalisation. For example 57% of French people associate globalisation with relocation, while the European Union (27) average on this issue is 35%.

Opinion of several European countries on the influence the European Union should have on globalisation (in %)

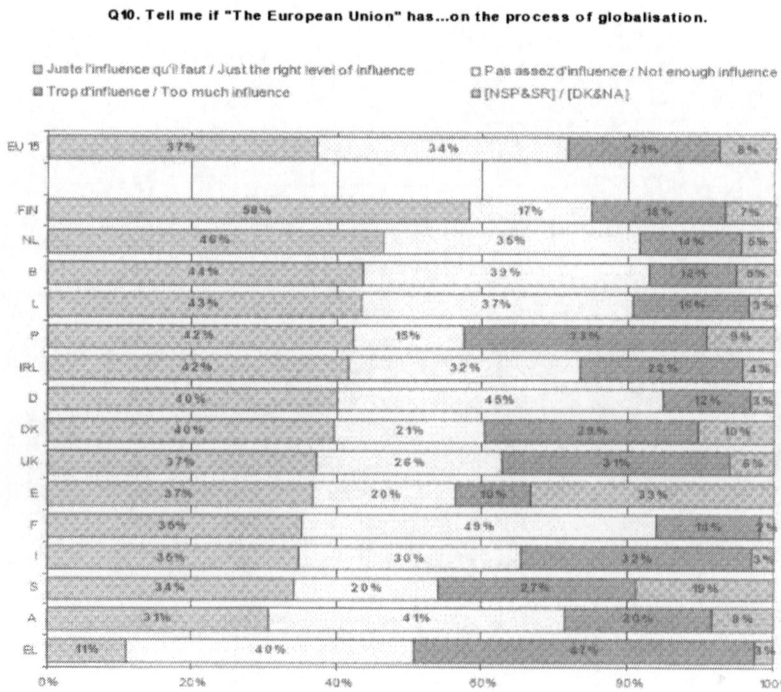

Source: European Commission (Flash Eurobarometer 151b – November 2003).

The French are the most numerous (49%) to consider that the influence exerted by the EU on the globalisation process should be reinforced.

Opinion of several European countries and of the United States on the benefit of international trade barriers (in %)

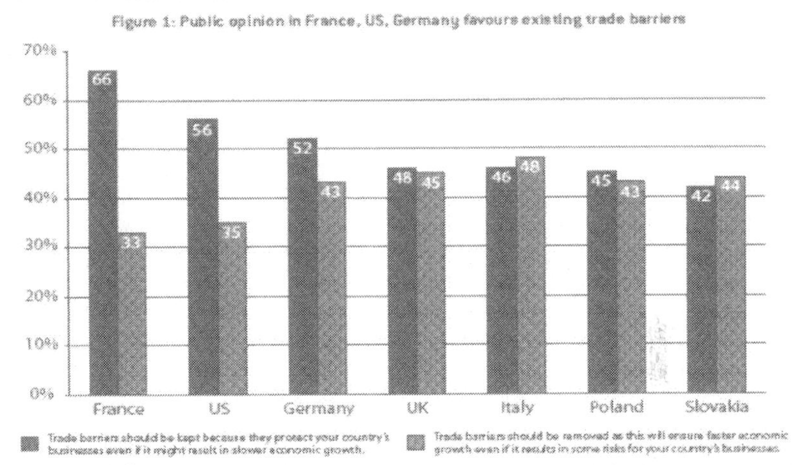

Source: German Marshall Fund (2006).

ANNEX 6

The Lisbon Treaty's Potential Contribution To a European Strategy For Globalisation

"Lisbon" is no longer just the name of a strategy, but more importantly today that of the new European treaty signed in December 2007 and ratified by 23 Member States as of August 2008. This annex highlights the most noteworthy innovations in favour of the goals of a European strategy for globalisation beyond 2010.

These innovations relate to institutions (I), the breakdown of competences (II), and the Union's policies (III).

I – Institutional Reform

1. Accelerated decision-making procedures

Although the implementation of the Lisbon strategy is primarily a matter for the Member States, the community dimension is far from absent. The improvement of decision-making procedures introduced by the new treaty will thus contribute to a more efficient deployment of a European strategy for globalisation.

a) Extension of qualified majority

By repealing unanimity, European integration can progress faster by accelerating the pace of implementation of the Union's policies. As was the case for each previous treaty revision, some fifty key domains are no longer subject to unanimity but to qualified majority voting.

Sensitive areas, such as taxation, social security, foreign policy, common defence policy, operational police cooperation, linguistic regime or the headquarters of institutions remain subject to unanimous vote. On the other hand, a certain number of existing or new areas will be governed by qualified majority.

The inclusion of matters relating to the freedom of movement for workers or to economic and financial issues will facilitate the development of policies necessary to the success of a European strategy for globalisation.

The following are among the most noteworthy areas to be governed by a qualified majority vote:

In the social sphere: freedom of movement for workers; social benefits; principles and conditions of functioning of services of general economic interest.

In the economic, financial and budgetary sphere: modification to some provisions of the statute of the European system of central banks; appointment of the ECB's chairman and board members; own resources system's implementation measures (however, the provisions relating to the own resources system itself remain subject to unanimous vote); common positions and unified representation on the international Eurozone scene.

In the field of police and judicial cooperation, immigration and administrative cooperation: administrative cooperation in the area of freedom, security and justice; border controls (except passports, identity documents and residence permits); asylum and protection of refugees and displaced persons; immigration; judicial cooperation in criminal matters; approximation of criminal norms, offences and sanctions; Eurojust; police cooperation in certain sectors (except for operational cooperation that remains subject to unanimous vote); Europol; measures that further crime prevention; civil protection; administrative cooperation.

In the sphere of foreign policy: decisions founded on a decision by the European Council or a proposal by the High Representative following a decision by the European Council; appointment of a special representative; measures that facilitate diplomatic and consular protection; appointment of a High Representative for foreign affairs and security policies; statute and headquarters of the European armaments agency; establishment of permanent structured cooperation in the area of defence; establishment of a start-up fund to finance tasks of the defence policy; humanitarian aid and the creation of a European voluntary corps.

In the framework of new competences assigned to the European Union: space policy, energy (market functioning, supplies, efficiency, renewable energy, interconnection); tourism; sport.

In the institutional sphere: list of the Council's configurations; review of rules relating to the composition of the Committee of the Regions and the Economic and Social Committee; the European citizens' initiative calling on the Commission to propose a change in European law; agreement on the withdrawal of a Member State; administration of the European Union.

Other spheres: high safety standards for medication and medical devices; measures in favour of protecting human health, in particular the fight against serious cross-border threats, tobacco and alcohol; intellectual property (creation of European titles and implementation of an authorisation regime, centralised controls at a European Union level) with the exception of the linguistic regime of titles of ownership.

b) New definition of double majority

In the framework of the mode of adoption of acts by the Council, the new definition of qualified majority voting retained by the Lisbon Treaty will make it possible to avoid, on the occasion of future enlargements, the difficult question of the number of votes allocated to each State. As this type of negotiation is singularly time consuming, it will enable the Council to focus on more important questions regarding the European Union's future.

The new definition of qualified majority voting, according to which the Union's acts are adopted when they are voted by 55% of Member States representing at least 65% of the Union's population, should simplify the decision-making process. Its legitimacy is supported by the fact that it is based on the objective criterion of population. Negotiations on this point were particularly difficult.

The Treaty is planned to come into full application in 2017.

c) Flexibility: the "bridge" clauses

Should the Member States decide to go further in a sphere covered by unanimous voting, (concerning the European strategy for globalisation, for example, this could be in the area of social security), they could resort to a bridge clause, a classic device adopted by the Lisbon Treaty.

The Lisbon Treaty provides for a general bridge clause, enabling the European Council to unanimously decide to transfer matters covered by unanimous vote to a qualified majority vote. The same reserve exists as for the flexibility clause, namely that this procedure covered by article 48 § 7 of the TEU cannot apply to decisions with military or defence implications. National parliaments must be informed of all initiatives in this area and have six months to oppose such decisions.

The Lisbon Treaty also provides for specific "bridge clauses" in certain spheres: common foreign and security policy (article 31 of the TFEU, with the exception of decisions with military or defence implications), some measures relating to family rights with cross-border implications (article 81 of the TFEU), the multiannual financial framework (article 312 of the TFEU).

Finally, it can be decided to switch from a special legislative procedure to an ordinary legislative procedure in certain spheres, in particular the rights of workers (article 137 § 2 of the TFEU), the environment and regional development (article 175 § 2 of the TFEU).

2. More efficient Community institutions

a) Reinforced European Parliament

The European Parliament has played an extremely important role in the past in relation to the Services Directive. The Directive was a central element of the 2005-2008 Lisbon community programme. The benefit of reinforcing this institution by the new Treaty, in the framework of the implementation of a European strategy for globalisation, is thus immediately perceptible.

The codecision procedure, that gives the European Parliament and the Council an equivalent role, is extended to the majority of areas governed by qualified majority voting. It has been renamed the "ordinary legislative procedure" by the Lisbon Treaty, thereby confirming its central role in the decision-making process.

The European Parliament's role has also been reinforced in relation to the adoption of the annual budget because it will have equal decision-making powers in this field with the Council that will therefore lose its "last word" prerogative on compulsory spending (in particular regarding the amounts allocated to the common agricultural policy). The Lisbon Treaty moreover abandons the distinction between compulsory and non-compulsory Structural Funds and internal policy expenditure in particular). Even if the European Parliament has the last word on budget, it will only be able to reject the budget by a majority of its members, and in the case of a budget rejected by the Council, will only be able to adopt it with three-fifths of the votes cast.

The prominent budgetary role given to the European Parliament confirms its significant position in the framework of the new budgetary deal required by a European strategy for globalisation.

A reinforced right of intervention has also been recognised for the European Parliament. It now has a right of approval in domains in which it had until then only been consulted: flexibility clause, adoption of the multi-annual financial framework, suspension of certain rights of Member States in the case of a serious breach of Union values, extension by the Council of the scope of criminal areas that can give rise to harmonisation, and a large proportion of international agreements. It also has the power to approve the authorisation of reinforced cooperation and likewise regarding the European Council's choice to revise treaties without the prior convening of a Convention.

Finally, the European Parliament will now be consulted in areas such as the diplomatic and consular protection of Union citizens, the linguistic regime of intellectual property titles, passports and other identity documents, etc.

b) Refocused European Commission

The Commission has an essential role to play regarding the implementation of the Lisbon community programme. The better it is organised, the more efficiently the policies necessary to a European strategy for globalisation will be implemented.

The Treaty provides for the improved coordination of the Commission's staff, and above all, the limitation, from 2014, of the number of commissioners to two-thirds of the number of Member States, a measure with important consequences and more complex conditions of implementation. Many of Lisbon's policies currently fall under the domain of competence of several commissioners, which complicates implementation. The implementation of a European strategy for globalisation can only benefit from this new configuration.

The Treaty does not modify competences. On the other hand, the role and political influence of the President of the European Commission are clearly asserted and reinforced by the Lisbon Treaty. The Commission's monopoly of power of initiative is clearly asserted and its decisive role in the launch of reinforced cooperation is recognised.

c) A genuine institutional regime for the European Council

Since the launch of the Lisbon strategy, the Council has played a significant role in its implementation and a European Council session, organised every spring addresses the Lisbon Strategy.

Now recognised as an institution of the Union, the functioning rules of the European Council have been substantially modified because it will elect, by qualified majority, a President for a two and half year term, renewable once. The European Council President will be, with the High Representative and the President of the European Commission, the "third man" at the head of the European Union. This three-headed "presidency" of the Union may call into doubt the Union's future effectiveness to speak with a single voice. The presidency of the Council's different configurations under a Troika format will persist. Interaction with the stable presidency of the Council may prove complex.

However, should the future President of the European Council seize the opportunity of a European strategy for globalisation, the visibility of the strategy will be significantly enhanced and result in substantial repercussions from the point of view of its national political appropriation at the very highest level.

II. The Union's Scope of Competences Is Reinforced by the Lisbon Treaty

1. Clarified breakdown of competences

The Lisbon Treaty clarifies the breakdown of competences between the European Union and the Member States. This clarification must encourage the implementation of the Lisbon strategy by distinguishing more clearly not only "national reform programmes" and "community programmes", but also national tools subject to the OMC and community action tools. Moreover, the transfer of technological research and development, formerly a support competence, to that of shared competence, will reinforce the community dimension of an essential policy in the framework of the success of the Lisbon strategy.

When the EU has ***exclusive competence*** (article 3 of the Treaty on the Functioning of the European Union[1], hereafter TFEU) in a specific area, only the Union may legislate and adopt legally binding acts, the Member States being able to do so themselves only if so empowered by the Union or for the implementation of Union acts. The Union has exclusive competence over the *customs union, common commercial policy*, the establishment of *rules of competition* necessary to the functioning of the internal market and *monetary policy* for Member States whose currency is the euro.

When a ***competence shared*** with Member States is granted to the EU in a specific area, the EU and the Member States may legislate and adopt legally binding acts in that area. Member States shall exercise their competence to the extent that the Union has not exercised or has ceased exercising its competence. Among these competences are the *Internal market*, *social policy* for aspects defined by the Treaty, "*agriculture* and fisheries with the exception of the conservation of marine biological resources", *transport*, *energy* and domains relating to *research*, *technological development* and space.

A third type of competence, ***support competence***, exists in areas where the EU can carry out actions to support, coordinate or supplement actions by Member States, without thereby superseding their competence in these areas. Legally binding acts of the EU adopted on the basis of the provisions of the Treaties relating to these areas shall not entail harmonisation of Member States' laws or regulations. This area of competence includes protection and improvement of human *health*, *industry*, *education*, youth, sport and *vocational training*.

NB: the coordination of economic and employment policies and common foreign and security policy are specific policies, poised between shared competences and support competences.

2. The "flexibility clause", a foundation of new European policies

At present, article 308 of the EC Treaty provides *"If action by the Community should prove necessary to attain, in the course of the operation of the common market, one of the objectives of the Community, and this Treaty has not provided the necessary powers, the Council shall, acting unanimously on a proposal from the Commission and after consulting the European Parliament, take the appropriate measures."*

This clause, maintained, has always been present in European treaties and has made it possible to implement policies essential to the European Union but not provided for in treaties, such as the environment policy, for example, or the

[1] The Treaty on the Functioning of the European Union is the new name the Treaty of Lisbon has given to the Treaty on the European Community.

premises of a European energy policy. The timid progress made in the energy area was also based on this provision.

The new article 308 however specifies in paragraph 2 that it cannot serve as the foundation for attaining an objective relating to common foreign and security policy. It will provide a pertinent legal base for the implementation of the new community policies required by a European strategy for globalisation.

3. External visibility of the European Union

a) Disappearance of the three-pillar structure and legal personality of the European Union

At present, the European Union is structured according to three pillars: the first pillar contains the European Community and is governed by the Community method, the second and third pillars respectively feature provisions relating to common foreign and security policy and to justice and internal affairs.

The Lisbon Treaty provides for the disappearance of this complex and somewhat illegible system. The three pillars will be merged into a single entity: the European Union. The EU will be endowed with a legal personality, which will represent a crucial innovation, particularly on the international scene because it will enable the Union to be a party to international conventions and agreements in its own right.

This improvement, from a point of internal legibility and international visibility, was essential for the European Union to be able to implement certain policies essential to globalisation, with an international dimension, such as the Union's commercial policy.

b) Reinforcement of the European Union's diplomatic role

The Lisbon Treaty provides for the appointment of a High Representative of the Union for foreign affairs and security policy, who will chair the Council of Ministers of Foreign Affairs, whilst also holding the position of Vice-President of the European Commission entrusted with external relations and the coordination of other aspects of the Union's external action.

The High Representative will be required to lead the Union's common foreign and security policy, to contribute to the development of this policy and to carry it out with the Council's mandate. His or her competence also extends to common security and defence policy, for which he or she will have the backing of a new "External Action Service" made up of the services of the European Commission and of Member States. This new European Commission Service seems quite promising in relation to the Union's external policy.

The High Representative will report to the European Council that will be able to dismiss him or her, but will also be a member of the European Commission, and will thus be subject to the investiture vote of the European Parliament. He or she can lose his or her position of Commissioner should the latter vote a motion of censure. In this way, and in the name of the principle of collegiality of the European Commission, he or she must thus obtain the backing of the majority of his or her colleagues for any initiative in the areas of his or her competence.

In light of the importance of the Union's external policies in the framework of the implementation of the Lisbon strategy and that of the strategy that will succeed it, in particular regarding the Union's difficulties in negotiating internationally, this innovation can only be beneficial.

III. Policies Necessary to a European Strategy for Globalisation Reinforced by the New Treaty

1. On a macro-economic scale

This is an essential dimension of a European strategy for globalisation, a domain in which European coordination suffers from a number of shortcomings. The Lisbon Treaty introduces several interesting modifications, particularly in terms of the representation of the Eurozone.

a) Economic policy

The European Central Bank has become a genuine European institution.

In terms of the implementation of the Stability and Growth Pact, the procedure relating to deficits changes very little. The Commission's role is reinforced because the Council will only be able to modify a proposal made by the Commission concerning excessive deficit by unanimous vote, while only a simple qualified majority of the Council suffices at present. This measure will enable more objectivity in the procedure.

Article 99 of the TFEU innovates in the field of multilateral surveillance and reinforces the role of all European institutions. Consequently, the Commission's role is reinforced should a state deviate from its budgetary adjustment trajectory compared with the Broad Economic Policy Guidelines (BEPGs). The Council will be able to make a recommendation to the State or make it public without taking into account the vote of the country concerned. Finally, the role of the European Parliament has been reinforced because it will jointly rule with the Council on the procedural modes of multilateral surveillance.

b) Monetary policy and the role of the Eurogroup

The amending treaty contains a section concerning the provisions relating to Member States whose currency is the euro and to the coordination of their economic policies, and sanctions the informal status of the Eurogroup (whose functioning is detailed in a protocol annexed to the Treaty). The provisions relating to the Eurogroup concern in particular the reinforcement of the budgetary coordination and surveillance of these States, and the development of economic policy guidelines that contribute to the proper functioning of the economic and monetary Union.

The treaty also features provisions relating to the external representation of the Eurozone and its role in international financial institutions. In this way the Council may, after a proposal by the Commission and consultation with the ECB, determine common positions on the representation of the euro. Furthermore, the Council, reduced to the Eurozone (*i.e.* only the States within the zone can vote), may adopt measures to "ensure unified representation" of the Eurozone.

2. Employment and social policies

The Lisbon Treaty is at the heart of the eponymous strategy, by undeniably reinforcing the social dimension of the European Union. This involves, in particular, the objectives assigned to the Union, the procedures that aim to ease the freedom of circulation of workers, the social clause or the legal basis granted to services of general economic interest.

New social objectives are assigned to the European Union: full employment, social progress, the fight against social exclusion and discrimination, justice and social welfare, gender equality, solidarity between generations and the protection of children.

At a general level the area of social security remains subject to unanimity. However, issues related to the social security rights of workers circulating in the European Union may be debated by qualified majority (article 42 of the TFEU). Should a Member State consider that the latter undermines its "*own social welfare system*", it will be able to appeal to the European Council. In practical terms, this takes the form of a right of veto.

The European Council can also resort to the qualified majority in a certain number of areas, in particular the adoption of measures that seek to improve cooperation between Member States regarding the protection of workers in the case of termination of employment, representation and collective defence of workers' and employers' interests and the labour conditions of nationals of third countries with a legal right of presence in the Union.

The Union is moreover under obligation, by way of a "social clause", to take into consideration objectives governed in part by the Lisbon strategy (in particular the promotion of high levels of employment, adequate social welfare and a high level of education and training, etc.) when defining and implementing its actions.

A legal base relating to "services of general economic interest" has been inserted into the treaties and can be used for the adoption of guidelines on this subject. One of the protocols annexed to the Treaty underlines the importance of services of general interest together with the role and extensive discretionary powers of national, regional and local authorities in the provision, carrying out and organisation of services of general economic interest. It recalls the diversity of these services, their high level of quality, security and accessibility, the equality of treatment and the promotion of universal access and rights of users. Finally, the protocol specifies that the provisions of the treaties may not undermine the competence of Member States to provide, carry out and organise services of general non-economic interest.

The legal value granted by the Charter of Fundamental Rights, which contains many social rights, contributes to the social dimension of the European Union. In particular, it recognises professional freedom and the right to work, the right to information and communication of company employees and the fact that European employees must be informed of the situation and decisions concerning their company.

The role of management and labour is sanctioned, as is the necessity of "preserving the diversity of national systems". The spring European Council is officially devoted to growth and employment.

The influence of the European Parliament is further reinforced because it is informed of agreements signed between management and labour and of actions taken by the Commission to facilitate cooperation between Member States.

The Lisbon Treaty also contributes to reinforcing European civil society by reinforcing democracy. This entails reinforcing the influence of the European Parliament, but also introducing a more participatory democracy, via the right to petition and the right to popular initiative, a genuine innovation of the constitutional treaty that enables citizens, providing they number at least one million and represent a significant number of states, to invite the European Commission to take measures in an area they deem requires intervention. The European Council and Parliament already feature this power of initiative, and as the European Commission also seems relatively open to this question, it is hoped that it will do likewise. The reinforcement of the role of national parliaments, particularly by ensuring that the principle of subsidiarity is respected, contributes to the democratic dimension of the European Union.

3. External policies of the European Union

a) Common trade policy

This is one of the main instruments of the Union's external policy and represents the counterpart to the customs union. The Lisbon Treaty does not modify in depth the common commercial policy, but modernises it by reinforcing certain aspects. As a result, the defence of intellectual property rights, services and foreign direct investments are now covered by this area (article 188 C of the

TFEU). The Lisbon Treaty generalises the qualified majority vote, except in relation to cultural and audiovisual services and welfare, education and health services.

At present, the external competences of the European Union are not explicitly defined, giving rise to controversy between the Commission and the Council. Article 300 of the EC Treaty grants the European Community competence to sign international agreements, which is a welcome clarification.

b) Common foreign and security policy

The current tasks of the European security and defence policy, known as Petersberg, are specified by the Treaty on European Union (article 17). They encompass: humanitarian missions and the evacuation of nationals, peacekeeping missions and tasks of combat forces in crisis management, including peacemaking operations. To these tasks, the Lisbon Treaty adds: disarmament, advice on military issues, stabilisation at the end of conflicts and the fight against terrorism, including in third country States.

The Lisbon Treaty also enriches the common foreign and security policy by a mutual defence clause and an antiterrorist solidarity clause, the launch of permanent structured cooperation between States that undertake certain commitments, and finally the creation of an armaments agency, the European Defence Agency, that was created by anticipation in 2004. The latter is required to develop the Union's defence capacities, set up cooperation in terms of armaments, develop the European defence market and assist research and technology in this area.

The improvement of the common foreign and security policy must regain a more prominent and visible position within the actions undertaken by the European Union. It is an integral aspect of the European strategy for globalisation.

4. New European policies

a) Technological research and development

This is key to the success of the European Union in terms of globalisation: the benefits of a united approach to this policy are huge. Technological research and development at a community-wide level are among the noteworthy innovations, in terms of policy, provided for by the Lisbon Treaty.

This policy becomes a shared competence of the EU and the Member States. Article 4 of the TFEU specifies that: "In the areas of research, technological development and space, the Union shall have competence to carry out activities, in particular to define and implement programmes; however, the exercise of that competence shall not result in Member States being prevented from exercising theirs."

The Lisbon Treaty provides a clear legal base for the foundation of European research area, indicating that: "The Union shall have the objective of strengthening its scientific and technological bases by achieving a European research area in which researchers, scientific knowledge and technology circulate freely, and encouraging it to become more competitive, including in its industry, while promoting all the research activities deemed necessary by virtue of other Chapters of the Treaties." As, up until now, the provisions concerning a European research area had no legal basis within the EC treaty, they were based on other provisions such as the freedom of circulation of workers or services.

Other elements of European research policy (such as RDFP for example) will continue to be adopted on the same basis and according to the same procedures as at present.

b) Energy policy

The Lisbon Treaty specifies and reinforces the Union's competences in order to ensure the proper functioning of the energy market, the supply of energy, the promotion of energy efficiency and sources of renewable energy. It is a core element of the European Union's security and competitiveness. Up until now, the few timid attempts to develop a European energy policy could only be based on the flexibility clause of Article 308 of the EC treaty. The provision of a "genuine" legal base to this policy is one of the points highlighted on the occasion of the adoption of the Lisbon Treaty.

This competence is shared between the Union and the Member States. Article 176 A of the TFEU specifies that the European Parliament and Council, ruling according to the ordinary legislative procedure, *i.e.* the codecision procedure, establish the measures necessary to reach these objectives. Even so, each State may determine the conditions of use of its own energy resources, its choice between different energy sources and the overall structure of its energy provisioning.

The treaty sanctions the concept of "solidarity between Member States", which must guide the Union's policy on this issue. Article 100 § 1 of the amending treaty endows the Council in particular with the competence to decide, on proposal by the Commission, in a spirit of solidarity between Member States, upon "the measures appropriate to the economic situation, in particular if severe difficulties arise in the supply of certain products, notably in the area of energy."

The TFEU does not specify any major changes concerning civil nuclear energy governed by the Euratom Treaty.

The emergence of a genuine European policy in this area is one of the critical aspects of a European strategy for globalisation.